RETHINKING RACIAL UPLIFT

RETHINKING RACIAL UPLIFT

RHETORICS OF BLACK UNITY AND DISUNITY IN THE OBAMA ERA

NIGEL I. MALCOLM

University Press of Mississippi / Jackson

The University Press of Mississippi is the scholarly publishing agency of the Mississippi Institutions of Higher Learning: Alcorn State University, Delta State University, Jackson State University, Mississippi State University, Mississippi University for Women, Mississippi Valley State University, University of Mississippi, and University of Southern Mississippi.

www.upress.state.ms.us

The University Press of Mississippi is a member of the Association of University Presses.

Chapter 2 is reprinted by permission from Nigel I. Malcolm, "Slaves to the Community: Blacks and the Rhetoric of 'Selling Out,'" *Journal of African American Studies* 19, no. 2 (2015): 120–34.

Any discriminatory or derogatory language or hate speech regarding race, ethnicity, religion, sex, gender, class, national origin, age, or disability that has been retained or appears in elided form is in no way an endorsement of the use of such language outside a scholarly context.

First printing 2023

∞

Library of Congress Cataloging-in-Publication Data

Names: Malcolm, Nigel I., author.
Title: Rethinking racial uplift : rhetorics of Black unity and disunity in the Obama era / Nigel I. Malcolm.
Description: Jackson : University Press of Mississippi, 2023. | Includes bibliographical references and index.
Identifiers: LCCN 2022033436 (print) | LCCN 2022033437 (ebook) | ISBN 9781496842640 (hardback) | ISBN 9781496842657 (trade paperback) | ISBN 9781496842664 (epub) | ISBN 9781496842671 (epub) | ISBN 9781496842688 (pdf) | ISBN 9781496842695 (pdf)
Subjects: LCSH: African Americans—Race identity. | Black people—Race identity.
Classification: LCC E185.625 .M327 2023 (print) | LCC E185.625 (ebook) | DDC 305.896/073—dc23/eng/20220824
LC record available at https://lccn.loc.gov/2022033436
LC ebook record available at https://lccn.loc.gov/2022033437

British Library Cataloging-in-Publication Data available

For Minnie P. Reed,

my grandmother,

who was always there for me.

CONTENTS

ACKNOWLEDGMENTS

Thank you to Vijay Shah for your interest in my work. I wish you all the best in your new endeavors. Thank you to Emily Snyder Bandy at the University Press of Mississippi for picking up where Vijay left off. I appreciate your carrying the baton and helping me to run this race until the end. Thank you to the anonymous reviewers for your feedback on my work. Thank you to Lisa McMurtray and all the many people at the University Press of Mississippi who make books possible.

Thank you to the Florida Education Fund, and Dr. Lawrence Morehouse, for your support these many years. Thank you to the African American Communication and Culture Division at NCA for providing a space for me to try out new ideas. Thank you to Keene State College for providing a sabbatical so that I could finish this work. Thank you to my colleagues who have also become friends.

Last, thank you to all my family, especially my wife, Sarah, for the trade-offs we make to support each other. Ian, Nya, and Nora, thank you for bringing unimagined joy to my life.

INTRODUCTION

We live in a different world from our predecessors. Both Blacks and whites in the post–civil rights era can attend the same schools, live in the same neighborhoods, and intermingle as they see fit. These things may not happen as much as they should or as much as we'd like them to, but the fact that they can happen is evidence of change in America. The distance between some Blacks and some whites has closed dramatically. We live in a world in which we must regularly assess whether the glass is half-full or half-empty. For some of us, the glass is perhaps three-quarters full, and for others it is overflowing.

This is a world in which Blacks can be both icons and pariahs. Some Blacks number among the wealthiest individuals and most successful individuals in the country. Others are middle-class, though, as Conley (1999) observed, lacking the wealth that makes their white counterparts solidly so. For at least another quarter of Blacks, life remains hard as they struggle to hold on to the short end of the stick in American society. They deal with what it means to be both Black and poor in a society in which many whites think that racism is a problem of the past, and some Blacks think that poor Blacks have only themselves to blame.

What, one may ask, are Black people to make of all of this? In the span of eight years, America went from electing in Obama its first Black president to electing Trump, whom Coates (2017) saw as "America's first white president" (344), one for whom "whiteness is neither notional nor symbolic but is the very core of his power" (343). One step forward and two steps backward may be the norm throughout American history, yet the road leading up to Obama's election appeared to signal for some the possibility that we had reached a new state of affairs in the relationship between Blacks and whites: a world in which George W. Bush provided us with two Black secretaries of state, and a Black secretary of education, despite Kanye West's assertion in 2005 that the president "doesn't care about black people." In 2018, Kanye later declared his love for Donald Trump and referred to him as his brother. While no one has yet figured out just where Kanye's head is at, it might be worth trying to see just where the heads of Black public intellectuals are at, given the head-spinning changes of the twenty-first century and even the last decade. For much of the twentieth century, Black intellectuals took their cues from Du Bois, but in the twenty-first century, that appears to be changing.

If for the iconic intellectual W. E. B. Du Bois (1969), "*The* problem of the twentieth century is the problem of the color-line" (54), then part of his solution to that problem lay in the creation of a group of people among Blacks that he deemed the Talented Tenth. For Du Bois (1986), "The Negro race, like all races, is going to be saved by its exceptional men" (842), and while women have always played, and continue to play, a role in racial uplift, the gendered nature of Du Bois's proclamation should be noted even if it is inaccurate. What matters most for my purposes is that Du Bois was an elitist and that he saw leadership among Blacks and racial uplift as derived from above. It was college-educated Blacks who he believed were capable of providing the race with the guidance it needed to surmount a history of slavery, segregation, and oppression in America.

Over time, Du Bois came to see that Blacks, like other humans, are capable of being selfish and self-interested. He reassessed his idea of the Talented Tenth and instead put his faith in a Guiding Hundredth (Gates and West 1996) before eventually turning away from such ideas altogether and leaving America for good to live in exile. Yet as I have argued in an earlier work (Malcolm 2008), the fact that Du Bois gave up on the Talented Tenth did not mean that the Talented Tenth gave up on themselves. Du Bois created the Talented Tenth through his own rhetoric, yet once the rhetoric and the group it created came into existence, both took on a life of their own. As Gates and West (1996) noted, "'The Talented Tenth' was held up as a model for the social, political, and ethical role of the members of what we might call a 'crossover' generation, those of us who, as a result of the great civil rights movement, were able to integrate historically white educational and professional institutions" (xi).

Nearly a hundred years later, Gates and West revisited Du Bois's idea because it still had power and held sway among Blacks in America. Even Randall Robinson (2000), when he wasn't talking about reparations and what America owed to Blacks, followed up with a discussion of what he thought Blacks owed each other (R. Robinson 2003). The idea of a debt that Blacks owe to the race, the idea of racial uplift with a Talented Tenth at the forefront, continues to hold sway for many Blacks.

Yet while some Blacks continue to believe that Blacks constitute a unified group and that members of the Talented Tenth owe a debt to the less fortunate masses, not everyone agrees. As hooks (2000) stated, "Collectively, black folks in the United States have never wanted to highlight the issue of class and class exploitation, even though there have always been diverse caste and class groups among African-Americans" (89). Hooks reminded us that "class matters. Race and gender can be used as screens to deflect attention away from the harsh realities class politics exposes" (7). Moreover, "That sense of solidarity was altered by a class-based civil rights struggle whose ultimate goal was to acquire more freedom for those black folks who already had a degree of class privilege however relative. By the late 1960s class-based racial integration disrupted the racial solidarity that often held blacks together despite class difference" (91).

Instead of seeing racial uplift as a debt the Talented Tenth owe the masses to ensure the success of all, racial uplift is now redefined as the Talented Tenth finding ways to elevate themselves and their children. My work suggests that success now has to do with one's own rise as the ties that bind the Talented Tenth to the lower classes are cut. As I will show, evidence for this change exists in the works of some contemporary Black writers whose books I have selected for analysis and critique. In this work, I argue that rhetorics of Black unity and Black disunity coexist today, and the appearance of both types of rhetoric in Black public intellectual discourse ultimately points to the divided state of Blacks in the post–civil rights era. I should note that while division has always existed among Blacks, both the need for and the appearance of Black unity have generally been advocated with a high degree of consensus even if such unity did not exist in reality. From Martin R. Delaney in the nineteenth century, to twentieth-century figures such as Washington, Du Bois, Garvey, Martin Luther King Jr., Malcolm X, Stokely Carmichael, "race women" such as Cooper, and the numerous women of the civil rights movement who put race before gender in the interest of group unity, debates between various individuals ensued, yet the belief in the necessity of Black unity remained strong. Even in the twenty-first century, we see efforts such as Shelby's (2005) to provide a philosophical bedrock for Black unity. A rhetoric of Black unity was a means to achieve the ends of racial justice. I define rhetorics of Black unity as those that envision Blacks as a unified group and stress the need for Blacks to work together as a collective, even at the expense of individual goals or self-interest. I define rhetorics of Black disunity as those that do not envision Blacks as a unified group and stress the need for Blacks to pursue individual rather than collective aims, even emphasizing commonalities across racial lines above loyalty to a perceived racial group. As I will show, examples of this exist in the work of Eugene Robinson (2010), who suggested that Blacks are broken up into four distinct subgroups; Touré (2011), who argued in favor of a post-Black identity that places individual needs before those of the group; and Cashin

(2014), who suggested that place should take precedence over race and that the wealthy Blacks can work against the interests of poor Blacks when higher education and social mobility are at stake. Yet what makes the subject of Black unity and Black disunity necessary to discuss today?

The success of the civil rights movement, as hooks (2000) noted, opens doors for some Blacks and allows others to be left behind. The totality of segregation and discrimination in the past was such a dominant scene that, to use Burke's ([1945] 1969) terms, it determined the actions Blacks could take. Yet when that scene changed, Blacks could act differently than they had in the past, and some chose to do so. Moreover, a change in the scene led to a change in how Blacks saw themselves as agents, both in the collective and in the individualistic sense. A change in the situation eventually produced a change in how Blacks identify with each other. The intermediating force for this change is rhetoric. As Bitzer (1968) wrote, "We need to understand that a particular discourse comes into existence because of some specific condition or situation which invites utterance" (4). I see the success of the civil rights movement as the condition that calls forth a change in the rhetoric of Black Americans. If the situation changes, then our rhetoric changes in response. Simply put, some Blacks no longer feel the need to appear unified, even in a rhetorical sense. My work combines insights from Bitzer (1968) about the rhetorical situation, Charland (1987) on the ways in which rhetoric helps constitute a people, Meyrowitz (1986) on the ways in which new media alter social environments in ways that change social behavior, and hooks's (2000) discussion of the changes in class relations among Blacks after the civil rights movement. In this work, I reveal how changes to the situation bring forth a change in rhetoric, which affects identity (both collective and individual among Blacks), leading to potential changes in behavior, which will themselves potentially affect the situation in which Blacks and other Americans find themselves going forward.

The post–civil rights era, and changes within this era, brings about a change in the rhetoric among Blacks related to unity and disunity. If unity among Blacks was based on historical necessity and circumstance, then changes in the situation in which Blacks exist historically open the door to changes in their rhetorical response to that situation. As Bitzer (1968) asserted, changes in the situation call forth a corresponding change in discourse. I suggest that shifts in rhetoric create, often intentionally, an opportunity for a new sense of identity among Blacks, both at the collective and the individual level. Eugene Robinson (2010) argued that four distinct groups now exist among Blacks, whereas Touré (2011) sought to move toward a post-Black identity at the individual level in ways that diminish group identity altogether. While my work, in discussing Touré's rhetoric, only partly reveals changes in behavior that would stem from changes to identity, I do assert that this is something that authors such as Cashin (2014) hope will happen when she argued in favor of "ardent integrators" who will help build multicultural alliances—a shift that I note takes Blacks away from Du Bois's notion of the Talented Tenth and their role among Blacks. Last, changes in the behavior of Blacks will have some effect on the environment or situation in which they exist. While whites are still the majority group and exert a great deal of power over our social world, Blacks throughout history have shown the ability to force alterations in social relations and the shared social world as well. Whites have always found it necessary to try to control the thoughts and actions of Blacks because those in power have always known that a change in one part of the system can alter the system as a whole.

The election of Donald Trump to the presidency is one such reaction to a shift in the system as a whole brought on by the election of Barack Obama. As Coates (2017) noted, "Replacing Obama is not enough—Trump has made the negation of Obama's legacy the foundation of his own. And this too is whiteness" (344). Obama's election to the presidency was something that not even Blacks really thought was possible until it happened. Who could have imagined that a biracial man who did not shirk from blackness but instead married into and celebrated it could defeat the Clinton regime, win the Democratic Party nomination, and ultimately the general election? Not many imagined it, and fewer still thought it possible. Yet Obama spoke of hope and change and enlisted Americans of all colors into a broader vision of what the country could and should be. He became the change he sought in the world, and America woke up one morning to see a Black family in the White House. Not everyone was comfortable with this new day in America, and some wanted to see it end as quickly as possible.

Yet for eight years that vision endured, and despite the racism Obama encountered both from other politicians and from many members of the public, he worked to save the world's financial system and to provide all Americans with some form of health care, even if half of them didn't appreciate the effort. The response to his good works was animosity, because good Negro government could not be tolerated. It was too much of a shock to the system. As Olson (2004) wrote, "White citizenship is the enjoyment of racial standing in a democratic polity. It is a position of equality and privilege simultaneously: equal to other white citizens yet privileged over those who are not white" (xix). Obama's election undermined white privilege, and after eight years of progress, a majority of white America decided to "make America great again" by attempting to turn back the clock to a time when minorities knew their place and the White House was for white people.

I mention the shift from Obama to Trump and the resurgence of white supremacy because all the books I critique were published from 2007 to 2015;

five of the six books overlap with Obama's term in office, and one was published while he campaigned for office in 2007. That said, these books constitute
a response to one of the most unprecedented events in American history, a
Black presidency. If ever there was a time when Black people could begin to
question the meaning of blackness and Black unity in the twenty-first century,
this was surely the time. Some of the works I critique display greater calls for
individuality than others. Some of the works attempt to double down on Black
unity at a time when Obama could attain the White House using race-neutral
politics, the endorsement of Oprah, and the legion of adoring white women
who constituted a faithful share of her television audience and continued
magazine readership.

What the authors whose works I critique would have written in 2016 upon
observing the election of Donald Trump and the racist campaign he embarked
on is not present in these texts. Perhaps some of them would have changed
their minds about just how far they thought Americans had really come as a
nation and the need, or lack thereof, for racial unity among Blacks. Yet what
interests me is what they did write and what it says about the shift in rhetoric
among Blacks in the post–civil rights era. This change did not take place all at
once, and no doubt other works also contain similar ideas. Yet all the works I
chose were popular and reached a national audience. Randall Kennedy's *Sellout* was reviewed in the *New York Times* and the *Washington Post*. Bill Cosby
and Alvin Poussaint's *Come On, People* reached number five on the *Publishers
Weekly* nonfiction best-seller list and was a *New York Times* best seller. Ta-Nehisi
Coates's *Between the World and Me* was a number one *New York Times* best
seller and won the 2015 National Book Award for Nonfiction. Eugene Robinson's
Disintegration was reviewed in the *New York Times* and the *Washington Post*.
Sheryll Cashin's *Place, Not Race* was reviewed in the *New York Times* and the
Washington Post and was nominated for an NAACP Image Award for Out-
standing Literary Work—Nonfiction. Touré's *Who's Afraid of Post-Blackness?*
was a *New York Times* and *Washington Post* notable book. These authors are
well-known, and one is now infamous, yet all for a time constituted part of a
modern-day Talented Tenth. What they have to say on the subject of race and
Black unity or disunity is important to consider.

Still, I find that extended analysis of the books such individuals produce
is mostly absent in the field of communication studies. Rhetoricians focus
on works of the past going back to abolition and advancing toward the civil
rights movement. While they study the speeches of social movement leaders
and Black politicians, less attention is given to the books of Black thinkers,
and fewer still discuss those books in concert with each other. Moreover,
when attention is paid, it usually concerns what the author has to say about

the relationship between Blacks and whites rather than the relationship that Blacks have with each other.

My fascination, however, is not with what one could call interracial communication but rather *intra*racial. What do Black people or members of any racial group say to each other? What thoughts cross their minds? What mutual interests are shared? What disagreements had? What resolutions to those disagreements found? Although my work cannot explore each of those questions to their full extent, these are the types of questions that motivate it. We often hear calls for interracial dialogue and greater communication between racial groups. Yet my contention is that before groups talk with each other, a conversation must first be had within those groups themselves. This intragroup conversation is primary, and just as important as the conversation that takes place between groups. Interracial conversations often proceed based on the notion that a single individual or a few persons can speak for an entire group of people. Yet who says that these are the right people, and for how long are they authorized to speak? Who says that a single person could even speak for an entire group unless some conversations within that group had already taken place and authority granted to a given leader or spokesperson? Disagreement among Blacks is in fact the norm. Why, then, should such productive disagreements not be explored and studied?

We value the rhetoric of whites talking primarily to other whites. Should not the rhetoric of Blacks talking primarily to other Blacks be equaled valued? Unlike whites, Blacks cannot pretend that whites do not matter or that they do not factor into the conversations that Blacks have with each other. Yet every conversation is not about white people, and every conversation is not addressed to them. Though whites may constitute a potential audience for Black rhetors, there are times at which white people are in fact secondary.

I believe that the conversations that Blacks have with each other about what it means to be Black in America and how Blacks should relate to one another are equally important to the conversations Blacks have with whites about race relations in America. My continued project is to explore this intraracial communication even while acknowledging that race is a sociological construct rather than a biological fact. Blacks have a shared history in America, and it is this shared history, along with the rhetoric and legal fictions of whites, that shapes our sense of blackness. Black thinkers spend a great deal of time writing their thoughts in books for other people to read. While Blacks have excelled in oral discourse, books take longer to produce and may reveal much more about the state of our thinking than a speech could. As Postman (1985) noted, the medium in which a thought is expressed can limit what is expressed. Just as Postman valued the type of culture the printed word could produce, I too

value the printed word and the use that Black authors make of it. Moreover, I
believe that the works of contemporary Black authors are worthy of exploration. As Rambsy (2016) observed, "Despite his popular acclaim, contemporary
writers like Coates seldom become central focal points in African American
literary studies" (196). In advocating for more attention from literary scholars
to the works of contemporary Black writers, Rambsy surmised, "Somewhere
out there in that vast body of data, we might discover answers to the riddle of
why so many black writers are met with indifference, while a select few enjoy
receptions that are quite remarkable" (203).

While some value lies in exploring works thirty or a hundred years after
their production, there is something equally valuable in critiquing the works of
authors who are writing about the present. The authors whose works I critique
are still alive, writing about today and the times in which they live. They are
actively attempting to shape the thoughts and actions of other Blacks and to
affect American society as a whole. To explore their work is to give it and them
the respect they deserve. It is my hope that, even while critiquing and at times
disagreeing with some of them, in paying attention to the works they have
produced, I show respect for these authors, the contributions they are making
to our society, and the shape that it may take in the future. Yet before moving on to the works I will critique, it is necessary to provide some discussion
of solidarity, unity, and linked fate, on the one hand, as well as disunity, class
stratification, ethnic/national origin, and generational divides, on the other, in
works that provide a foundation for my own. While I will at times diverge from
these authors, their insights are nevertheless of great value to my own study.

RETHINKING BLACK UNITY

Dawson (1994) explored the reasons for Black solidarity in the past and the
possibility of it breaking down in the future. Blacks, he argued, are not nearly as
unified as they might seem, and their presentation of solidarity is a response to
racism and discrimination from whites. Given that Blacks were discriminated
against as a group, and the chances of individual Black advancement were
limited, Dawson posited that Blacks engaged in a phenomenon he labeled the
Black utility heuristic, in which it "was more efficient for them to use the status
of the group, both relative and absolute, as a proxy for individual utility" (10).
The status of Blacks in relation to whites is what mattered, and if the group
did not fare well, then the prospects for an individual were regarded to be the
same as that of the group. Dawson went on to explore his concept of linked
fate, "which measure[s] the degree to which African Americans believe that

their own self-interests are linked to the interests of the race" (77). As Dawson showed, contrary to what one would expect, the degree of linked fate increases, rather than declines, with the socioeconomic status and education of Blacks. It is the Black middle class that benefited the most from the civil rights movement and professes a greater belief in linked fate. Yet the politics of this group and that of the Black lower class vary greatly, as the Black lower class favors economic redistribution, Black political parties, and autonomy from whites, none of which resonate with the Black middle class. Indeed, as Dawson pointed out, survey research, given its emphasis on interracial conflict and differences, often masks the intraracial differences that exist among Blacks.

Blacks engage in creating the illusion of a united front to combat racism. Different groups among Blacks work together at times to protest injustice or to elect a Black politician, but this does not mean that they think alike or share the same interests. Unity is in fact the anomaly, and the question for political theorists is why Blacks continue to appear so unified in ways that other groups do not. Dawson wrote, "The puzzle for researchers and political observers is why, given the growing economic cleavage among black Americans, political unity among blacks appears to remain fairly strong" (45). Indeed, in a pluralist society, one would expect that, as a result of integration, Blacks would begin to function more as individuals seeking common cause with other Americans in place of pursuing racial interests. Yet given the ongoing economic subordination of Blacks, and in particular the disparities between Blacks and whites, the degree of political heterogeneity that one would expect to see has not occurred.

Dawson argued that this is in part a function of the limited options that Blacks have within a truncated two-party political system, as well as the ties that more educated and prosperous Blacks have to family members who are neither educated nor prosperous. However, as members of the Black middle class gain their educations, work for predominately white institutions, and move out of Black neighborhoods, their links to the Black community lessen. According the Dawson, "As perceptions of racial group interests become less able to predict individual utility, perceptions of racial group interests are less likely to be considered" (65). Moreover, "Affluent African Americans with weak ties to the black community are likely to have biased calculations in favor of the individual calculus" (67). Without something to bind upwardly mobile Blacks to the Black community, "one should expect to see a decline in group consciousness in this stratum" (59).

One of the reasons why we have failed to see the divisions that exist among Blacks is that, according to Dawson, survey research itself may not be the most useful tool in gaining insight into this phenomenon. Most surveys focus on the differences between Blacks and whites rather than those that occur among

Blacks. The very questions that most surveys ask do not deal with the questions that are of concern to the Black community. Blacks agree that racism needs to be fought, but they differ on which strategies to employ and which leaders to support. Moreover, the Black poor, Dawson notes, tend to be least represented in surveys, yet their views differ significantly from those of middle-class Blacks.

Dawson advocated the use of more qualitative research methods to better illuminate the differences that exist intraracially among Blacks. As Dawson observed, "Political responsibility to the African-American community was considered a higher good than the individual's right to act on his or her own preferences if those preferences were considered harmful to the black community" (99). Blacks' belief that "individual salvation can occur only within the framework of collective salvation" (100) has for some time limited the possibilities of Black politics. Yet that may be changing, and Dawson argued that we can see more political heterogeneity among Blacks under certain circumstances.

Blacks usually put race ahead of class in their calculations, but this does not always have to be the case going forward. Dawson observed in his work that "as perceptions of interracial disparities declined and as individual African Americans' perceptions of linked fate declined, class distinctions became more pronounced" (197). Shelton and colleagues (2016) reached a similar conclusion in their follow-up study to Dawson's work, noting, "It appears that favorable evaluations of race relations undermine commitments to black unity and solidarity" (95). "In short," they wrote, "there is strong reason to believe that class-based cultural and attitudinal differences have become a normative feature of contemporary Black experiences" (82). So the present and future of race relations will not necessarily resemble the past, and various possibilities emerge. In what Dawson (1994) termed a pluralist scenario, we would see "both the racial and economic environments steadily improve" (208). While Dawson believed this scenario to be unlikely, it would lead toward the assimilation of Blacks and free them to pursue their own individual interests. In another scenario he termed "unite and fight," the economic climate would remain the same or worsen, while the racial climate improved. This would bring class to the foreground for Blacks, as "class identity would take the place of racial identity as the primary factor influencing black politics" (209). The Black and white middle class in this example could unite to defend their own interests against those of the lower classes.

While Dawson believed that Blacks should work toward improved conditions for all members of the racial group, he nevertheless admits that this will be difficult to achieve for two reasons. The first is "the environment in which black politics must operate," and the second is "the political divisions within the black community" (211). He stated, "The emerging black middle class may see the relentless fight for the rights and survival of the poor as 'futile'" (212). Dawson concluded, "The future of African-American politics may well depend on how the racial and economic environment of twenty-first-century America dictates which African Americans perceive that their fates remain linked" (212). It is this question that I believe my work sheds light on, but not in the ways that Dawson might expect. I believe that a critique of the rhetoric of Black public intellectuals reveals the extent to which linked fate has lessened among middle-class Blacks. The divisions among Blacks are more apparent when one looks at what they are writing and saying to each other rather than in their responses to survey questions that focus more on how Blacks differ from whites. If one wants to understand intraracial division among Blacks, then one needs to take a closer look at the rhetorical struggles that are taking place among us. We are not all on the same page, and if we examine the pages of the books that Black public intellectuals are producing, this becomes clear.

Masuoka and Junn (2013) borrowed Dawson's theory of linked fate and extended it further using their analysis of data from the 2004 National Politics Study. The authors' noted that "perceived linked fated" captures "the extent to which respondents believe their individual fate is connected to that of others in their racial group" (112). All Americans exist within a racial hierarchy, and the authors argued that "the concept of linked fate as a measure of racial group identity . . . best captures racial group position and exclusion from the nation" (105). Blacks occupy the lowest position in a racial hierarchy in which whites are at the top, followed by Asians, then Latinos lower in the order, with Blacks at the very bottom. This racial order is socially constructed, but its effects on the life chances and outcomes for each of those groups and the individuals in them are very real. As the group at the bottom of the racial hierarchy, Blacks are most aware of the impact of racism and discrimination in our society. It is a reality that most find hard to ignore.

Given that the treatment of their racial group affects them as individuals, Blacks have historically maintained a strong degree of political cohesion because of the disadvantages they face given their placement at the bottom of the racial hierarchy. Moreover, Blacks "have the highest degree of racial-group identity of all racial groups" (Masuoka and Junn 2013, 108). Other groups such as Asians and Latinos show lower levels of racial group identification, and reasons given for this range from "the high degree of ethnic or national origin diversity" (108) to "numerous social and economic opportunities they experience compared the blacks" (109). While ethnic diversity also exists among Blacks, Masuoka and Junn pointed out that this is generally ignored in the literature on group identity.

Masuoka and Junn argued that a connection exists between "stronger racial group identity in linked fate" and "more cohesive political attitudes" (106). As the perception of linked fate weakens, the heterogeneity of viewpoints increases, and "it is more likely that individuals will consider their own fate ahead of that of the group" (106). Moreover, "groups experiencing quicker socioeconomic success are more likely to view society as open and accepting rather than excluding on the basis of race" (109). This perception of openness is more common among Asian Americans and to some degree Latinos, who "may mirror blacks in their relatively low economic status, but they have experienced relatively faster inroads into mainstream society" (109). Both Asians and Latinos express lower degrees of racial solidarity and less support "for racially redistributive policies" in comparison to Blacks (109).

Although all the previously mentioned facts are true, they do not tell the whole story and paint an incomplete picture of the puzzle we are facing as a nation and in particular among Blacks. Masuoka and Junn, in their analysis of the 2004 National Politics Study, emphasized the differences between Blacks and other racial groups. However, I focus on another part of their analysis that they did not spend time on, as it provides a foundation for my own work on the importance of understanding changes that are occurring among Blacks. Of all groups, Blacks express the highest degree of linked fate at 31 percent. Compare that to whites at 15 percent, and both Latinos and Asians at 18 percent each (Masuoka and Junn 2013, 113). In contrast, 38 percent of whites express a low degree of linked fate, believing that what happens to others in their group does not affect them at all. Interestingly, 53 percent of Latinos, more than any other group, lack a sense of linked fate. Asians came in at 31 percent. Blacks, as I will emphasize, had a response similar to that of Asians at 31 percent in lacking a sense of linked fate. What this means is that an identical percentage of Blacks express a lack of linked fate despite their place at the bottom of the racial hierarchy as do Asians, who fare much better, rank just below whites, and are more accepted by whites. Again, 31 percent of Blacks express a strong degree of linked fate, while the *same percentage* of Blacks, at 31 percent, express no sense of linked fate at all. What this shows is that, despite our common perceptions of solidarity among Blacks, a division among Blacks exists that is rarely addressed.

As I noted earlier, even Masuoka and Junn did not focus on this point, even though it was plain from their own analysis. The overall percentage of Blacks who expressed that what happened to other Blacks affected them either not at all or not very much was 39 percent when the two responses are combined. In comparison, the combined responses for Asians expressing little to no sense of linked fate was 40 percent. So, despite the large number of Blacks who express a high degree of linked fate, an equal number of Blacks express none at 31 percent; and overall, 39 percent of Blacks express little to no sense of linked fate at all.

Additionally, 29 percent of Blacks express some sense of linked fate with other Blacks. When we aren't flipping coins on whether we share a sense of linked fate with other Blacks, 29 percent said they sometimes do, and a full 39 percent aren't seeing how what happens to other Blacks affects them much at all. In this measure, Blacks are similar to Asians at 40 percent and trail whites, 38 percent of whom believe that what happens to other whites does not affect them, and 10 percent of whom do not believe that they are affected much at all. Negative responses to linked fate total 48 percent for whites, 39 percent for Blacks, 40 percent for Asians, and 57 percent for Latinos (Masuoka and Junn 2013, 113). What this means is that our perception of solidarity among Blacks is skewed. We emphasize the top 31 percent while ignoring the bottom 39 percent, and 29 percent of Blacks think we are linked only sometimes.

Why does this matter? It matters because we can feel close to other members of our group (for example, 54 percent of Blacks, 38 percent of Asians, 50 percent of Latinos, and 39 percent of whites do so [114]) while still not feeling that our fate is linked to other members of the same group. As Masuoka and Junn pointed out, linked fate and racial group closeness are two different measures. Furthermore, only our sense of linked fate matters when it comes to perceiving discrimination in society. As the authors pointed out, "71 percent of Blacks with high perceived linked fate perceive a lot of discrimination against African-Americans, compared with 38 percent of those with low perceived linked fate" (115). The same pattern regarding linked fate and perception of discrimination existed for Asians and Latinos, though the strength of the connection was weaker. Whether or not Blacks have a strong sense of linked fate matters, as it is "related to the belief that minorities cannot only blame themselves for failures and to opposition to racial profiling and support for affirmative action" (117). I believe that the differences among Blacks regarding linked fate also correspond to different kinds of rhetoric.

A Black person with a high degree of linked fate and a Black person with little to no sense of linked fate will not sound the same. We often focus so much on those with a high degree of linked fate and the rhetoric that they produce that it blinds us to the equally present rhetoric of those who do not perceive themselves to have a linked fate with other Blacks. Blacks with a lower degree of linked fate may see the United States more as Asians do, emphasizing individuality, education, social mobility, and the perceived openness of American society. This is not to say that Blacks as a group are not still at the bottom of the American racial hierarchy. That has not changed. What has changed is the perception among Blacks that we are all linked together. This is no longer a shared perception but rather a bifurcated one in which an equal number of Blacks believe that we do not share a linked fate as those who believe we do.

Blacks without a sense of linked fate will focus more on the opportunities that America provides for them and will encourage others to do so as well. They will accentuate the positive by arguing that the negatives of racism and discrimination are not as powerful as they once were and that they do not apply to all Blacks equally.

While scholars in political science have explored the concept of linked fate, its importance has not been previously explored in communication studies. In particular, the ramifications for a change in the perceptions of linked fate on Black rhetoric have never been explicated. What I seek to do in my study is to show what a change in the perception of linked fate among Blacks looks like rhetorically. In examining the work of Black public intellectuals, I will provide evidence for a broader spectrum of discourse than is usually the focus of our analysis. While I do not claim that Blacks as a group will lose their sense of linked fate entirely, I can show that changes that have taken place in the post–civil rights era have left their mark on us rhetorically. As Bitzer (1968) argued, "Rhetorical discourse comes into existence as a response to situation" (5), and as the situation of Blacks has changed to some degree, so has our rhetoric. We are not all in the same boat politically, socially, or economically to the degree that we once were. As such, we no longer speak with one voice, even though some may attempt to make their voices heard more than others. I do not seek to endorse one set of voices over another, only to show that there are different parts being sung even if we have not always listened closely enough to hear them.

Blacks are divided by transnational and ethnic lines (e.g., Africans, Caribbeans, and native-born Blacks in the United States), class lines, and adherence to a collective versus an individualistic ethos (i.e., believers in Du Bois's mandate for the Talented Tenth versus American individualism). As I will show, Black rhetoric in the post–civil rights era exists along a continuum. In this work, I critique various texts that illustrate this continuum using the rhetoric of Black public intellectuals as examples. The works I critique were written in the Obama era, which I argue provided a moment for Blacks to reexamine their connections to each other as what seemed impossible became a political reality with the election of a Black man to the presidency.

Kim (2000) provided us with a new understanding of the racial order in American society and the ways in which Blacks and other racial groups find themselves embedded in it. Kim posited that racial groups are positioned along two axes: superior/inferior and insider/foreigner. Whites, for example, are seen as superior insiders at the top of the racial order, while Blacks are seen as inferior insiders at the bottom of the racial order. Other groups, such as Asians, are positioned as superior foreigners, while Latinos may be positioned above Blacks but below Asians and may be seen as foreigners depending on the salience of immigration. What Kim showed us is that conflict between Blacks and Koreans during the Red Apple boycott of 1990 in Flatbush, New York, was not an instance of racial scapegoating of Koreans but rather "the 'bitter fruit' of deeply entrenched patterns of racial power in contemporary American society" (2). While native-born Blacks along with Haitian immigrants sought to conduct an antiracist campaign of social protest, Korean immigrants, with support from other Asian groups, sought to uphold their place in the existing racial order as "model minorities" who were simply attempting to live the American dream. Although the conflict took place between Blacks and Koreans, whites positioned themselves as neutral while favoring the interpretation of the conflict that Korean immigrants offered because it suited the color-blind narrative that whites preferred despite their long history of benefiting from racial power in American society.

For my purposes, what I find most interesting in Kim's work is the extent to which it revealed how both Blacks and Koreans attempted to create solidarity among themselves by arguing for the importance of linked fate. Native-born Blacks sought to bring Haitian immigrants under the Black Power umbrella and make them aware of their oppression as Blacks. However, Haitian immigrants see themselves as Haitian rather than as Black and resist being classified in the same category as native-born Blacks. Still, given that this is how whites see them, and, as Kim argued, how the racial order functions, Haitians have little power to resist this classification despite their own emphasis on a transnational identity in which they remain tied to Haiti. In the Red Apple boycott, Haitians worked with Blacks because it suited them while at the same time remaining independent of them. Even among native-born Blacks, tension existed between moderates and the militant December 12th Movement that took control of the boycott.

Moderates chose either to distance themselves from militants without criticizing them publicly or, in the case of some groups such as the NAACP and CORE, to oppose the December 12th Movement publicly, arguing that the group violated the tenets of racial solidarity and brotherhood on which the integrationist activists of the civil rights movement based their struggle for racial justice. Oddly enough, members of the NAACP and CORE, along with some Black clergy, marched with Koreans against fellow Blacks in arguing for an end to the boycott and in some cases willingly crossing the picket lines. These groups put pressure on Mayor Dinkins to come out against the boycott and ultimately pushed him to cross the picket line in an attempt to avoid further damage to his administration. Despite being elected the city's first Black mayor with the help of Black militants who organized for him in communities where he did not have a strong base, Dinkins eventually distanced himself from them, and in turn many Blacks and Latinos distanced themselves from him, contributing to his failed reelection bid as white Democrats overwhelming voted for the Republican candidate Rudolph Giuliani..

Korean immigrants also saw themselves as transnational with links to Korea rather than seeing themselves as Asian Americans. Yet again, they had little control over their placement in the American racial order or the interpretation white Americans, along with other Asian groups, gave to their narrative about the boycott. The Red Apple boycott was deemed to be anti-Asian, not anti-Korean. Both interpretations were incorrect, as Blacks continued to shop at other Korean grocery stores during the boycott and solely targeted two stores that were the boycott's focus. Still, Koreans used the boycott as a means to become more politically active and resist what they saw as racial scapegoating, rallying members of their community to unify and defend themselves against perceived aggression from Blacks while defending their own place in the racial order. Korean disrespect of Blacks and the alleged beating of a Haitian immigrant in the Family Red Apple store were overlooked, while a narrative of color blindness was put forward along with an emphasis on Koreans as model minorities who simply wanted to live the Korean American dream.

Neither Blacks' attempt to create racial solidarity among themselves while bringing Haitian immigrants into the fold nor Korean immigrants' attempt to convince first- and second-generation Koreans to see eye to eye on the boycott succeeded. Still, Black moderates and the Black media often refused to criticize the boycott publicly even while not agreeing with the December 12th Movement's goals and refusal to negotiate an end to the boycott. Second-generation Koreans tended to have a greater understanding of the racial order in American society, and the mistreatment of Blacks by Korean merchants, yet also chose not to publicly criticize the counterprotest of first-generation Korean immigrants.

What this shows is that for both Blacks and Koreans, solidarity is often an illusion. Especially in the case of Blacks, organizations and individuals fight among themselves while publicly putting forth a facade of unity in the face of white oppression. Notions of linked fate are used to galvanize members of each group, yet those attempts are not entirely successful. Although Black militants voted for a moderate Black Democrat for mayor after more than a decade of racism from the Koch administration, they soon parted ways with Mayor Dinkins when he crossed their picket line. Militant Black organizations were at odds with more moderate civil rights organizations such as the NAACP and CORE over the boycott and were opposed by them and even challenged in court as moderate Blacks sought to break a boycott instituted by militant Blacks. Second-generation Korean Americans acknowledged the validity of concerns on both sides of the boycott and "sought to avert future conflicts by building bridges between Blacks and Korean Americans" (185) while at the same time avoiding public criticism of the tactics first-generation Korean immigrants employed in dealing with the boycott. Kim's work showed that racial solidarity is an illusion, and groups and individuals within racial groups employ a rhetoric of linked fate in an attempt to create solidarity and mobilize individuals into collective action. This rhetoric is not entirely effective and can be resisted on various fronts. Not all Blacks see themselves as connected, even though they may choose to work together for their own purposes if it suits them. Such coalitions, as the effort to elect New York City's first Black mayor shows, are often short-lived, as are the coalitions that form between different social movement organizations in an effort to resist racial oppression.

Beltrán (2010) examined racial unity among Latinos and found it to be more illusion than reality, at best more temporary than permanent. She noted that everyone from scholars to journalists to Latino interest groups to Latino politicians is invested in the idea of Latinidad, seeing Latinos as one cohesive group, a sleeping giant that is always in the process of emerging. Yet Beltrán challenged this narrative, arguing instead that "there is no sleeping giant—only political subjects whose variegated actions and intentions are obscured by this limited vision of Latino empowerment" (9). Latinos, as Beltrán observed, are a heterogeneous group whose diversity is downplayed or ignored in the interests of creating the impression of homogeneity, which is seen as a precursor to the exercise of power within a political environment in the United States centered on group interests.

Latinos, Beltrán noted, both admire and attempt to compete with Blacks, and Latino politicians obscure the racial, class, and ethnic diversity among Latinos in an effort to position the group as the new majority-minority in the United States. Such attempts, however, mirror the radicalism of the 1960s and 1970s, in which group unity was presumed both as a given and as a necessity, and internal division punished and seen as a lack of proper socialization. Still, Beltrán suggested that "Latinos are not so much an electorate as an aggregate. If this is the case, then as this population grows, terms such as 'Latino interests' and 'Latino issues' will become increasingly meaningless" (127). In short, "the language of civic Latinidad may obscure more than it reveals" (127).

Despite this fact, Beltrán noted that scholars have for too long taken terms such as "Latino" as a given along with the unity they suggest rather than questioning both and the ways in which "the Latino electorate may actually consist of segments that are growing and dispersing in different directions" (126). Unity, Beltrán noted, has never been the case, as activists during the 1960s and 1970s sought to create a sense of Latino identity through public displays such as "rallies, teatros, and poetry readings" while attempting "to downplay and avoid agonistic deliberation and legitimate democratic debate" (15). Yet it is only in embracing the diversity of the Latino population and the ways in which "Latino interests are multiple, crosscutting, and periodically opposed to one another" (165) that new possibilities for Latino politics can emerge.

In reviewing the 1992 Latino National Political Survey results, a number of interesting findings emerged that undermine the notion of Latinos as a unified group. Latinos don't see themselves as sharing "common political concerns" (112). "No more than 14 percent of any group reported that another Latino group was 'very similar' to themselves." The largest three groups among Latinos "did not interact with other Latinos other than their own national origin group," and "affinities between Latino subgroups proved to be even lower than with other racial or ethnic groups" (112–13). Rather than viewing each other negatively, Latinos regard other Latino groups in neutral fashion (113). All these data point to the heterogeneous nature of Latinos and the ways in which both scholars' and Latino politicians' perceptions of the group differ from those of the people they claim to represent. As Beltrán observed, the "ethos of civic Latinidad is ideological, not preexistent. It represents a vision of political solidarity that is less found than forged" (127). Most important, "Latino interests are not only varied but actively in competition and in conflict with one another" (127). The same, I argue, can be said of Blacks, particularly in the post–civil rights era.

Blacks have never been a homogeneous group or a completely unified one. Yet Blacks have had ample reason to portray themselves as such and to coordinate their actions as a means to fight against segregation, discrimination, and the totality of racism in America. Beltrán suggests, "Approaching Latinidad as action—as something we do rather than something we are—this definition sees Latino politics as inherently coalitional" (19). I believe that the same logic should be applied to Blacks. As authors such as Eugene Robinson (2010) suggested, we should think of Blacks not as a single group but as a number of groups: "These four black Americas are increasingly distinct, separated by demography, geography, and psychology" (5). Differences not only of class but also of increasingly ethnic and transnational identities divide Blacks in ways that are greater than they once were. Influxes of individuals from both the Caribbean and increasingly Africa continue to push and stretch the boundaries of what it means to be black in America. Robinson wrote, "There is no longer one black America. . . . But there remains one black racial identity that the majority of African Americans—Mainstream, Abandoned, Transcendent, and Emergent—still share" (236). Where I differ from Robinson is in the suggestion that a single Black racial identity exists, or that it has any coherent meaning for its constituent groups. Just as the term "Latino" lacks specificity, so too does the term "Black" tell us less and less about the people or person to whom it is applied.

Just as Beltrán (2010) did "not seek to resolve the heterogeneity implicit in Latinidad" and had "no wish to create unity out of diversity" (9), I seek to do neither in regard to the term "Black." Instead my work seeks to illustrate the changing meanings of that term, and the ways in which these changes lead to tensions that various rhetors seek to address in their works. Some pull against this tension, while others attempt to push it forward in ways they deem more liberating of us as individuals. It is this tension between the group and the individual that makes the changing meaning of the term "Black" both problematic and full of potential, depending on one's point of view. I do not seek to endorse either perspective, only to show the increasing spectrum, the diversity of Black thought about what it means to be Black in the post–civil rights era. Some call for greater unity among Blacks, while others push for individual freedoms that lead in the direction of disunity. While unity itself was always something of a fiction, the reality of a Black president, along with the changing economic, social, and ethnic localities of Blacks, reveals tears in the social fabric that once appeared to hold many Blacks together. Arguments in favor of Black unity and Black disunity exist along a continuum, and it is this continuum that my book explores. Exploring Black unity and disunity forces us to engage with people's attempts to both limit and expand the meaning of blackness, because to be Black was to appear to be unified in thought, or at least to give that appearance to those outside the group. Now, in the post–civil rights era, we see blackness made visible in ever-increasing shades and complexities. These complexities defy our traditional understandings and challenge both the nation and Blacks as individuals to reexamine commitments based on racial group interest and loyalty. If the meaning of blackness is changing and expanding, then so too can Black politics, and the ways in which we live Black lives.

Shelby (2005) recognized from the outset that Black political unity is linked to social justice. However, this unity is based both on Black identity and on a shared history of racial oppression. The link between identity and oppression, Shelby wrote, "is often taken for granted and treated as a matter of common sense" (1). Yet in his work Shelby sought to separate the two, seeing the latter as more important than the former for Blacks. He stated:

> I seek to identify a basis for black political unity that does not deny, downplay, or disparage individual or group differentiation within the black population. I insist that there are many, perhaps incommensurable, ways to be black, none more "natural" than the others. Yet I also defend a conception of black solidarity that is not only, or even primarily, concerned with questions of identity, but that urges

a joint commitment to defeating racism, to eliminating unjust racial inequalities, and to improving the material life prospects of those racialized as "black," especially the most disadvantaged. (3–4)

Shelby's work advocated in favor of Black solidarity not on the basis of identity but out of political necessity. He observed, "This would be a form of political solidarity that would subordinate questions of who blacks are as a people to questions about the ways in which they have been and continue to be unfairly treated" (4). This put him at odds with Blacks who favor the formation of a strong, unified Black identity as a means to achieve racial and social justice. Moreover, Shelby argued that "black unity must operate across multi-racial political organizations; it must recognize that the sources of black disadvantage cannot all be reduced to racism; and it should acknowledge the need for a decentralized network of black advocacy" (22). In doing so, I believe Shelby pushes Blacks to look outward rather than inward and moves us away from the politics of race leadership and specifically Du Bois's notion of the Talented Tenth.

Shelby's work examined black nationalism, strains of which, he stated, "have become, for all practical purposes, a constitutive component of the self-understanding of a substantial segment of the African-American population" (25). Shelby distinguished between what he called strong Black nationalism versus weak Black nationalism, the former based on calls for Black separatism, and the latter focused on a political means to resist oppression. Shelby also referred to these two positions as classical Black nationalism and pragmatic Black nationalism, and Shelby's own position is of the pragmatic kind. He specifically noted that he saw Du Bois as "a classical nationalist about culture—as an advocate of Black cultural integrity as an end in itself—but as a pragmatic nationalist about politics" (67). Shelby observed that solidarity is based on identification, and this "solidarity requires special concern, in particular a disposition to assist and comfort those with whom one identifies" (68). This does not rule out concern for others outside one's group, but it does point to a partiality toward members of one's own group. In contrast to Du Bois, Shelby argued against cultural nationalism, noting that "black political solidarity should be understood as Black collective action in the interest of racial justice, not on behalf of an ideal of blackness" (151). Like Du Bois, Shelby observed that most Blacks will not make personal sacrifices that do not favor themselves or their children (115). Furthermore, Shelby attempted "to enlist the help of black elites while ensuring that they do not have a disproportionate influence on leadership or the construction of the black agenda" (119). Again, this moved Blacks away from Du Bois's focus on leadership from above and specifically his notion of the Talented Tenth, which held sway for much of the twentieth century.

My work is similar to Shelby's in that we both see Black collective action and racial unity from a pragmatic rather than a classic Black nationalist perspective. Our works differ in that Shelby sought to find a philosophical foundation for Black solidarity, whereas my own work examines the dissolution of that sense of solidarity both in a cultural, and often in a political, sense. I explore the rhetorics of Black unity and Black disunity, noting the ways in which even rhetorics of Black unity provide evidence of disunity. Shelby's work advocated in favor of Black solidarity, as that was his goal. My work, on the other hand, is more agnostic. I seek only to show what I see, revealing the break that exists within the Black population, judging it as neither entirely positive nor negative. I see Black solidarity as a response to white racism and in particular the limiting effects of segregation on the Black imagination and social advancement in the United States. As the civil rights movement opened doors that had previously been closed, new opportunities emerged. One such opportunity was the potential for reexamining the utility of Black unity at a time when more opportunities than ever before existed for Blacks as individuals. As Shelby observed, "Black Americans are a people—an intergenerational community of descent that is tied by the stigma of race—but not a cohesive cultural or national unit" (252). What holds us together is the need to fight racial oppression, and as that aim begins to be achieved, even if only partially, we will see breaks in the line among us. Shelby concluded:

> Pragmatic nationalism is a form of black solidarity that aims, ultimately, to transcend itself. Its objective, indeed its raison d'etre, is to bring about a racially just social order. Once this has been achieved, black political solidarity as such would be no longer necessary, and perhaps even counterproductive. (254)

We are not yet at the point where a racially just social order exists, but we have reached a time when Blacks can become billionaires and even president. This is historically unprecedented, and such changes, both for the Black elite and even among the Black middle class, give us reason to revisit notions of Black solidarity that previously remained unquestioned. While economic, political, and social equality have not been achieved for everyone, they have been achieved for some. Whether those individuals continue to work on behalf of Blacks as a group for pragmatic reasons, especially when doing so may call for personal sacrifice, remains to be seen. Yet historically that has not been the case, as commentators from Du Bois to West have noted. Even Barack Obama, the twenty-first century's most iconic example of a Black man achieving the impossible dream, for the most part pursues race-neutral politics and only speaks about race when the situation requires that he do so. Were Obama a classical Black nationalist, there is no way he could have achieved the presidency. Yet while still seeing himself as Black, Obama is a politician as well, and this may get in the way of the extent to which he will publicly advocate for pragmatic Black nationalism. Instead he puts his faith in the dream of a color-blind future, one in which Americans of all shades and colors can see themselves as Americans first, if not on par with being people of color.

Rhetorics of Black unity rest on the assumption that Blacks are set apart from other Americans in an environment that continues to be hostile toward them. Moreover, the advancement of the group is paramount, as individual Blacks operate from the assumption that the fate of one Black person is linked to that of another. Du Bois's rhetoric of the Talented Tenth linked more educated and privileged Blacks to their less fortunate brethren, charging the Talented Tenth with the mandate to uplift the entire race. Yet as the limitations that segregation placed on this group lessened, so too, I argue, does their need to see racial uplift as tied to group advancement, in particular that of the underclass. It becomes apparent that the fortunes and fates of the Talented Tenth are no longer linked to those of poorer Blacks to the extent that they were in the past. Division among members of the Talented Tenth comes to the fore, as some continue to advocate for Black unity, while others begin to explore identifications based less on race and more on class. As I have stated before, class divisions have always existed among Blacks, and even during the civil rights movement, the group was never truly unified. Nevertheless there was a generally accepted consensus on both the need for unity and the appearance of unity—a rhetoric of unity in the face of discrimination and oppression. With the demise of legalized segregation, changes in the social, political, and economic position of some Blacks create an opportunity for changes in the rhetoric of Black unity. I believe that one site where we can see these changes is in the works of Black public intellectuals, and it is these works that I investigate in this study. Blacks no longer feel the need to pretend to be unified, and the emergence of rhetorics of Black disunity signal a change both in the position of Blacks vis-à-vis one another and in their understanding of what racial uplift means in the post–civil rights era. Whereas racial uplift is traditionally identified with raising up the most disadvantaged, my work suggests that it now connotes a celebration and focus on individual advancement as the Black underclass is left behind, not only by white Americans but also by many Black Americans as well.

THE STRUCTURE OF THE BOOK

In chapter 1, "Race, Class, and Fear in Twenty-First-Century America," I critique Ta-Nehisi Coates's book *Between the World and Me*. Coates writes for two audiences, one Black and the other white. In his work, Coates provides his white readers with more than a glimpse of what the lives of Blacks (or more specifically, as I will argue, poor Blacks) are like in America. I argue that Coates's work reveals not only the gap that separates Blacks from whites, according to the author, but also the distance that separates Blacks from each other. While Coates's aim is to address the subject of race and what it means to still be a problem in twenty-first-century America, his work also reveals issues of class that exist among Blacks and the ways in which this creates separate communities that may go unseen or unacknowledged even among Blacks themselves.

In chapter 2, "Slaves to the Community: Blacks and the Rhetoric of Selling Out," I critique Randall Kennedy's book *Sellout*. In the post–civil rights era, Blacks can achieve a great deal as individuals. However, the tension between the aspirations of the individual and the demands of the racial group create internal pressures (Touré 2011) that bring forth a divided self that mirrors the one Du Bois wrote about at the beginning of the twentieth century. This is the result of a color line, drawn by white citizens in the past, but now solidified and reified by Blacks in the present (Dickerson 2004). As I will argue, the rhetoric of "selling out" functions as a mechanism of social control meant to keep Blacks on "their side" of the color line. It does so at the very moment it becomes possible for Blacks to cross the threshold and become part of the American mainstream.

In chapter 3, "Black Man's Burden: The Rhetoric of Racial Uplift," I critique Bill Cosby and Alvin Poussaint's work *Come On, People*. While the reputation of one of the authors is now destroyed, that of the other remains intact. When their coauthored book was published, it garnered a great deal of attention, and the message it delivered was well received by many Blacks. The idea that poor Blacks should pull themselves up by their bootstraps is not new. Yet when examined in light of Du Bois's idea of the Talented Tenth, this self-help rhetoric now functions to provide absolution to the Talented Tenth for their failure to fulfill their historical mandate to lift up the masses of poor Blacks. Cosby and Poussaint are well-educated Blacks, the very individuals that Du Bois singled out to provide leadership of the race. As I will argue, the authors embrace their role as "fathers" to the race and seek to guide their wayward children onto the path of enlightenment. Moreover, while urging poor Blacks to look after their children better, Cosby and Poussaint rhetorically position the Black underclass in the role of children and themselves in the role of parents. The Black underclass is seen as possessing the ability to move away from their status as "victims," but lacking both the knowledge and the willpower that would make this move possible. Cosby and Poussaint attempt to provide poor Blacks with a dose of self-help/bootstraps rhetoric, yet this self-help remedy comes with a side of castigation for the "sins" that some Black people have committed. I argue that their rhetoric does work, but not on the audience they suggest. It is the Black middle class that most benefits from the soothing balm that Cosby and Poussaint provide. It is the shame of their failure to fulfill Du Bois's mandate that is washed away as the authors provide them with reason enough to wash their hands of the Black poor.

In chapter 4, "Identification, Division, and the Rhetoric of Black Disunity," I critique Eugene Robinson's work *Disintegration*. Robinson argues that Blacks no longer comprise one cohesive racial group in America but rather four distinct groups: Mainstream, Transcendent, Emergent, and the Abandoned. The rise of a rhetoric of Black disunity seeks to replace the rhetoric of Black unity that held sway throughout slavery and segregation. I argue that this rhetoric of Black disunity can best be understood through the lens of identification and division. Identification among Blacks is no longer based on race, as class and position in society are now seen as more important factors. Class and position were always present among Blacks, but they were previously never put forward as a reason for division among Blacks. The rhetoric of Black disunity is in fact a marker for the success of integration. Yet I note that it also indicates a profound change among Blacks in regard to notions of racial solidarity and advancement in America. The individual, rather than the group, is now deemed most important, and the individual is no longer defined by his or her location within the group.

In chapter 5, "Divided Loyalty: Race, Class, and Place in the Affirmative Action Debate," I critique Sheryll Cashin's *Place, Not Race*. Cashin's book provides more than a different way to look at affirmative action policy in the United States. I argue that a closer reading of the text in light of Du Bois's notion of the Talented Tenth provides us with a new understanding of the conflict that now exists between the Talented Tenth and members of the Black lower class. While Du Bois posited that the role of the Talented Tenth was to provide leadership and lift up the masses of Blacks, I find that Cashin's text provides evidence that the Talented Tenth may work alongside whites to keep poor Blacks in their place at the bottom of the social hierarchy.

In chapter 6, "Blacks and the Rhetoric of Individualism," I critique Touré's work *Who's Afraid of Post-Blackness?* In the post–civil rights era, some Blacks wish to live free of restrictions that attempt to tell them not only who to be but also how to be. Touré is one such individual, and his book examines the lives of many others who, rather than trying to redefine what it means to be Black in a singular sense, wish to explore the plurality of ways in which individuals can enact their own notions of blackness. I argue, however, that the post-Black identity Touré advocates for is more likely to be embraced by the Mainstream and Transcendent groups rather than the Abandoned, who continue to occupy a place at the bottom of America's social hierarchy, even among other Blacks. As I will show, problems with the post-Black identity exist. Still, some may see this as a trade-off they are willing to accept, especially if they see class as a more important marker than race. Nevertheless, the post-Black identity is problematic for Blacks, both as a group and as individuals.

In the conclusion, I summarize the rhetorics of Black unity and disunity discussed throughout the book. I then discuss how both types of rhetoric ultimately point to the divided state of Blacks in the post–civil rights era. If for Du Bois in the twentieth century, the color line that separated whites from Blacks was the focus of his discourse, then for Blacks in the twenty-first century, issues of class that separate one Black from another are now a subject of concern. Over the course of a century, the subject of Black discourse has changed, as disunity is both acknowledged and, for some, seen as potentially desirable. Integration is both a sign of success in terms of the civil rights movement and also the catalyst for disunity among Blacks in the post–civil rights era.

RETHINKING RACIAL UPLIFT

CHAPTER 1

Race, Class, and Fear in Twenty-First-Century America

Du Bois (1969) wrote, "To the real question, how does it feel to be a problem? I answer seldom a word" (44). In *Between the World and Me*, Coates attempts to answer this question for readers, and one senses that his book addresses two audiences: one Black and the other white. Although Coates addresses the book to his son, its primary audience is not just the author's son but other Blacks as well. Yet the secondary audience is white America (D. Williams 2016; Smith 2016; Dahl 2017; Carney 2017), as the author knows that white people will likely make up part of the readership. According to Carney (2017), "White readers are offered the opportunity to eavesdrop on an essential conversation" (450), as Coates, like Baldwin before him, positions himself between "Black and white communities in similar ways" (448). Some, such as Lewis (2016), saw this as problematic, in that "Coates is among the few that have the stage at the present moment" (195). Coates's "opinion is seen as the *only* opinion because black folk do not control the message or the mechanisms by which it is delivered" (196). One could argue that some whites, especially liberals, have a fascination with Blacks and tales of what it means to exist in a world where, as Du Bois (1969) wrote, "one ever feels his twoness,—an American, a Negro; two souls, two thoughts, two unreconciled strivings; two warring ideals in one dark body, whose dogged strength alone keeps it from being torn asunder" (45). Dana Williams (2016) noted that "like Baldwin, Coates has been celebrated among white liberals in spite of and because of his willingness to speak candidly about race" (182). Coates provides his white readers with more than a glimpse of what the lives of Blacks (or more specifically, as I will argue, poor Blacks) are like in America. As Williams (2016) wrote, "Importantly, Coates makes no claims of speaking on behalf of the race" (182). I argue that Coates's *Between the World and Me* reveals not only the gap that separates Blacks from whites, according to the author, but also the distance that separates Blacks from each other.

First, this approach differs from the work of other rhetoricians such as Mack and Alexander (2019), who used Coates's work to "analyze the rhetoric of memoir and also to carve out for memoir a more central place in rhetorical studies than it has yet occupied" (51). Similarly, Guerrero (2017) stated, "Black critical memoir in the 21st century narrates and navigates the struggle for racial salvation and what the possibility of deliverance means in this post-racial world" (415). Second, my approach differs from that of Dahl (2017), who saw the work as "an avowed and explicit exploration of black masculinity" that warrants "attention to its gendered and sexual particularity" (321). In focusing on Coates's work as "a deep theoretical reflection on the moral and political problem of 'black disembodiment' as a condition of unfreedom" (320), Dahl's reading and focus differ from my own. While I argue that Coates aims to address the subject of race and what it means to still be a problem in twenty-first-century America, his work also reveals issues of class that exist among Blacks and the ways in which this creates separate communities that may go unseen or acknowledged, even among Blacks themselves. Smith (2016) briefly noted "the book's resistance to class-consciousness" (184), adding that "the neonationalism that is central to his project is certainly a response to perceived crises of the post–civil rights–era black community and solidarity that were addressed quite differently by the prominent crop of black academics that emerged in the 1990s" (185). Coates's work "is in the first instance, meant for a black readership" and "is meant to be understood as a soulful specimen of intergenerational black family discourse" (186). As pertains to my project, Smith suggested that Coates is "invested in the (re)animation of black corporate identity in America" (186) in response "to a neoliberal era witnessing intensified fracturing of black community along class and generational fault lines" (186). Moreover, Smith posited that "Coates establishes a conceptual field that allows him to address those experiential gaps that splinter the coherence of an imagined black community while asserting distance from his middle-class white audience" (186).

It is this imagined black community that is the subject of my critique, and the ways in which Coates's work attempts to divide Blacks from whites while rhetorically identifying all Blacks with each other. To do so, Coates ignores the class division among Blacks that I suggest his work speaks to, as class is rarely the focus of other readings of his work. Montoya, Matias, and McBride (2017), while still focused primarily on race rather than class in their discussion, observed that "Coates provides, albeit unstated, educators with a pedagogical tool to better understand urban students and the racialized lives they are forced to live by" (57). Perhaps few focus on the class dimensions of Coates's work in part due to the author's own focus on the division between Blacks and whites rather than among Blacks themselves.

In Coates's world, the Black body is one that is continually subject to violence, both from police and from parents. It is a world of fear, one where police are the enforcers of white oppression toward brutalized Black bodies, often without cause. It is a world where Black parents enact violence on their children to supposedly protect them from the violence they will later feel at the hands of police should they even appear to have committed any infraction. It is a world where brutalized children commit acts of violence against each other on street corners for simply looking at each other the wrong way, wearing the wrong colors, or nothing more than being in the wrong place at the wrong time. It is a world with its own logic and its own rules, a world that Blacks did not create but are forced to live in nonetheless. As LaMothe (2018) wrote in examining the emergence of a melancholic self in Coates's work and others, "Sadly, in the case of an African American child the public world is filled with daily humiliations and dangers, though a child's awareness of this is at first, limited" (663). Yet what is not mentioned is that the world Coates describes is one perhaps rooted just as much in class as it is in race.

Not all Blacks are repeatedly subject to police violence. Not all Blacks beat their kids out of fear of such violence. Not all Blacks engage in violence on street corners. No, this is the world of what Eugene Robinson (2010) termed the Abandoned, and it is the world of one specific group among the four that Robinson argued exist in Black communities in America. As Robinson observed, "These four black Americas are increasingly distinct, separated by demography, geography, and psychology" (5).

The problem with Coates's work is that both the author and his readers may take the world he depicts to represent that of all Blacks. I believe that readers would have good reason to do so, since Coates has a distinct viewpoint, having lived among the Abandoned. Despite having achieved what he calls "the velocity of escape" (Coates 2015, 21), he nevertheless relates his experience as a member of the Abandoned as if it is representative of the Black world in its entirety. I believe he does so because he either does not see distinctions among Blacks or does not ultimately believe that such distinctions are relevant. As Smith (2016) observed of Coates's text, "One of its chief nationalist goals is to eliminate perceived distances between black people. . . . No matter location, no matter social circumstance, black bodies are essentially united in mortal vulnerability" (187). Put simply, "Coates's project . . . tends to homogenize black time and space, thereby muting discourses of intraracial difference" (188).

First, for Coates, Blacks are one people. Second, all Blacks live in fear. This becomes apparent early on in his text. Yet the failure to discuss and acknowledge the specificity of his discussion of life among the Abandoned causes him to present a narrow picture of what it means to be Black in America today. In this he differs from Cruse (1967), who wrote, "I do not claim to represent the thinking of all the people in America who are called Negroes, for Negroes are certainly divided into classes—a fact white liberals and radicals often overlook when they speak of 'the Negro'" (4). If Cruse could acknowledge differences in the late sixties, then we should not be surprised that individuals such as hooks and Robinson continued to notice them as well. As Hochschild (1995) observed:

> Polarization is also occurring in the likelihood of being a victim of crime. . . . The pattern holds for both Blacks and whites, although the former are always more likely to be victims of violence than the latter. Poor Blacks not only began the period with the highest rates of victimization from violence, but they are also suffering from the greatest increase. (50)

In focusing on violence against Black bodies, Coates conflates the lives of the Abandoned with that of the Mainstream, Emergent, and Transcendent groups among Blacks that Eugene Robinson discussed. Yet as hooks (2000) reminded us, "Class matters. Race and gender can be used as screens to deflect attention away from the harsh realities class politics exposes" (7).

While Coates could have zoomed in on the issue of class and the disparities it creates in regard to being the subjects of violence, he did not choose to do so. Given that he sees Blacks as a unified group, he discusses violence as if it is something that all Blacks are equally subject to, thus failing to make any distinctions among them on the basis of class. While Henry Louis Gates Jr. did have a confrontation with the police in front of his own home, the resolution to that problem was much different from the ways in which police deal with members of the Black underclass. Gates may have been arrested, but poor Blacks are killed. The issue is not that Coates discusses violence against Blacks but rather that what many of the victims he lists have in common is that they are poor Blacks or were mistaken for being poor. White people treat poor whites differently, and one can expect that they treat poor Blacks differently as well. Yet in failing to make the necessary distinctions among Blacks, Coates creates a world where Blacks as a group are set apart from whites. He creates a world where Blacks as a group are the victimized, and whites as a group are the victimizers. This is not to say that institutional oppression and racism do not exist or that they have had no effect on Black lives. As Feagin (2000), Massey and Denton (1993), and Conley (1999), among others, have noted, the effects of institutional racism and oppression are evident. Rather, the experiences of oppression differ, and the effects on Blacks' lives differ, and these differences matter and should be acknowledged.

The myth of a homogeneous and unified Black community is as damaging to Blacks as the idea that whites constitute a homogeneous and unified group. If this myth were true, then there would have been no white people involved in abolition, the founding of the NAACP, or the civil rights movement. Whites are no more united in upholding racism than Blacks are in confronting it. Where Coates errs is to assume that the effects of racism are the same for all Blacks regardless of class.

AN AMERICAN NIGHTMARE

One way in which Coates's failure to distinguish among Blacks makes a difference is in his discussion of fear. Coates (2015) speaks of the "confrontation with the brutality of my country . . . the sheer terror of disembodiment" (12). Whites, he asserts, are allowed to live the dream. "The Dream smells like peppermint but tastes like strawberry shortcake" (11). It is life in the suburbs, free from violence, never having to wonder if, or assert that, white lives matter. Blacks, however, cannot live this dream, "because the Dream rests on our backs, the bedding made from our bodies" (11). Yet while in general much of America was built on the backs of Blacks, and even their bodies were ground to dust, one must admit that life for many Blacks in the post–civil rights era has changed, and they too can live the American dream. As hooks (2000) noted, "That sense of solidarity was altered by a class-based civil rights struggle whose ultimate goal was to acquire more freedom for those Black folks who already had a degree of class privilege, however relative. By the late 1960s class-based racial integration disrupted the racial solidarity that often held blacks together despite class difference" (91).

Early in his life, Coates was denied the ability to live the dream not because of race but rather because of class. Racism still exists, and many Black people may not receive parity in earnings or get what they deserve in regard to promotions, and so on, despite their efforts. Still, class can serve to lessen the sting of racism, and class can modify and change the ways in which racism is experienced. Black nationalism and the like obscure these differences and in so doing create as false a picture as the one Coates paints of white life. Surely he now knows that not all whites live in suburbs or experience the privileges of being white in the same way. Many whites would likely argue that they do not feel privileged at all, and economically that is true for many of them.

Nevertheless, Coates sees whites as privileged to the extent that they do not have to live in fear. He writes, "Somewhere out there beyond the firmament, past the asteroid belt, there were other worlds where children did not have to regularly fear for their bodies" (20). Coates writes of the fear he regularly experienced growing up in Baltimore and the way he "obsessed over the distance between that other sector of space and my own" (22). In Coates's world, he had to survive the streets and the other Black bodies that inhabited them. Other young Black men looked like him yet would do him harm; both parties engaged in "a lifestyle of near-death experience" (22). Yet it is whites whom Coates blames for creating the world that he and others are forced to inhabit, doing their best to survive and protect their bodies from violation while simultaneously violating the bodies of others through physical violence. As he observes, "My understanding of the universe was physical, and its moral arc bent towards chaos and concluded in a box" (28). He notes earlier, "I had no sense that any just God was on my side" (22). In stating this, he puts himself in opposition to the thoughts of Dr. Martin Luther King Jr. As a reverend, King believed in justice and a just God. As both a minister and a social movement leader, he sought to help his fellow humans be more just with one another. Yet the world that Coates inhabits is a physical one, lacking in morality; only the code of the streets exists for him, and the wider world he sees as being created and maintained by whites has no place for him.

The schools are a place for which he has even more contempt than the streets. The streets at least seem to have their own logic that he understands. Yet the schools pretend to educate but for the most part send Black youths back to the streets, where they will be subject to violence and eventual imprisonment. The only escape is death at the hands of other Blacks or, in some cases, the police. The streets inflict violence on the Black body while the schools do violence to the mind. Coates was taught subjects he believed he would never use and about places he believed he would never visit. He states, "I was a curious boy, but the schools were not concerned with curiosity. They were concerned with compliance" (26). The schools were not seen "as a place of higher learning but as a means of escape from death and penal warehousing" (26). They were a short-term holding pen, a way station on the road to prison. The schools he attended were unfit, and he saw himself as unfit for the type of education they offered.

One example of this is his discussion of the philosophy of nonviolence that Blacks were taught during Black History Month. Each year he saw videos of civil rights marchers being beaten while marching for rights that whites could take for granted as God-given. Blacks sacrificed their bodies and at times their lives to a God who they hoped would one day offer deliverance and change the hearts of evil men. Yet Coates cannot see himself in this philosophy. He believes in no God, and this lesson of nonviolence conflicts thoroughly with what he has learned from the streets, as well as about the wider world that his country dominates, all of which speak a "primary language—violence" (30). He states that those civil rights martyrs held up as heroes in the school system "struck me as ridiculous and contrary to everything I knew" (3). Instead Coates turned to the lessons he could absorb from books and the lives of his grandfather and father. Rather than Dr. Martin Luther King Jr., Coates found a hero in Malcolm X, who spoke a truth about material existence that squared better with the world that Coates knew.

The preference for Malcolm X is understandable, given that he came from the streets and experienced prison life. Malcolm X rose from what Eugene Robinson called the Abandoned, or what others call the Black underclass. King, however, was a member of the Mainstream that Robinson describes, and one might even argue that he became a member of the Transcendent class, despite attaining neither a political position nor wealth during his lifetime. King believed, as the Bible states, that we should love our enemies, yet Malcolm called an enemy an enemy and argued that there was nothing wrong with self-defense. Self-defense is a basic human right, and people only seemed to have a problem with the idea when it was applied to or by Blacks. Coates, like Malcolm, judges people by their actions and notes that "'good intention' is a hall pass through history, a sleeping pill that ensures the Dream" (33). By this he means that whites exonerate themselves of the world they have created and blame Blacks for the difficulties they have in overcoming it. Coates sees whites as people who look the other way and at the end of the day "will do all they can to preserve the Dream" (33). Yet members of the Abandoned see the nightmare that Malcolm X described. They cannot pretend that the world is something other than it is and must instead keep it real, because realness is all they have. There are no illusions in the streets, and the violence of both the block and the nation "was not magical, but was of a piece and by design" (34). Coates's task is to continually ask questions to better understand both himself and the world around him.

Yet in asking these questions and searching for answers, Coates lands on Black nationalism and essentialism. He reveres Malcolm X and the Black Panthers, and his discussion of the mecca of Howard University is filled with nostalgia and mythology. He writes, "The Mecca is a machine, crafted to capture and concentrate the dark energy of all African peoples and inject it into the student body" (40). Again, we see that Coates views Blacks as one people. Moreover, they are imbued with some kind of force that sets them apart from whites. There is an essentialism to Coates's viewpoint, in that he believes that Blacks should make no effort to look like whites, because the physical differences of Blacks are important to him. To straighten one's hair or do anything that might be perceived as an attempt to look white or assimilate would likely be a betrayal for Coates. According to Greeson (1982), people may see membership in a racial group as subject to betrayal. Appiah and Gutmann (1996) distinguished between race consciousness and color consciousness, the former being based on essentialism, and the latter being based on history and superficial distinctions between groups. Coates's rhetoric reveals him to be an essentialist who believes that natural differences exist between racial groups. Moreover, he believes that these differences ought to be preserved, stating, "We are all our beautiful black bodies and so we must never prostrate ourselves before barbarians, must never submit our original self, our one of one, to defiling and plunder" (36). To do anything perceived as such would likely subject a person to the label of sellout that Kennedy (2008) discussed in his work. For Coates (2015), "'The black race' was a thing I supposed existed from time immemorial, a thing that was real and mattered" (45).

Early on, Coates admits that differences exist among Blacks in terms of nationality, but he still sees them as one racial group. In discussing what he saw at the yard at Howard University, he writes, "All of them were hot and incredible, exotic even, though we hailed from the same tribe" (42). He begins to see Black as something more than the opposite of white, but nevertheless subject to whites. He observes, "The power of domination and exclusion is central to the belief in being white, and without it 'white people' would cease to exist for want of reasons" (42). Coates seeks evidence of a time when Blacks too had power, and he finds it both in books and in the personhood of Malcolm X. Over time, however, his professors cause him to question his understanding of blackness and his unified theory of oneness. His own readings reveal not "a coherent tradition marching lockstep but instead factions, and factions within factions" (47).

This shows one of the first instances in which Coates must come to terms with the fact that distinctions exist among the many people identified as Black. He learns that these distinctions exist not just in history but in the present as well. In Prince George's County, he learns of a Black enclave that mirrors the televised images of whiteness he was exposed to as a child. Yet he also learns that in Prince George's County there "were black people who elected their own politicians, but these politicians, I learned, superintended a police force as vicious as any in America" (53). Coates's understanding of blackness is shattered, and he has to come to terms with the importance of class and the reality that, as Eugene Robinson (2010) discussed, there are various groups of Blacks distinct from one another and potentially at odds. As Hyra's 2006 study of intraracial class conflict among Blacks in New York and Chicago revealed, class carries more weight than culture in the eyes of middle-class Blacks. Many middle-class Blacks "feel ambivalent toward or disdainful of low-income residents" (81). The longtime but poorer residents of these neighborhoods may "perceive individuals promoting redevelopment as 'sellouts', 'race traitors', and 'Uncle Toms'" (85). In the case of Prince George's County, the poor are simply kept out of the area from the beginning, and the police function as a barrier between well-off and poor Blacks, keeping the poor separate because they are seen as unequal.

Coates (2015) learns in the classroom that what he seeks, he will not find. He writes, "My history professors thought nothing of telling me that my search for myth was doomed, that the stories I wanted to tell myself could not be matched to truths" (53). Eventually he lets go of his race-conscious stance and his belief in essentialism and instead comes to be color conscious, recognizing that blackness is a social construct of historical rather than biological significance. He accepts that "there was nothing holy or particular in my skin; I was black because of history and heritage . . . and there was no inherent meaning in black blood" (55). He admits, "My great error was not that I had accepted someone else's dream but that I had accepted the fact of dreams, the need for escape, and the invention of racecraft" (56). Until this point, rather than working against racist notions that whites perpetuated, he was instead working in concert with them. To believe in essentialism, to be race conscious, was not the opposite of racism but just another variant of it from the other side of the color line. As McPhail (1994) noted, for the most part, researchers, like those they observe, often fall prey to a politics of complicity in which they reify the very structures of racism they seek to tear down. Through an essentialist discourse, scholars can "fail to consider the extent to which these phenomena [race and racism] are negotiated through participatory social interaction" (344). McPhail (1998) critiqued the rhetoric of both Eurocentricity and Afrocentricity to illustrate the ways in which the latter is complicit in the former. Rather than challenge the underlying epistemological assumptions of Eurocentricity, McPhail argued that "Afrocentricity reifies the same exclusionary tendencies it condemns in Eurocentricity" (124). McPhail aimed to show the ways in which the two can be seen to engage in "a dynamic interplay of complementaries rather than a conflict of essentially competitive worldviews" (115). It is this discovery that Coates began to make early in his life as his teachers challenged him and he continued to question what he was reading on his own.

Coates, then, is left not with an understanding of the world in black and white but rather with a more nuanced understanding of blackness. He begins to see that "perhaps too the Irish had once lost their bodies. . . . Perhaps being named 'black' was just someone's name for being at the bottom, a human turned to object, object turned to pariah" (55). In this he echoes Goffman (1974), who observed that "there are the tribal stigma[s] of race, nation, and religion, these being stigma[s] that can be transmitted through lineages and equally contaminate all members of a family" (4). Yet for Coates, to identify blackness with "being at the bottom" shows that he still viewed the world more from the perspective of the Abandoned. Someone whom Eugene Robinson (2010) would identify as a member of the Transcendent or even the Mainstream would likely have a different point of view. Gates (1997) wrote, "Of course, the paradox is that the cultural centrality of the African-American—this is a country where Michael Jordan and Shaquille O'Neal look down from every billboard—coexists with the economic and political marginality of the African-American, most especially of the African-American male" (xv). As Touré (2011) stated, "To experience the full possibilities of Blackness, you must break free of the strictures sometimes placed on Blackness from outside the African-American culture and also from within it" (4). It is doubtful that Blacks living in Prince George's County saw themselves as being at the bottom, even while acknowledging the social stigma of race and the attempt of white Americans to keep Blacks at the bottom throughout much of our nation's history. Yet again there is a glimpse of this understanding in Coates (2015) when he writes, "But perhaps too I had the capacity to plunder, maybe I would take another human's body to confirm myself in a community" (60). Still, he returns to the perspective of the Abandoned once again in stating, "On the outside black people controlled nothing, least of all the fate of their bodies" (62). Only when he observed Blacks dancing in a nightclub did they appear "to be in total control of every step, every nod, every pivot" (62). The instances where Coates sees Blacks as in control appear primarily when they are on street corners or dance floors. This is the perspective of someone raised in the underclass, whose gaze was at least initially lowered, perhaps as it was meant to be in a country that for centuries subjugated Blacks. Yet as Griffin and Calafell's (2011) critique of the NBA revealed, "While complicit, black athletes are packaged, disciplined, and dehumanized under the gaze of whiteness as objects for voyeuristic consumption" (129). Thus Black subjugation can take place before our very eyes even while we believe ourselves to be witnessing evidence of the physical power and economic elevation of some Blacks.

The subjugation of Blacks is not simply a matter of history but a state that continues into the present, as Coates reveals in his work. He had earlier spoken of Prince George's County, an enclave for wealthy Blacks that nevertheless has a repressive police force that was no friend to nonresidents who were poor and Black. Coates relates the story of how his friend from college Prince Jones died at the hands of an officer from Prince George's County. He was killed for having committed no crime but simply being Black not far from his own family home in Virginia. There is irony in the story of a man Coates sees as a Black prince, named Prince, killed by an officer of the law from Prince George's County. There is greater irony in the fact that Prince Jones was the child of a Black doctor, killed by an officer of the law who was hired to protect privileged Blacks from their poorer brethren. Prince Jones was mistaken for just an ordinary Black, and the story of his death reveals how death can find any Black person in a country where police hired by wealthy Blacks can kill their own children as well. The police make no distinctions between poor and wealthy Blacks, between the law-abiding and the criminal, between those who believe in a just god and those who do not. In the post–civil rights era, wealthy Blacks have assimilated into mainstream society to the extent that they too can participate in the oppression of poor Blacks or anyone mistaken for one. Race matters, but so does class when it provides some with the same twisted privilege of oppression that whites have enjoyed for centuries.

No matter how many slave auctions over the centuries, no Black body can ever approach the same worth as that of a white one. The very fact that a Black body was up for auction nullifies this possibility from the start. Black bodies and the persons who reside in them have always been seen as less than whites and disposable no matter how hard they work, how high their aspirations, or how honorable their family lineages. As Cose (1993) revealed, "Despite its very evident prosperity, much of America's Black middle class is in excruciating pain. And that distress—although most of the country does not see it—illuminates a serious American problem" (1). Coates (2015) himself relates that he too had been stopped by an officer of Prince George's County for no reason and left to wonder if he would become yet another statistic. As he observes, "At that point in American history, no police department fired its guns more than that of Prince George's County. . . . The police chief was rewarded with a raise" (76). Coates sees the police as nothing more than an extension of American society itself, and in particular white America. As he states, "The truth is that the police reflect America in all of its will and fear, and whatever we might make of this country's criminal justice policy, it cannot be said that this was imposed by a repressive minority" (78–79). Moshin and Jackson (2011), in their critique of the Oscar-winning film *Crash*, observed that it "excuses individual White racist acts and performances" (215) and "forgives Ryan his racism, and we forgive him his sexual assault on Christine" (228), and ultimately "Ryan, who is responsible for some of the most virulent racism in the film, walks away a hero" (228). Asante (2005) opined that "it is the society itself that dictates the way the filmmaker will respond to the artistic and entertainment environment" (34). America on the whole is still racist, and what one sees in Coates's depiction of the Black enclave of Prince George's County is that wealthy Blacks can be racist as well as classist, using the police to do their bidding in the same way that wealthy whites do.

Although the discussion of police killing Blacks provides commentary on law enforcement and American society as a whole, it also sheds light on the divisions that separate some groups of Blacks from others. Both the Transcendent class that Eugene Robinson speaks of and the Mainstream class are separate from the Abandoned. In this separation, one finds that both the life chances of these groups and their perspective on life differ as well. Coates depicts life from the perspective of the Abandoned, and thus he focuses on the extent to which Blacks can lose their bodies to violence. Yet this loss is much more likely to occur for members of the Abandoned than for other groups of Blacks. Coates (2015) writes that "all are not equally robbed of their bodies, that the bodies of women are set aside for pillage in ways I could never truly know" (65). Yet this same statement could be made in reference to different classes or groups among Blacks. The Transcendent and the Mainstream cannot truly know the fear that Coates describes living as a member of the Abandoned. They will never dwell on what it means to merely survive, because they have the opportunity and the means to thrive. They can "claim the whole world, as it is" (68), which for Coates was only a desire he had for his newborn son. Coates believes, like Bell (1993), that Blacks live at the bottom of America's racial hierarchy.

Yet what neither Coates nor Bell focuses much on are the differences that separate one Black person from another. Few members of the Transcendent or the Mainstream would agree with the idea that they live at the bottom of American society. While they might acknowledge that Americans do still have a racial hierarchy, they can nevertheless attest to the fact that, as individuals, their education and income allow them to rise above it. Even the terms by which they are identified speak to this status. The Transcendent have transcended race, and the Mainstream have blended into mainstream white society to such an extent that little separates them from many of their white neighbors save wealth, as Conley (1999) pointed out, and the color of their skin, which neither they nor their politically correct neighbors will remark on except to say that it doesn't matter or they don't see color. Yet in the world that Coates (2015) bequeaths to his son, he must advise him, "You have to make your peace with the chaos, but you cannot lie. You cannot forget how much they took from us" (71). Coates cannot forget that "we were enslaved in this country longer than we have been free" (70), and even now, Black bodies are still not entirely free, nor are those who possess them free to the extent that whites are free to live without fear, and nothing Blacks do can "save them from the mark of plunder and the gravity of our particular world" (81).

If even someone like Prince Jones could die at the hands of police, then no Black is safe. Coates's story reveals to readers that while an individual Black may be exceptional, there is no such thing as an exceptional Black for whom the rules of race and racism might not apply on some unfortunate evening. As Abramowitsch (2017) observed, Coates "pushes against both the notion that in the present post–civil rights world other identities or forms of privilege might supersede blackness or that blackness offers a common human experience all readers might identify with" (463). As Coates (2015) speaks of his son, he says, "You are all we have, and you come to us endangered" (82). Black lives are ever more endangered in a world where the simple assertion that Black lives matter is met with scorn and charges of reverse racism. As Greeson (2004) explained, "We must understand that white pain, a form of mourning, has given way to a series of 'determined actions' that I call recovery strategies. These actions have achieved a certain consolation for whites, but at the expense of those who sense that some injustice has been perpetrated on them" (118). The lack of concern for Black pain and Black lives greatly affects the Abandoned, who Coates (2015) observes must "fear not just the criminals among them but the police" (82), whether they are white or Black, as was the officer who killed Prince Jones.

BLACK-ON-BLACK CRIME

Crimes against Blacks, according to Coates, are talked about as if they are as natural as earthquakes, natural phenomena that cannot be stopped yet have immense destructive force. In discussing television news, Asante (2005) noted that "we become participants, experiencing the deaths of the dead or mutilated Africans in confrontations with police. In some strange way we are victimized again by the crimes against the civil rights movement when we see the brutality measured out to Africans on the streets of our cities" (54–55). Yet what makes the crime against Prince Jones particularly important is not just its personal importance for Coates but also that it was perpetrated by Blacks. The officer, the politicians, and the community of Prince George's County are Black. What they seek is protection from other Blacks who are not of the same social class or group as they are. Coates, given his upbringing as a member of the Abandoned, is an outsider; but Prince Jones, as the son of a doctor, should have been an insider. Still, in the end, a Black cop could not or did not see anything more than a Black man whose body could be taken and disposed of like any other. As Coates (2015) learned later, "The black citizens of PG County were comfortable and had 'a certain impatience' with crime" (84). One might say that they and the officer had the same level of comfort and impatience as white citizens and enjoyed the same privileges. The primary privilege and duty of white Americans, from Coates's perspective, is the destruction of the Black body, for their entire world, he believes, is based on it. As Coates states, "In America, it is traditional to destroy the black body—it is heritage" (103). Yet whites do not have to see or acknowledge this fact for what it is, while poor Blacks in particular are still subjected to the brutal reality of it.

For much of Coates's life, he found it difficult to see beyond the confines of Baltimore. Even when he moved to New York City, he still found himself in Flatbush, a neighborhood quite similar to the one he had left. He still lived in fear of those around him, and when he traveled to other parts of the city, he was as much of a tourist there as any visitor, yet feeling more uncomfortable and less carefree. As he observes, "The lack of safety cannot help but constrain your sense of the galaxy" (85). Coates realizes that like himself, his son may walk and talk in ways that belie his status at the bottom of America's racial hierarchy. He cannot help but look at little white boys and little white girls and think of how "the galaxy belonged to them" (89). They live in a world without fear as masters of the universe, while Blacks "need to be always on guard" (90). Yet once again Coates generalizes to all Blacks, when in fact his statement is more specific to the fears of the Black underclass. The well-off Blacks of Prince George's County pay police to stand guard for them so that they can live and walk in their neighborhoods without fear—without fear that other Blacks, the wrong kind of Blacks, will mistake their neighborhood for one they too can feel safe in. Members of the Mainstream and Transcendent classes are the kinds of Blacks who "spent semesters abroad," and as Coates admits, "I never knew what they did or why" (86). What we see here is evidence of the distance that separates Coates from two worlds: the world of whites, and the world of Blacks who are now privileged enough to participate in it as something akin to members in a global fraternity.

Coates, however, can feel little but disdain for this larger white world. He admits that he could not mourn when the Twin Towers were struck, because no one mourned for Prince Jones and because Blacks feel terror every day and no one seems to care. "Looking out upon the ruins of America, my heart was cold. I had disasters all my own" (86). If 9/11 was a tragic event that brought many Americans together, then it also exposed the divisions that lay between members of the Abandoned like Coates and everyone else. How could one be expected to mourn an assault on a nation that one sees as assaulting one's body and soul on a daily basis? Coates can feel no sense of belonging because he has never been allowed to feel that he *does* belong. He writes, "Hell upon those who tell us to be twice as good and shoot us no matter" (86). "Black, white or whatever, they were menaces of nature . . . which could—with no justification—shatter my body" (87). For Coates, "Perhaps the defining feature of being drafted into the Black race was the inescapable robbery of time because the moments we spent readying the mask, or readying ourselves to accept half as much, could not be recovered" (91). Blacks and whites don't just live in separate neighborhoods; from Coates's perspective, they live in separate worlds.

Yet Coates observes that he has at times forgotten the place he occupied in American society. As a member of the Abandoned, he could never feel completely safe or assimilated into the mainstream. He recounts a trip to the mall when a white woman pushed his child, the words he said to her, and the white man who took her side, and the words this man spoke to him when Coates pushed him. The white man reminded Coates that he could simply call the police, and Coates would be arrested or worse. Coates was reminded of his place at the bottom of the social hierarchy and reminded that he was endangering his son because he had forgotten both that he was no longer in Baltimore and that he was a Black man subject to the violence of white society—violence that must always be justified by citing the error of the Black person in question, because "people who believe themselves to be white are obsessed with the politics of personal exoneration" (97). As Greeson (1995) noted, "An ironic twist has occurred in race relations and related areas involving historically oppressed collectivities: the oppressor is now the oppressed, and the victim is now the villain" (163). White innocence and Black guilt are the recurring theme of America's past and present as told by whites. Coates (2015) seeks to speak his truth because white America seeks to deceive not only itself but Blacks as well. Americans, he writes, "try to enlist you in your own robbery and disguise their burning and looting as Christian charity. But robbery is what this is, what it always was" (101). Members of the Abandoned, as Coates once was, never received their forty acres and a mule, no reparations, no affirmative action, and no white-collar jobs or white picket fences to go along with their mortgages.

White America, Coates observes, has stolen both Black Americans' wealth and their bodies, because for much of American history, wealth was measured in Black bodies. American society, Coates argues, is based on breaking "the black body, the black family, the black community, the black nation. The bodies were pulverized into stock and marked with insurance." Moreover, "The right to break bodies was the mark of civilization . . . the meaning of their sacred equality" (104). Blacks have always been at the bottom of American society because American society is built on the bodies of Blacks, both dead and alive. While Blacks in general suffer from racism, no Blacks in America would experience the crushing weight of it more than the Abandoned, or what some call the Black underclass. Yet "for their innocence, they nullify your anger, your fear. . . . It is truly horrible to understand yourself as the essential below of your country" (106). While Coates speaks of all Blacks in this statement, it speaks more to the understanding of the Abandoned than to that of the Mainstream or the Transcendent. Terms such as "Mainstream" and "Transcendent" speak to different groups among Blacks that no longer understand themselves as being at the bottom of American society. The Mainstream have reached the middle, and the Transcendent soar above it all.

BLACK, SEPARATE, AND UNEQUAL

One of the ways we can draw a distinction between the Abandoned, whose perspective Coates represents, and that of the Mainstream and the Transcendent is in their relationship to what he refers to as "the Dream." While Coates spends much of his time discussing how this dream constitutes daily life for whites in suburban enclaves and his own distance from it, that is not necessarily the case for all Blacks. First, there is the relationship of Blacks to America's history of slavery and segregation. Second, one must consider the extent to which Blacks are able or willing to participate in this dream themselves.

In regard to America's history of slavery and segregation, one must address the question of whether or not all Blacks still feel the sense of twoness, of separation from the rest of American society, that Du Bois spoke of. For members of the Abandoned, that is still the case, as they are separate both geographically from mainstream society and psychologically in that they have reason to feel estranged. The police do not protect them but rather subject them to violence. The schools are not meant to educate them but rather serve as temporary holding pens on the way to prisons that are meant to house them. As Tuck (2010) observed, "The problem of race in the twenty-first century remain[s] the embedded gap between Black (and Latino) Americans and white Americans on virtually every socioeconomic indicator, from incarceration and unemployment rates to home ownership and educational achievements" (419). This, however, is less the case for members of the Mainstream and the Transcendent than it is for the Abandoned. The Mainstream and Transcendent groups have, for the most part, integrated into the society at large and enjoy many of its benefits. Still, one must admit that racism exists and that better-off Blacks do not share equally with whites in our democratic system and capitalist society. Nevertheless, members of the Mainstream and the Transcendent are likely to strive to continue to move the country past the issue of race in the hopes that one day it will be of little relevance. This, for them, would mean success and the culmination of the civil rights movement's continuing struggle.

Yet members of the Abandoned are disenfranchised and dispossessed still today. They cannot move past race because they are reminded daily of the impact of race on their daily lives. They are, as Coates reminds us, at the bottom of the racial hierarchy in America and as such are more likely to see themselves as a group, whether it be for race-conscious or color-conscious reasons. In Coates's own writing, we see him move from being race conscious to color conscious as he realizes that what separates Blacks from others is "not anything intrinsic to us but the actual injury done by people intent on naming us" (120). Still, Coates's status as a member of the Abandoned makes it impossible for him to ever embrace the dream of white America or even to long for it. He sees the dream as a lie, and exposing this lie to himself and to others becomes the goal of his life. Although he understands the falsity of race biologically, he cannot look past the reality of race and racism as "a legacy of plunder, a network of laws and traditions, a heritage" (110) that leads to the death and destruction of Black bodies. While disembodiment "pushed the black middle-class survivors into aggressive passivity" (114), Coates can never be truly comfortable in this world, even when his economic situation begins to change. He is not fully part of the middle class that West (1993b) described as "more deficient and, to put it strongly, more decadent" (36) than ever before. Coates knows and feels too much what life is like as one of the Abandoned, and it is only when he leaves the country on a trip to France that he can for the first time feel what it is like not to bear the weight of oppression.

BLACK AMERICAN IN PARIS

Coates finds it difficult to participate in the dream in the way members of the Mainstream and Transcendent are able to. As he said earlier, he did not participate in study abroad and had no idea what other Blacks did when they went abroad. Race and place were still intertwined for him as a member of the Abandoned and remained so for much of his life. Only in middle age did he first travel abroad to France, and it was there for the first time in his life that he felt some sense of freedom. He writes that "for the first time I was an alien, I was a sailor—landless and disconnected. . . . I had never felt myself so far outside of someone else's dream" (Coates 2015, 124). "How much I would have loved to have a past apart from the fear" (125).

What Coates experienced is not a sense of being American in terms of inclusion in the mainstream while abroad, but rather a sense of what white Americans and some Blacks may experience both in America and abroad. Coates, however, was "marked by old codes which shielded me in one world and then chained me in the next" (125). One could take a member of the Abandoned out of the hood, but it is difficult to take the memories of the hood out of the Abandoned. Coates writes to his son that he was "ashamed of my fear, of the generational chains I tried to clasp on your wrists" (125), for Coates finds it difficult to truly feel free, haunted by the ghosts of his past, expecting to find the specters of Baltimore around the next corner in Paris. He observes, "We will always be black, you and I, even if it means different things in different places" (127).

This feeling, I argue, is more a function of Coates's membership in the Abandoned than it is solely of race. Not all Blacks may feel the weight of race at all times and all places. Having lived abroad as a military dependent, I can say that I never felt more American than when I lived in Japan. This statement too reveals its own issues in regard to America and the treatment of Blacks, but at the same time it reveals the possibility of feeling included in a way that eludes Coates. When Coates alludes to the prison-industrial complex, he remarks that "our bodies have refinanced the Dream of being white. Black life is cheap, but in America black bodies are a natural resource of incomparable value" (132). Once again this is a statement with greater relevance for the Abandoned than for the Mainstream or the Transcendent. It is the bodies of the Abandoned that are most likely to be deemed expendable, as possessing their greatest value not in their software but in their hardware.

SHATTERED DREAMS, BROKEN PROMISES

When Coates visits Prince Jones's mother and talks with her about his death, the contrasts between the Abandoned and the Mainstream become more evident. While Coates seeks to use her upward mobility to highlight the contrast between Blacks and whites, what one also sees in the discussion is the difference between her life as a doctor and that of other lower-class Blacks. She lives a life of privilege, given her profession and income, and she raised her children in privilege as well. Her children's lives resembled that of their white classmates, and the death of her son at the hands of a police officer is a tragedy that was unfathomable until it occurred. This separates members of the Mainstream from members of the Abandoned, who must face the prospects of death at the hands of the police or criminals as a fact of life. The tragedy in Prince Jones's death is that it was not supposed to happen to one so privileged, to one who never knew the dangers of a low-income neighborhood.

The gap between Prince Jones and others shows in his mother's plans for him to attend Harvard or Yale, or the like, not Howard. Her aspirations for him may have soared as high as the Transcendent class, at least educationally. His choice to attend Howard was perhaps an act of rebellion against these aspirations and an attempt to embrace an idea of blackness that he had not known living in a world that was predominantly white. Until college, he had attended an elite magnet school and was the only Black child in his class. Coates admits to Prince's mother that he had not really known her son well and wants to understand more about him. In seeking to understand Prince Jones, Coates is coming to understand more about the life of privilege of someone born into the Black Mainstream. Yet while Coates would use Prince Jones's death as a marker for the fragility of Black life in general, the story of Prince Jones shows that his death was exceptional, not par for the course for someone from the Mainstream. It was in death that he suffered the same fate as someone from the Abandoned, but in life he lived far above them.

Coates de-emphasizes this difference because he believes that all Blacks are in the same boat, "surrounded by the majoritarian bandits of America" (146), who can plunder Blacks bodies and lives at will. As Guerrero (2017) wrote about Coates's work, "This uniqueness in the certainty of black death in America comes from the way in which it is not unexpected as death generally is in society's imagination of it; in the black imagination black people prepare for death like battle" (422). Yet this is not the perspective that Prince Jones's mother has of her country. She saw America as a place where upward mobility is possible and a place in which the officer who killed her son would be punished for his crime. Hers is a mentality that more closely resembles that of the white majority than that of the Black underclass, because she has more in common with the former than the latter. Coates stretches to create connections that do not exist between the Mainstream and the Abandoned. That he did not really know Prince Jones well may signify Coates's lack of knowledge of the Mainstream and the gap that exists between the Abandoned and this group. Even when the Abandoned attend college with the Mainstream on a campus filled with Blacks, a distance remains between the two, despite the superficial markers of sameness.

What distinguishes the Mainstream from the Abandoned is the extent to which the Mainstream have integrated into American society and found some measure of acceptance. Coates's perspective on America is more akin to that of the Abandoned, and he sees the interests of whites and Blacks as separate. Whites, in Coates's (2015) eyes, have plundered the lives of others and continue to plunder the planet as a whole. The separation between Blacks and whites is something he passes on to his son in stating, "You must live—and there is so much to live for, not just in someone else's country" (146–47). It is here that Coates views America as not belonging to him, not belonging to Blacks. Yet one could argue that this perspective encapsulates the standpoint of the Abandoned more than that of the Mainstream. Mainstream Blacks have integrated into the middle class, and while they may not enjoy equal pay or treatment in all cases, they nevertheless would take issue with someone stating that they were something other than American. I note that Colin Powell, a member of the Transcendent class of Blacks, titled his autobiography *My American Journey.* Yet one need not reach transcendent status to see oneself as an American. As Coates wrote of Prince Jones's mother, "She spoke like an American, with the same expectations of fairness, even fairness belated and begrudged" (144). Yet Coates finds his own solace in opposition, stating, "This power, this black power, originates in a view of the American galaxy taken from a dark and essential planet. . . . They made us into a race. We made ourselves into a people" (149). Coates sees something special in blackness, stating, "And black power births a kind of understanding that illuminates all the galaxies in their truest colors" (149). As Stewart (1997) stated of Stokely Carmichael's use of the term "Black Power" in 1966, "The civil rights movement would never be the same in tone, demands, tactics, and relationships" (434). To be Black, Coates believes, is not to be lesser but to be something more. Yet this is just an inversion of white notions of superiority, now put forth with a Black hue. Coates sees Blacks and whites not as together but instead as engaged in a struggle that Blacks are losing. He writes, "I do not believe that we can stop them[,] Samori, because they must ultimately stop themselves. And still I urge you to struggle" (Coates 2015, 151). This notion of Black life as continual struggle in opposition to the misdeeds of whites is but another side of the coin of fear that Coates states is always a part of him. Simply driving by the ghetto brings up the old feelings of powerlessness for him and illustrates that although he may have become a member of the Mainstream, he nevertheless is not to the manor born. His perspective is that of the Abandoned, and it appears that no amount of money or success changes that for him. Yet that perspective, I argue, is a particular one that is not shared among all Blacks.

CONCLUSION

While Coates aims to illustrate the distance that separates Blacks from whites in twenty-first-century America, I argue that his work also reveals the separation that exists among Blacks as well. Specifically, Coates's work depicts the life and times of a member of what Eugene Robinson called the Abandoned far more accurately than it represents Black life in general. Coates's work, as Smith (2016) wrote, "represents a nostalgic longing for black communal solidarity" (191). This is America as seen from the bottom, and it is informed by class as much as by race. The fear that Coates attributes to all Blacks is in fact more synonymous with life among the Abandoned than that of Mainstream Blacks who have integrated into society.

Early on in his work, Coates depicts fear as emanating from three places. The first source of fear is the police, who act as enforcers of white America's desire to keep Blacks in their place. The second source of fear is Black parents, who are violent toward their children in an effort to preempt future violence that they might suffer at the hands of the police. The third source of fear is Black youths, who terrorize each other for as little as being in the wrong place at the wrong time or looking at someone in the wrong way. Yet, as Coates's own work reveals, these sources of fear are more an issue for the Abandoned than they are for members of the Mainstream. The fear Coates feels is rooted in class far more than it is in race. The children most likely to suffer violence at the hands of the police are the children of the Abandoned. It is the Abandoned who therefore preemptively strike at their own children to ward off any infraction that might later subject their children to violence at the hands of the police. Last, it is the children of the Abandoned who live in a world of violence both at home and in their neighborhoods. They live in fear of those who protect and serve others at their expense, and they engage in violence toward each other given that this is much of what they have experienced in life. Yet while Coates accurately depicts life among the Abandoned, I argue that he conflates the lives of the Abandoned with that of the Mainstream, Emergent, and Transcendent groups among Blacks that Eugene Robinson (2010) discussed.

When discussing his experience with the educational system, Coates sees the school system as inflicting violence on his mind. Yet this feeling, I believe, is based on class difference far more than it is rooted in race. In stating that compliance, rather than curiosity, was the focus of the schools he attended, Coates reveals more about the type of schools he attended as a member of the Abandoned than he does about the type of education all Blacks receive. Coates's disdain for being taught the philosophy of nonviolence and his preference for Malcolm X over Dr. Martin Luther King Jr. reveal a class distinction as much as a desire to engage in self-defense. Malcolm X was a member of the Abandoned and saw an American nightmare, whereas Dr. Martin Luther King Jr. was a member of the Mainstream and sought to participate in the dream that Coates disparages. King championed integration, whereas Malcolm X spoke of the separation that existed between the Abandoned and the rest of American society. Yet in the post–civil rights era, we see evidence of the success of the civil rights movement's push for integration, though this success has not come without its costs.

As Mainstream Blacks integrate into American society, they also separate themselves from members of the Abandoned. As Wilson (1997) argued, deindustrialization, coupled with the flight of middle-class Blacks from urban areas, contributed to a rise in poverty and the culture many associate with it. No longer forced to live side by side with the poor because of residential segregation, Mainstream Blacks integrate with white communities and in some cases create communities of their own. Coates (2015) focuses on one such community, Prince George's County, that has "a police force as vicious as any in America" (53). Yet one is left to wonder who the recipients of this vicious behavior are. The answer, it appears, would be other Blacks, and poor Blacks in particular. It is in Prince George's County that Mainstream Blacks can seek separation from members of the Abandoned, and the Black-on-Black violence that takes place via the police force is evidence of class conflict among Blacks. It is in Prince George's County that Coates's friend, the son of a doctor, lost his life because he was mistaken for just an ordinary Black, a member of the Abandoned rather than the Mainstream. It is in the use of the police as an instrument of violence toward other Blacks that one sees the extent to which the Mainstream has come to identify with white America. If, as Coates writes, "in America, it is traditional to destroy the black body—it is heritage" (103), then one now sees evidence of the extent to which the Mainstream too participates in this heritage. The well-off Blacks of Prince George's County pay police to protect them from other Blacks, the wrong kind of Blacks, the Abandoned. Coates sees the dream as a lie because it doesn't reflect his lived experience. Because he is a member of the Abandoned, race and place are for him still intertwined, but as he learns when talking to Prince Jones's mother about her son's death, that is not the case for all Blacks.

The death of Prince Jones at the hands of a police officer was unfathomable until after it occurred, because not all Blacks feel the weight of race at all times and places. As a doctor, Prince Jones's mother had dreams of Harvard and Yale for her son. She saw the possibility of him rising ever higher, perhaps to become a member of the Transcendent class of Blacks. She believed in the dream and, even after her son's death, believed that those responsible would be punished for their actions. This mind-set resembles that of the white majority far more than that of a member of the Abandoned. Ideas like liberty, justice, fairness, equality, and opportunity have far more meaning for Mainstream Blacks than they do for the Abandoned. Coates sought in his work to illuminate what separates Blacks from whites, but if one looks closer, his work shows that not all Blacks live in darkness. The darker cousin that Langston Hughes spoke of no longer eats in the kitchen when company comes but instead has a kitchen of his own. Moreover, it is just as likely that for members of the Mainstream, company may be white as well as Black, because associations are based as much on class as they are on race in the post–civil rights era. The Abandoned, however, still reside far outside the confines of the warmth and safety that other Blacks enjoy inside houses they were once not allowed to buy. It is this separation between the world of the Abandoned and that of Mainstream Blacks that Coates's work reveals, even if that was not its intended aim.

CHAPTER 2

Slaves to the Community:
Blacks and the Rhetoric of Selling Out

At the beginning of the twentieth century W. E. B. Du Bois wrote of the difficulties of being Black in America. The sentiments he expressed still reverberate and find resonance in the hearts and minds of Blacks living in the twenty-first century. Although we have witnessed the election and inauguration of the nation's first Black president, issues of race and racism still exist. In the words of Du Bois (1969), "One ever feels his twoness,—an American, a Negro; two souls, two thoughts, two unreconciled strivings; two warring ideals in one dark body, whose dogged strength alone keeps it from being torn asunder" (45). The pressure exerted on Blacks as they attempt to reconcile race and nationality is often thought to be due to external factors such as discrimination from whites. When Du Bois wrote of double consciousness, segregation was the accepted norm in the United States and would continue to be so for six decades. It was then that Dr. Martin Luther King Jr. challenged the nation in his "I Have a Dream" speech to make real the promise of life, liberty, and the pursuit of happiness for all of the nation's citizens, regardless of color.

In 2008 many hoped that the election of Barack Obama would allow the nation to move past issues of race and racism. Yet while President Obama may have transcended race in the eyes of some, race is nevertheless a factor in everyday life for many Black Americans. The difference now is that the external pressures of discrimination play less of a role than they did in 1903 or in 1963. Conditions among Blacks in America diverge significantly along economic lines as some move forward while others are left behind (Dawson 2001; Gates and West 1996; hooks 2000; E. Robinson 2010). If the election of the nation's first Black president has shown us anything, it is that Blacks can achieve a great deal as individuals (E. Robinson 2010, 140). However, the tension between the aspirations of the individual and the demands of the racial group create internal pressures (Touré 2011) that bring forth a divided self that mirrors the one Du Bois wrote about at the beginning of the twentieth century. This is the result of a color line, drawn by white citizens in the past, but now solidified and reified by Blacks in the present (Dickerson 2004). As I will argue, the rhetoric of "selling out" functions as a mechanism of social control meant to keep Blacks on "their side" of the color line.

This rhetoric works on the basis of a few assumptions. First is the notion that Blacks are a group defined by race. Whether race is defined as biological or a sociological construct is less important than that those adhering to the concept see it as something "real." As Stubblefield (1995) wrote, "We are born into society with labels already affixed from the moment of conception" (352). Second is the notion that membership in the racial group is something that one can betray (Greeson 1982). Membership in the racial group has its obligations, and each member is expected to fulfill them (Goffman 1974, 38). Those who fail to live their lives in a way befitting a "Black" person are singled out for having defied the social norms of the group. Third, application of the label "sellout" is the primary means by which individuals who violate group norms are stigmatized. Stigmatization functions to eliminate threats to group cohesion by rhetorically excommunicating "heretics." Excommunication denies agency to those labeled "sellouts" and, just as important, denies agency to other members of the racial group, who learn from these negative examples that silence and conformity, rather than freedom of expression and individuality, are to be expected.

In the twenty-first century, the struggle is less one between Blacks and whites than between one Black and another. Gates and West (1996), in their discussion of the status of Blacks as a racial group, observed: "Economists have shown that fully one-third of the members of African-American communities are worse off economically today than they were the day that King was killed. If it is the best of times for the Black middle class—the heirs of Du Bois's 'Talented Tenth'—it is the worst of times for an equally large segment of our community" (xii). The Talented Tenth, the authors admit, "were able to integrate historically white educational and professional institutions" (xi). While some Blacks move ahead, others remain behind, and the tensions that this disparity generates, and the significance it holds, have not gone unnoticed. According to West, the gap between better-off Blacks and less fortunate members of the race will only continue to widen in the future with detrimental outcomes for cooperation among Blacks (109–10). As Hochschild (1995) observed, the pace at which lower-class Blacks are falling behind is greater than that of their white counterparts (48).

All of this creates what Burke ([1950] 1969) would call "an invitation to rhetoric" (25). On one hand, Blacks are asked to identify with each other as members of a racial group. In the past, this identification was strengthened as a result of slavery, segregation, and other forms of discrimination (R. Robinson 2000). However, in the absence of the totalizing segregation that existed before the civil rights movement, and the increased mobility of some Blacks in previously all-white neighborhoods, institutions of higher learning, boardrooms, and political chambers, division, rather than identification, becomes increasingly noticeable both to and among Blacks. As a result, one hears calls for greater group cohesion at a time when opportunities for individuals to break away from the group abound. According to Burke, "Identification is affirmed with earnestness precisely because there is division. Identification is compensatory to division. If men were not apart from one another, there would be no need for the rhetorician to proclaim their unity" (22).

Realizing the difficulty of holding Blacks together as a racial group, some rhetors have found it useful to target individuals judged guilty of breaking away from the collective in thought, word, or deed. This targeting does not generally result in physical harm, but the psychological and sociological impact of these rhetorical volleys should not be overlooked. Individuals judged to be guilty of "selling out" are shamed, ostracized, and possibly made to feel guilty over their supposed betrayal. Those refusing to toe the line, or fall back in line, face the possibility of excommunication from the group.

The result of this is that no Black in America is free. A web of rhetoric entraps them all. Blacks may have been freed from the physical chains of slavery, but the rhetorical chains of community bind them to each other. It is not that community is undesirable but that within a community the freedom of the individual should still remain paramount. Yet in the Black community, this is not the case. The community takes precedence over the individual. For this reason, Blacks are caught in a bind. They live in the land of the free, knowing that they are slaves to each other.

RHETORIC AND GROUP IDENTITY

Both the formation and the maintenance of group identity have their roots in rhetoric. Defining, naming, or labeling the group exerts such a powerful force in creating identification that it can also be a source of division. The question of what the descendants of former slaves, as well as those who enjoyed freedom much earlier, should be called is a source of controversy. As Martin (1991) suggested, "Naming—proposing, imposing and accepting names—can be a political exercise" (83). He noted that leaders in the Black Power movement sought to stress the primacy of the group over the individual in a society where individuals were discriminated against because of group affiliation. If in America race mattered more than character, then race counted for more than character in the political arena. Rather than see themselves as Negroes, those of African ancestry were asked to identify as Blacks. As Martin observed, "Until the late 1960s, black was an insult for many Negroes . . . and the term posed a test for conformity for both Negroes and whites" (90). The purpose of mandating a new name was "to strengthen group loyalty by renewing a sense of differences from and grievances toward outsiders" (91).

This goal was largely achieved, as "Black" replaced "Negro" as the appropriate label to the extent that even members of the Black middle class embraced it. Embracing this label allowed for downward identification with poor Blacks and division from the white middle class: "Middle-class Negroes were required to adopt cultural values of lower-class urban blacks as marks of racial loyalty" (93). Alienation from the white mainstream has occurred to such an extent that "blacks with college experience are more likely than others to perceive widespread discrimination and blame whites for blacks' circumstances" (100). This sense of division from the mainstream is evidenced in the attempt to exchange "Black" for "African American," a term in which "African" is still seen as more important than "American" in a way that it is not for other ethnic groups. As Martin wrote, this was "in part . . . a reassertion of the primacy of black moral claims on American society" (86).

Yet labeling can function just as powerfully internally as externally. Stubblefield (1995) noted that "by identifying a person as a 'member' of a racial group, we semantically trick ourselves into believing that the group itself is a pre-existing entity" (345). This trick allows individuals to engage in essentialist notions of race that run counter to nonessentialist conceptions that argue for the irrelevance of any differences that may exist between groups. Once individuals identify both themselves and others as a member of a racial group, they may believe that this connection creates mutually binding obligations between members.

According to Stubblefield, the problem with identification on the basis of race, or "labeling," is that it "is harmful to the person being labeled," as he is viewed as "a representative of the category in which I have placed him, rather than as a complete, unique person" (345). Given that individuals are viewed as representatives of a category, it is likely that the limitations and obligations this categorization places on individuals are stressful for both the individual and the group to which he or she is said to belong. The act of labeling says more about the person doing the labeling than it does about the person who is being labeled, "indicating something about her perceptions and values" (348).

Furthermore, "The act of labeling creates a barrier between mutually satisfactory interaction between people" (350). Last, "Label-specific social norms, which dictate behaviors that conform to the social meanings of the related label, place excessive demands on people to whom that label is applied" (350). Labels constrain communication, curtail behavior, and function as a means of socialization (350).

Given the power of labels to help us socially construct reality, it is no wonder that individuals find their lives circumscribed by them. To label an individual as Black, for example, is to subject that individual to whatever that label implies without his or her consent. The label creates an assumption that individuals who share skin color also share other characteristics and must abide by the same social norms and obligations. When these individuals attempt to live life outside the confines of the label, they may find themselves branded as "sellouts" or traitors to the group, especially if their behaviors defy group norms and expectations. Yet these group norms and expectations do not exist outside the minds of the individuals who create them. These group norms and expectations are no more real than the essentialist notions of race on which they are based. Still, they can serve as a means to rhetorically sanction individuals who defy these norms.

Russell (1997) discussed the ways in which Black attorneys may find themselves bound by the demands that race places on them. Even the selection of what area of law to practice has implications for whether or not an individual is deemed to be fulfilling his or her obligations to the race. The choice to practice corporate law, for example, could be seen by some to be a denial of one's obligation to the group rather than simply the choice of an individual to practice his or her profession in the most personally fulfilling manner. Russell argued that Black attorneys face difficulties that do not exist for whites engaged in the legal practice. Black attorneys must deal with either being labeled as "sellouts" or being accused of "playing the race card," "whenever issues of race are even potentially relevant in a particular case" (3). Blacks must either claim that race is irrelevant and therefore be labeled "sellouts" or make race salient for individuals who often choose to deny its importance, and face charges of "playing the race card." Yet, as Russell noted, race is always an issue when the attorney or judge is Black, as Blacks are deemed by whites to be less impartial than whites on the issue of race. In the legal profession, "the presumption is that 'minority' group loyalties will taint professional ethics in a way that 'majority' affiliations will not" (5). Obligations among minorities are believed to exist in ways that they do not for members of the majority group. Members of the white majority believe that Blacks are in fact subject to group loyalties and that such loyalties override not only individuality but also professional obligations. If

Black attorneys adhere to these group loyalties, then they are not loyal to their profession. If Black attorneys attempt to uphold professional obligations and appear to be color-blind, then they will be accused of selling out their race.

McDermott (2001) examined the relationship between class status among Blacks and the degree to which they adhered to integrationist or separatist beliefs. She noted that most research tends to examine the Black middle class as a monolithic entity; however, she argued that differences exist within this group, depending on the nature of the work that individuals do. A majority of the Black middle class works in the public sector, and those with "expert credentials" are more likely not only to work in the public sector but also to live among members of the white majority rather than in primarily Black neighborhoods (11–12). As might be expected, they are more likely to embrace an integrationist ethos rather than the separatist belief system that appeals more to the Black proletariat. Those in expert supervisory or worker positions do not embrace separatist beliefs but are not as strongly opposed to it as individuals in expert manager positions (14). Much of the Black middle class lives and works among the white majority; however, they do so in positions that are less secure, and they have not accumulated wealth comparable to that of their white counterparts. As such, they must deal with the stress of trying to maintain their class status while potentially struggling with the stress of maintaining a coherent racial identity. As McDermott concluded, "Social structural position can exercise an influence upon attitudes, particularly those relating to issues of identity" (17).

The attempt to bridge the gap between one's class status and one's racial identity may prove successful for some Blacks. Class status and the benefits that accrue from it can be seen as a means to not only sustain one's identity as Black but also fulfill a perceived obligation to support and maintain Black culture. Banks (2010) sought to understand "how middle class blacks articulate racial unity through the patronage of black visual art" (272). In keeping with Du Bois's call for the Talented Tenth to provide leadership of the race, some middle-class Blacks see their support of Black art "as a collective project of black cultural advancement" (273). While class status may be seen as something that separates middle-class Blacks from other members of their racial group (Hochschild 1995; Gates and West 1996; hooks 2000), the individuals whom Banks interviewed saw it as a means to affirm their identities as Blacks (Banks 2010). Black patrons saw supporting Black artists and Black institutions as a means to address racial inequality in the art world (276) and a lack of inclusion in "the artistic canon" (278). While Gates and West (1996) saw division among Blacks due to class status (109–10), Banks (2010) observed that "fundamental to the belief that blacks are a cohesive group is the idea that a shared culture unites them. Black visual art is seen as a form of culture that binds blacks together" (280). It is through their actions as consumers of Black art that middle-class Blacks demonstrate their identification with poor Blacks who function as creators of Black culture. Perhaps in response to Cruse's (1967) critique of "the failure of the black bourgeoisie as a class, to play any social role as patron or sponsor of the arts" (454), these individuals answer the call to be supporters of Black culture.

While some members of the Black middle class may see patronage of the arts as a way to support Black artists and to identify with Black culture, a willingness to share culture does not necessarily translate into a willingness to share a neighborhood. Hyra's 2006 study of class conflict among Blacks in New York City and Chicago points to the ways in which class carries more weight than culture in the eyes of middle-class Blacks. More well-off Blacks see the revitalization of poor Black neighborhoods as a form of "'racial uplift' advancing the interests and goals of the entire race" (272) while at the same time engaging in the "displacement of the poor" (78) in the interests of rising property values. According to Hyra, many middle-class Blacks "feel ambivalent toward or disdainful of low-income residents" (81). The longtime but poorer residents of these neighborhoods may "perceive individuals promoting redevelopment as 'sellouts,' 'race traitors,' and 'Uncle Toms'" (85). The Black middle class's attempts to mirror the white middle class and move into the mainstream leave them open to charges of having betrayed their debt to the race. The behavior of the Black middle class is in keeping with that of other Americans. However, unlike the white middle class, well-off Blacks have a more difficult time "sustaining their tenuous class status" (86), and their efforts to do so leave them open to charges that they are selfish individuals who put their own needs ahead of those of the group as a whole.

Lusane (2001) observed that Black members of Congress are not immune to similar charges. Some Black constituents believe their officials "have betrayed the objectives of the grassroots movement in exchange for voting rights and black representation in elected office" (16). Frustration with Black elected officials is understandable, given the difficulties that many in the Black community face, such as high poverty rates, a lack of adequate education, and single-parent households. As Lusane noted in his discussion of the Congressional Black Caucus, "The perceived power of the CBC is greater than its real power" (18). Couple that with ideological tensions among CBC members, gender issues, and the need for some representatives to please powerful party officials at the expense of group cohesion, and the ability of the CBC to influence Black life fails to meet expectations. Furthermore, "Some black candidates have employed the strategy of deracialization that advocates a 'non-racial' or 'race neutral' approach to politics" (22). This approach may work well for individual politicians, but many question whether it serves the Black community well as a whole. As Lusane concluded, "Both unity and struggle will remain constants in the life and times of African American members of Congress" (26). As we shall see, the struggle for unity also remains a constant among Blacks as a group.

THE MAKING AND UNMAKING OF BLACKNESS

Randall Kennedy (2008), in his book *Sellout: The Politics of Racial Betrayal*, begins an examination of the history of the term "sellout" and its use and abuse in the Black community. Yet, from the outset, I cannot help but question both the use of the term and Kennedy's attempt to justify it.

We are told early on that Blacks are afraid of the corrupting power of whites over other Blacks. We are told that Blacks fear whites' ability to "promote black free riders and defectors who sap solidarity and discourage effective strategies for resisting subordination" (3). We are told that "every social group . . . confronts the challenge of exacting loyalty to the collective in the face of self-interest, hardship, or even danger" (3). One can see right away that since Blacks are perpetually at war with "the system," always fighting against "the man," no Black person can ever be free of the tyranny of the collective. As Kennedy provides us with analogies of the IRS pursuing tax evaders and the Department of Justice pursuing traitors, we come to see that being born Black involves taxes one is required to pay to the community, the greatest of which I see as a renunciation of one's own individuality. Yet given that, in Kennedy's eyes, the group always had a claim on any and all Blacks, we are not much more than property. To assert one's humanity, to assert one's right to individuality, is a problem. It appears that being born Black in America makes one a vassal of Black America more than a citizen of the United States of America. In the United States of America, individuality is a prized commodity. In Black America, it is a lesser good and at times is seen as the greatest of evils (McWhorter 2000).

Don't take my word for it; take Kennedy's. No sooner have we learned of the allegiance that Blacks owe to the community than we learn of all the ways that Blacks can become traitors to the race. Being successful "in a multiracial setting" outside of athletics (7); marrying white; pretending to be white; acting, speaking, or thinking white; even claiming to be "multiracial" (Kennedy 2008) all can get a person a one-way ticket to exile island and excommunication from the true religion of blackness.

Does Kennedy see anything wrong with this? He notes a few significant problems but ultimately decides, "If there is going to exist an imagined community known as Black America, there must also exist some point at which a citizen of Black America can rightly be charged with having done something that betrays that polity" (9). The question of who decides when one is guilty of having committed this crime is not specified. What we do know from Kennedy's observation is that these charges are leveled too often and that accusers should be subject to the same penalty as the accused if the charges are baseless. Yet again, one is left to wonder who decides guilt or innocence. Is it some Black elite? Or are the accused simply left to the justice of the masses—a situation in which neighbor can accuse neighbor, and the "community" can decide who is innocent and who is guilty of violating the racial status quo?

The question of who determines the innocence or guilt of individuals accused of selling out is not the only one that is left without a satisfactory answer. In Kennedy's own words, Blacks do not even have a satisfactory answer to the question of who is Black. As Kennedy writes, "The answer is uncertain" (29). Kennedy and other Blacks may not be certain of who is Black, but Kennedy appears to be quite certain of at least two things when it comes to blackness. The first is that being born Black, at least in terms of verifiable skin color, makes one a trusted member of the group until said individual "shows his 'true colors'" (5) by betraying the group in some way. Yet if being born with a given skin color is all it takes to make one Black, then the decision to be Black is one that no person chooses; one simply is Black. If being Black is something beyond one's control, governed by nature, genetics, and even lineage, then there is nothing to choose. Blackness requires no choice because it is seen as deterministic fact, not a sociological construct over which one can exercise some degree of choice in creating one's reality.

However, when it suits Kennedy and others to do so, they make blackness into something that can be taken away. How else can one understand the notion of being labeled a sellout and henceforth subject to excommunication from the race? Simply put, other Blacks are somehow given the choice to kick one Black or another out of a group that he or she had no choice in joining in the first place. Those doing the deciding seem to be telling other Blacks and the world that you are Black by default, but you remain Black only as long as we say you are—whoever this unidentified "we" may be, the elites, the masses, or a combination of both, perhaps. Blackness is predetermined when it is convenient for Blacks as a group. It is a choice when it becomes necessary for the group to revoke someone's pre-issued race card. Blacks as a group apparently have the power to override what is written on one's birth certificate.

Earlier, I noted that being born Black makes one a member of the race, according to the consensus. As Kennedy writes, "When conflict arises between looks and lineage, it is the former that usually emerges as the more influential of the two" (20). However, in the case of individuals with mixed ancestry, choice appears to be part of the equation. Despite the one-drop rule that continues to hold sway over American society (Cose 1997, 4), people like Tiger Woods and Barack Obama can exercise choice in whether or not they want to identify themselves as Black. Leaving out the supposed controversy over whether Obama qualifies as an African American or is an American of direct African descent (meaning one whose ancestors did not experience slavery in the United States), the fact remains that Obama can be physically identified as Black according to prevailing standards. Nevertheless, Kennedy finds it convenient to emphasize that because Obama's mother was white, and he was not raised in a Black community, a choice was involved in Obama's becoming Black. His choice of what church to attend, his choice of what neighborhood to live in, and his choice of spouse (31) appear to affect the degree to which Obama can claim his racial bona fides. Despite being more phenotypically identified as Black, the fact that his mother was white seems to force him to make a choice about what group to belong to racially. Blackness becomes a choice for those of mixed ancestry in a way that it is not for those of a supposedly more homogeneous extraction. (I say supposedly, since few Blacks in this country can claim to be free of any European or other ancestry.) This choice is made evident in the decisions that a person makes in regard to social life.

According to Kennedy, these same choices, when made by those who are "born Black," are enough to result in the revocation of one's race card if said choices are not made according to the demands of Black America. As Kennedy notes, "Allegations of selling out are currently triggered by a wide range of actions" (9). Yet if these choices are enough to make one supposedly unfit to remain a member of the race, and one is in fact judged on those choices, then blackness is in fact more of a sociological construct than it is a deterministic fact. To the contrary, if blackness is somehow inherent in individuals from the moment of birth, then it cannot be taken away; not today, not tomorrow, not ever, no matter what one does.

Any individual who believes that he or she has the right to revoke another's race card should afford said person the latitude of deciding whether or not to be Black in the same way that he or she does for those of mixed ancestry. If the Black elite or the Black masses can choose to unmake someone's blackness, then that same individual has the right to claim it or not as he or she forms an identity in society. Blacks as a group cannot have their cake and eat it too. If one is Black from birth, then no one can take away one's membership in the group. If belonging to the group is something that one must choose, then being displeased with the choices a person makes as an individual should not invoke the term "sellout." If one never chose to belong to a group, then one cannot be accused of betraying it.

Still, Kennedy spends a great deal of time on the question of who qualifies as a sellout in both the past and present. One comes to understand that in the early 1800s, Blacks who did not "participate actively" in the freedom struggle merited the term (34). The option to simply "be free" and live one's own life was not acceptable. Du Bois may not yet have written of the Talented Tenth and its debt to Black America, but it is obvious from Kennedy's perspective that free Blacks at the time were in fact bound to the race. Any attempt to exercise one's free will or embrace one's individuality would have merited the term "sellout."

RACE CONSCIOUSNESS AND RACIAL BETRAYAL

As I noted earlier, one of the first terms that we find tied to Kennedy's notion of selling out is the word "fear." Fear underlies Kennedy's, and ostensibly Blacks', understanding as a whole of the term "sellout." Kennedy writes that "blacks fear that whites will favor and corrupt acquiescent Negroes" (3). Fear of white power predominates: fear of whites' ability to bestow privilege on those Blacks who acquiesce to their desires; fear of whites' ability to corrupt Blacks.

Yet one should note that corruption implies some purer state of blackness. It implies the idea that blackness is in fact an essence, part of our fundamental nature. White influence, it seems, poses a threat to this essence, which then must be a somewhat unstable substance. Blacks may not become white, but they may be seen as "Oreos," Black on the outside but white on the inside.

Fear surfaces in another way as well. As Kennedy continues, "African Americans fear that whites will promote black free riders and defectors who sap solidarity and discourage effective strategies for resisting subordination" (3). Free riders are individuals who benefit from the common good, or the commons, without making any contribution to it. Blacks are seen as engaged in a collective struggle against racism, and in Kennedy's rhetoric, it is taken for granted that all Blacks should contribute to that struggle for the benefit of the group. Those who choose not to do so, or who work against the struggle, are deemed "defectors." Any Black who chooses not to engage in the collective struggle would be both a free rider and a defector, given that failure to engage in the struggle would seem to make one less Black. It does so because engaging in the struggle against racism appears to be part of what makes one Black. It is part of one's obligation as a Black. Kennedy implies that being born Black comes with certain responsibilities. As Kennedy states, "A 'sellout' is a person who betrays something to which she is said to owe allegiance" (4). He notes, "'Sellout' is a disparaging term that refers to blacks who knowingly or with gross negligence act against the interests of blacks as a whole" (4). Yet simply refusing to do one's part, being a free rider, to use Kennedy's term, might appear to be enough to merit the term. For Kennedy, a sellout "is (or is thought to be) a member of the family, tribe, nation, or race. The sellout is person who is trusted because of his perceived membership in a given group—trusted until he shows his 'true colors'" (5). What unites Blacks in Kennedy's mind is the idea that they are part of the same racial group.

Kennedy's use of terms such as "family," "tribe," and "nation" is problematic. All Blacks are not part of the same family in terms of lineage. Nor are they part of the same tribe, as many tribes exist in Africa. We are not all of the same nation, as many nations exist in Africa, and those of us born in America hold US citizenship and likely no other. Were we to claim nationality as a unifying factor, it would create identification rather than division with other Americans. The only thing that unites one Black with another, that allows one Black to identify with another and no one else, is the unscientific idea that we are part of the same racial group. Race is the substance that creates identification between one Black person and another. Yet in relying on race as a ground for identification, Kennedy invokes a rhetoric of race consciousness rather than color consciousness.

Appiah and Gutmann (1996) differentiated between race consciousness and color consciousness, noting the significance of each term. "Race consciousness is the kind of consciousness that presumes the existence of separate human races and identifies race with essential natural differences between human beings that are morally relevant" (163). "Color consciousness entails an awareness of the way in which individuals have historically come to be identified by superficial phenotypical differences—such as skin color and facial features—that serve as the bases for invidious discriminations and other injustices associated with race" (163–64).

Kennedy's (2008) rhetoric is race conscious rather than color conscious, as evidenced in his discussion of selling out. He refers to the usefulness of "identifying and stigmatizing a real menace: the black race traitor" (6). For Kennedy, the Black race is separate and distinct from the white race, but the borders of blackness must be policed. This is why individuals such as Obama are troublesome for him. One reason for having one's racial loyalty questioned stems from ancestry. Obama's blackness is questioned due to his having a white mother. A second reason for having one's racial loyalty questioned is being approved of by too many white people. As a politician who does not emphasize race or run as a Black politician, Obama finds broad approval. Yet some question whether this approval stems not only from the way he campaigns but also from his being biracial.

Even when ancestry is not a part of the picture, the issue of class surfaces. What becomes apparent in Kennedy's work is that the problem of selling out is a problem of "blacks who attain success in a multi-racial setting" (7). Success can mean nothing more than attaining middle-class status. Middle-class Blacks who marry outside the race or in any way are seen as identifying too closely with mainstream, or white, America through their behaviors, speech, thought, choice of residence, or profession (9) may be accused of selling out. Although admitting that diversity exists among Blacks, Kennedy nevertheless adheres to the belief that using the term "sellout" is both legitimate and necessary. Rather than challenge the meaningfulness of the term, he argues that it should be applied more carefully.

Kennedy's adherence to race consciousness rather than color consciousness explains why the idea of selling out remains meaningful for him. His discussion of just who is or is not Black illustrates his attempt to grapple with how to determine what amount of blackness is enough to make one Black. Individuals of mixed-race ancestry such as Obama are seen as choosing to be Black in ways that other Blacks do not. Yet Obama's understanding of what makes him Black, I argue, is based on color consciousness rather than race consciousness. While noting Obama's discussion of "his appearance, the response of onlookers to his appearance, and his shared experience of those responses to others also perceived to be 'black'" (12), Kennedy misses the ways in which Obama's understanding of blackness differs from his own. Obama's understanding of race acknowledges the "superficial phenotypical differences" and the "invidious discriminations" that are made because of those differences (Appiah and Gutmann 1996, 163–64). A shared history of discrimination, rather than an essentialized understanding of race, is what makes Obama and others like him identify as Black. Moreover, it is the response of other individuals to his color that makes him Black. Were Obama to have the same parents but appear to be white to those around him, he would be classified as white. Most likely he would also escape discrimination, as individuals who historically chose to pass as white did.

Race, from this point of view, is a categorization that rests in the eye of the beholder. This perspective defies the one-drop rule that Kennedy and others may adhere to. The one-drop rule is based on the notion that blackness is so powerful that even one drop is enough to classify an individual as nonwhite. Yet this understanding of race was meant to support white supremacy and racial purity. Efforts by Blacks today to classify others as Black on the basis of "one drop" are attempts to create racial unity while ironically acknowledging a lack of racial purity. Kennedy (2008) admits that "the one-drop rule is now embraced by some devotees of black unity as a way of reinforcing solidarity and discouraging exit by 'blacks' who might otherwise prefer to reinvent themselves racially" (14). That Kennedy puts "blacks" in quotations shows that even he reluctantly admits the contingent and questioned status of some individuals marked by others as Black. He goes on to note that mulattoes have been classified at various times as separate from Blacks or as Blacks. Even when they have been classified as Black, they have at times "insisted upon distinguishing themselves from 'real' Negroes" (16). Perhaps worse in his eyes, "some people resolutely refuse to identify themselves racially at all, believing the very concept of race to be a mischievous delusion" (24–25).

Yet race is, in fact, an unscientific concept, despite Kennedy's attempt to ridicule the idea that one can simply belong to "the human race" (25). Kennedy's inability to accept the idea of a single human race without racial division stems from his own race consciousness and a rejection of the perspective that stems from color consciousness. Kennedy sees race as real in a way that those who are color conscious do not. It is for this reason that he misreads Obama's reply that he did not choose to be Black. Kennedy states, "Perhaps Obama wanted to convey the message that his connection to blackness is indissoluble, rooted in something beyond his control and thus beyond withdrawal" (31). Yet this misreading of Obama's intent is due to Kennedy's own race consciousness and his own inability to connect with or understand Obama's color consciousness. A color-conscious perspective allows us to see that Obama's blackness can be something that he did not in fact choose, while at the same time not being "indissoluble" or essential. Obama identifies as Black because other individuals see him as Black and act toward him on the basis of this categorization. As Appiah wrote:

> In fact, where my ascriptive identity is one on which almost all my fellow citizens agree, I am likely to have little sense of choice about whether the identity is mine; though I can choose how central my identification with it will be—choose, that is, how much I will organize my life around that identity. (Appiah and Gutmann 1996, 80)

Kennedy's race-conscious perspective, however, embraces the idea of racial citizenship. Individuals are born into a racial group. Yet it is their choice whether or not to remain a member of that group in the social sense. He writes, "In my view, Negroes should be voluntary Negroes, blacks by choice, African Americans with a recognized right to resign from the race" (80). Yet this puts individuals in a position to resign from a racial group they had no choice in joining, but to which they are assumed to belong, and toward which they are expected to show loyalty. Choosing to resign is an option, but that choice will be seen as a form of disloyalty or racial treason. Individuals who do not consciously choose to resign their citizenship in Black America may have it revoked by other Blacks, if they choose "a course of conduct that convincingly demonstrates the absence of even minimal communal allegiance" (80).

Ostracism, Kennedy argues, is good. For example, "ostracism of racists, misogynists, fascists, and purveyors of other hateful ideologies" (82). Yet these examples are misleading in that all the individuals who espouse these ideas focus on superficial differences among people in an effort to make one group appear superior to another. It is a focus on difference that Kennedy shares in common with individuals who espouse these ideologies. Both Kennedy and an individual advocating racism both share a belief in the idea of race. The crucial difference is that the racist attributes a degree of superiority to his or her own group that Kennedy does not argue for. He does, however, seem to embrace the idea that there are different races and that they should be kept separate. Miscegenation is seen as racial treason to both the racist white and the advocate of Black racial unity. According to Kennedy, individuals who fail to promote ostracism of sellouts yet "want to perpetuate black communities, but eschew any internal monitoring of these communities, . . . want a sociological impossibility" (84). In his eyes, "Solidarity always poses a problem of balance between collective unity and individual freedom" (85).

Given this dialectical opposition, Kennedy comes down in favor of collective unity. The freedom of the individual must be suppressed if collective unity is to be maintained. Free speech may be a constitutional right that all Americans share in mainstream society. However, Kennedy believes that it cannot exist in the Black community if the racial group is to maintain cohesion. As he observes, "The identification and stigmatization of taboos, including betrayal, are simply inescapable, albeit dangerous aspects of any collective enterprise" (84). Therefore, all that can be done is to "regulate rather than abolish that rhetoric" (85).

Throughout Kennedy's text, one finds no evidence of a desire to do away with the idea of selling out. He does not attempt to argue against the ostracism of individuals who are deemed to have betrayed or sold out the race in some manner. All one finds is an attempt to justify, via both historical and contemporary examples, the reasons why such ostracism is necessary. Kennedy wants to perfect the aim of those who would ostracize, so that they can hit their targets more accurately.

Yet the question of what makes an individual a sellout or what constitutes selling out is not as easily determined as Kennedy would like it to be. He brings forth what some might see as obvious examples of attempts by Blacks to do harm to the Black community, such as hatred toward the group, and attempts to prevent racial uplift. Still, the real difficulty with the idea of selling out and its use as a rhetorical weapon stems from its relationship to other ideas. The first is the idea of racial patriotism, "that one ought to define one's obligation's or commitments by reference to racial characteristics" (75). The second is the idea of racial loyalty, as "most blacks want to retain for the foreseeable future, if not permanently, a sense of group solidarity and its attendant manifestations in social, cultural, and political life" (76). If one objects to the idea of racial patriotism and therefore does not exhibit racial loyalty, then one can and will be labeled a sellout.

The determination of what constitutes patriotism or loyalty is made by some unnamed individual or group of individuals within the Black community, or seemingly left up to the Black community as a whole. Yet given that no polls or votes are ever taken to determine these issues, it appears to be primarily a matter of whether one's accuser can make the accusation stick. Unlike in American jurisprudence, in which one is innocent until proven guilty, in Kennedy's Black America, individuals accused of selling out are most likely guilty until they can prove themselves to be innocent. This subversion of the burden of proof puts the onus on the accused rather than on those who seek to prosecute them in a court of public opinion. In any other context, it would be both unlawful and unjust, but in Black America, it appears to be no more than business as usual, so much so that Kennedy assures us that the practice has been going on for some time now. If ostracism has happened in the past, then it must surely be necessary in the present. The circular argument is that everything happens for a reason, and the reason that individuals are accused of selling out every once in a while is because it is necessary. It is necessary, in Kennedy's world, to sacrifice the individual for the good of the group. Yet who determines what is in the group's best interests or who has violated those interests is up for grabs.

CONCLUSION

Kennedy's rhetoric and that of others who argue in favor of labeling individuals as sellouts is based on race consciousness rather than color consciousness. The distinction between these two conceptions of race is vital, as it makes a difference in one's understanding of the degree to which choice is involved in prescribing racial identity. As Appiah and Gutmann noted, race consciousness is an essentialist conception, whereas color consciousness recognizes that differences between individuals are superficial. The former sees race as natural and the latter as artificial. If race is real, then it is what we are. However, if race is socially constructed, then it is what we choose or historically were forced to be. To the extent that one can call the current era postracial, it is only because we are becoming more aware of the degree of choice that individuals have in choosing their own racial identity or lack thereof. As individuals today exercise more choice in regard to their own identity, we might proclaim ourselves postracial to the degree that essentialist notions no longer hold sway to the extent they once did. Yet it is this very choice that Kennedy and others find problematic, as it undermines the fictional belief that race is essential and that one is obliged to demonstrate both racial patriotism and racial loyalty. Individuals like Barack Obama and Tiger Woods show the degree to which people of mixed ancestry have choice in contemporary America. In exercising this choice, they reveal the degree to which race is a fiction in which we choose to participate. This makes people even traditionally thought of as Black free to explore their own identities as Blacks or simply as people.

The civil rights movement ultimately led to more freedom for Blacks, both socially and economically. For a long time, to be Black was to be poor, as "the man" was always keeping us down in an era of segregation. Now a Black person can not only dream of becoming wealthy but can actually become wealthier than most white Americans. Yet the rhetoric of selling out does not require that one attain millions or even a billion dollars. It begins as soon as one crosses the threshold into the middle class. This is a sad occurrence, given that Blacks fought for so long to be able to be recognized and rewarded for their abilities in the same manner as other Americans.

The rhetoric of selling out is antithetical to the dreams and aspirations of the civil rights movement—a movement that sought to erase the color line that Du Bois wrote of over a century ago. The rhetoric of selling out moves that line back and marks it in bold at just the moment when all things have begun to seem possible for so many long held in check by racism. Ultimately, in trying to keep Blacks together on "their side of the line," those who support notions of selling out create division rather than identification among Blacks. The more one seeks to prescribe and control Black identity, the fewer people one will find who ultimately claim it. Given that there are so many ways to "sell out," one may find that there is no longer anyone left who wants to "buy in" to the idea of blackness, especially when it appears to run contrary to their opportunities as an American.

It has always been difficult to be both Black and American. Initially, much of that difficulty came from the white side of the color line. In the post–civil rights era, much of the continued difficulty is due as much to Black hindrance as to white hindrance. So-called Black leaders are making it difficult for many of the hardest-working and most educated Blacks to realize the dream. At the very moment it becomes possible for Blacks to cross the threshold and become part of the American mainstream, members of the civil rights clergy are telling the congregation to back away from the door. Yet the only unifying thread that can tie together this vast network of racial, ethnic, and cultural identities is a sense that, above it all, we are all American. One should not have to choose between being Black and being an American. One should also not have to put being Black before being an American. This is the land of the free, so let us as Blacks be brave and allow each other to walk freely without shackles forged in oppression and in response to it. Freedom is an inside job, and we now have the opportunity to rid ourselves of all that confines us to an existence that is less than it should be. Being free doesn't make us white; it makes us free. That's what we really need to remember.

CHAPTER 3

Black Man's Burden:
The Rhetoric of Racial Uplift

Revelations that Bill Cosby drugged and raped numerous women throughout his career render his image and, from a rhetorical standpoint, his ethos irredeemably damaged. How can any statement he made or book he wrote be taken seriously when the credibility and moral authority of its author is in ruin? On April 26, 2018, Cosby was convicted of sexual assault, further marring our image of the man who was once America's most famous fictional dad. We remember the man who gave America a new image of Black masculinity and fatherhood on *The Cosby Show* while now being forced to juxtapose that with the reality of the nightly news and newspaper articles portraying him as a sexual predator for decades.

We can never look at Cosby in the same way, so why should we be bothered to look at his works? Would they not only remind us of our own feeling of having been taken in by him, seduced by his words, and drugged by someone who preyed on our own vulnerabilities and desires? While we could turn away from our pain, I believe there is another way. We can look it straight in the eye and see if we can learn something by examining it.

Humans are complex and flawed creatures, some more than others. Both angels and demons can occupy the same ground in the same person. Cosby has fallen from a great height, but one should still acknowledge that he achieved a level of success in America that at one time did give him standing to advise others on how they too could achieve their dreams. Moreover, while difficult, it may nevertheless prove fruitful to separate the now-tarnished image of the man from the messages he once gave us. To do otherwise is to engage in an ad hominem attack, focused on the man rather than on the message he sought to deliver. I seek to attack not the man but the message itself. I ask the reader not to suspend disbelief, as when reading fiction, but rather to believe that in reality it is still worth our time to examine the words and deeds of flawed men. For example, a critique of Clinton's NAFTA need not begin with a discussion of his relationship with Monica Lewinsky. The policy may stand as good or bad irrespective of the sexual proclivities of our former president. While preachers may have affairs with members of their congregation, and priests engage in pedophilia, we do not throw out our Bibles because the person delivering the scripture is filled with sin. I realize that making such a distinction may be too much to ask of some. However, for those of you willing to believe that even the worst of us might still have attempted to do some good, I ask you to focus for a short time on the message rather than the messenger.

One reason for doing so is that, in this case, the text under examination had two authors, Cosby and Poussaint. The reputation of the first is in tatters, but that of the latter remains intact. If the book under consideration had been written solely by Poussaint, we would not shirk from its message. Both men, I point out, agreed on the message they sought to deliver, and while we may hold one of the messengers in low regard, the message itself remains the same. If we want to dismiss the message, then let us do so after examining it closely. Persuasion consists of three parts: ethos, or the credibility of the speaker; logos, or the argument itself; and pathos, or emotional appeal. While ethos is undeniably important, we can still ask ourselves if the logos, the argument, is still intact, even when the credibility of the speaker is not. I believe that to be possible, and for this reason, an examination of Cosby and Poussaint's rhetoric is still worthwhile. It is with this belief that I begin my analysis of their text, an analysis written years before Cosby's wrongdoing became known and when his reputation was still intact.

Du Bois (1969) wrote that "the Negro race, like all races, is going to be saved by its exceptional men" (842). In 2007 two such exceptional men, William H. Cosby Jr. and Dr. Alvin Poussaint, attempted to fulfill their obligation as members of the heralded "Talented Tenth" with the publication of their book *Come On, People: On the Path from Victims to Victors*. That Cosby is the author of best-selling books such as *Fatherhood* and Poussaint is a noted psychiatrist are relevant credentials in that their aim is to diagnose and treat what ostensibly ails the Black community. Yet it is not the entire Black community that suffers the maladies that Cosby and Poussaint discuss but rather a specific segment of the Black population. It is the Black underclass and the culture of poverty that concern the authors most, although they are careful not to make the issue of class too salient. Nevertheless, class is an issue that separates the well-off authors from the poor Blacks whose behavior they address, as well as the middle-class Blacks who are likely to read the book.

Cosby and Poussaint are well-educated Blacks, the very individuals that Du Bois singled out to provide leadership of the race. As I will argue, they embrace their role as "fathers" to the race and seek to guide their wayward children onto the path of enlightenment. Moreover, while urging poor Blacks to look after their children better, Cosby and Poussaint rhetorically position the Black underclass in the role of children and themselves in the role of parent. The Black underclass is seen as possessing the ability to move away from their status as "victims" but lacking both the knowledge and the willpower that would make this move possible. Cosby and Poussaint attempt to provide poor Blacks with a dose of the self-help/bootstraps rhetoric that becomes more popular among Blacks during times of economic distress and benign neglect on the part of the government. Yet this self-help remedy comes with a side of castigation for the "sins" that some Black people have committed. According to Dyson (2006), Cosby "wrongly locates the source of poor black suffering—and by implication its remedy—in the lives of the poor" (5).

As members of the Talented Tenth, the authors remind Black people of the shame that exists among us but is not caused by all of us. Cosby and Poussaint take up what I will call "the Black man's burden," one that obligates them as members of the Talented Tenth to address the shame that the Black underclass creates for other Blacks. While members of the Talented Tenth may focus on the positive goal of racial uplift with a focus on the Black poor, they are also concerned with the problem that the culture of poverty among the underclass creates for Blacks attempting to find and maintain success in mainstream America. The social status of upper- and middle-class Blacks is continually undermined, despite their own best efforts, by the actions of the Black underclass.

While Blacks may make and understand that class distinctions and divisions exist within the group, they are at the same time aware that white Americans, and others, often fail to make such distinctions. The actions of the Black underclass are seen as bringing shame on all Blacks, whether upper- and middle-class Blacks like it or not. As a result, upper- and middle-class Blacks may see themselves as burdened with both the shame of poor Blacks and the responsibility to change them, if only to protect their own self-interest and self-esteem.

If embracing the Protestant work ethic and living "biblically" makes one moral, then the Black underclass cannot help but be seen by the nation as a group of sinners. Their "lifestyle" is, in a word, "ungodly," and it is a sermon of repentance and reform that the Talented Tenth, as reluctant shepherds, are obliged to provide to their wayward flock. As Du Bois (1995) wrote, "They are ashamed and embarrassed because of the compulsion of being classed with a mass of people over whom they have no real control and whose actions they can only influence with difficulty and compromise and with every risk of defeat" (78). The Talented Tenth find themselves in the difficult position of being unable to leave the flock behind without being branded as "sellouts" while at the same time being unable to lead the flock in a direction other than the one in which the flock wishes to go. The Talented Tenth finds itself struggling with a "can't leave, can't lead" dialectical tension that makes racial uplift problematic. Nevertheless, those attempting to fulfill their historical debt to the race will attempt to lead even when followers are few.

Before Cosby can begin to provide the guidance he believes the Black poor need, he finds it necessary to justify himself not as a Black leader but as a Black man. The book begins with a quote accusing Cosby of not being Black. "For forty years, Bill Cosby has never shown that he is black or said that he was black" (xv). That Cosby chose not only to include this quote but also to open the book with it speaks to the uncertainty that exists for Blacks who succeed in mainstream America (Kennedy 2008). In the eyes of some, the integration of middle- and upper-class Blacks creates a separation between them and the majority of Blacks (hooks 2000). Given that the Black Power movement located the essence of blackness with poor Blacks, those who have moved away from poverty may be accused of having lost their center. As Steele (1991) noted, Black Power championed the notion "that the purest black was the poor black" (101).

Cosby's response to this attempt at an ad hominem attack is to turn the focus away from whether or not he is Black enough to whether or not Blacks as a group have progressed enough. He notes the dire statistics related to marriage and divorce rates among Blacks and states that "the numbers speak for themselves" (xv). Yet he realizes that it is not enough to stop there, as the message may only be heard if the people are willing to listen. Still, unwilling to spend too much time debating whether he is Black enough, Cosby asks whether Malcolm X, Dr. Martin Luther King Jr., W. E. B. Du Bois, and Louis Farrakhan are Black enough, noting that they have discussed the same problems that he and Dr. Poussaint wish to address. References to Malcolm X, Marcus Garvey, and Du Bois were made previously during a speech in Pittsburgh in 2004 (J. Williams 2006, 190). Finally, Cosby reminds those who question his blackness that, in the eyes of white people, he has always been Black, and "the people of my generation suffered the kind of indignities that people of yours can barely even imagine" (xv–xvii).

NO SHAME IN THEIR GAME

The locus of the contemporary problem, according to Cosby and Poussaint, is the Black male. Although they write that "no one has suffered more than our young black men" (1), it becomes clear that Black men are the cause of much of the suffering among poor Blacks. In many ways, poverty among Blacks can be attributed to the actions of Black men. While the authors do not desire to blame the victim, it is evident that Black men can be both victims and victimizers. Black men are seen as responsible for the devolution of the two-parent family among Blacks and the fact that large numbers of Black children are born into poverty as a result. Their homes are both broken and broke.

Black males, according to Cosby and Poussaint, have acted shamelessly. They have brought shame on their families, the young women they impregnate, and themselves. Failure to live up to their obligations as parents has contributed to the breakdown of societal norms among Blacks. Two-parent homes have given way to single-parent households. Yet the authors argue that "parenting works best when both a mother and a father participate. . . . A house without a father is a challenge. A neighborhood without fathers is a catastrophe, and that's just what we have today" (3). The solution, we are told, is to go forward by turning back the clock. "In 1950, we still feared our parents and respected them" (2). It is the absence of this fear and respect, particularly in poor Black communities, that the authors see as a problem, rather than deindustrialization coupled with the flight of the Black middle class from urban areas (Wilson 1997) or American apartheid (Massey and Denton 1993).

The self-help rhetoric that Cosby and Poussaint provide is based on conservative values and gender norms. For example, the authors write, "A mother can usually teach a daughter how to be a woman. But as much as mothers love their sons, they have difficulty showing a son how to be a man" (4). Moreover, we are told, "There is another thing that little boys don't do any more: go to church" (4).

It's not that there is anything wrong with two-parent homes, traditional gender norms, or going to church. These suggestions would find ready acceptance across the heartland of America, particularly among the religious conservative base of the Republican Party. What is interesting is that these ideas, from the perspective of the authors, appear to be foreign to the Black poor although Blacks as a people are known for singing the Gospel and worshipping under the Christian faith. The contemporary Black poor appear from this perspective to be godless heathens living in sin. They are guilty of breaking both the religious covenant and the secular covenant that is said to bind us together as Americans.

Work and family are two indispensable values, as any politician running for office knows. Yet if these values are absent among the Black poor, then they may be seen by other Americans as something other than American, not second-class citizens but individuals left out of the social fabric altogether. Blacks during segregation may have been second-class citizens, but they had little doubt that they had many of the same values as white Americans. Now both middle-class Blacks and whites may wonder whether poor Blacks, trapped in a culture of poverty, have not become a separate group within the nation. Hacker (1995) wrote that "Black Americans are Americans, yet they still subsist as aliens in the only land they know" (3). While middle-class Blacks now enjoy the fruits of integration, poor Blacks remain segregated and unequal.

Cosby and Poussaint, however, do not see segregation as the primary deterrent to Black youth getting an education. Rather, in the case of Black boys, many of them drop out or are kicked out of school. As the authors suggest, "When the boys get suspended or expelled—admit it parents—there is usually a good reason" (6). Although poor Blacks are often looked at as victims, the only way for them to move to the status of victors, in the eyes of the authors, is to accept some responsibility for their own failures.

Poor Blacks occupy a position outside the American mainstream in part because they have failed to take the necessary steps on the path to integration and acceptance. One of those steps, according to the authors, is mastering the English language. As Cosby and Poussaint note, "Many of our kids don't want to speak English" (7). They speak it "as if English were a second language" (7). This echoes McWhorter's (2000) position that Ebonics is just bad English and that Blacks fail in school because of a cult of anti-intellectualism. According to Touré (2011), "Many Black students are faced with the choice of either getting good grades or being accepted by their Black peers—they cannot have both. And the better grades they get the more shunned they'll be" (157).

America may have been founded on the ideals of life, liberty, and the pursuit of happiness, but Cosby and Poussaint state that "these boys don't really know what the word *future* means" (7). To have a future, one must be oriented toward it and engage in what psychologists refer to as delayed gratification. What poor Black males suffer from is the tyranny of the now, and this makes it difficult for them to envision much beyond the street corners that Cosby and Poussaint state they can be found on. The authors admit, "If we seem hard on our brothers, it is only because we know how hard they will have to work to regain control of their destinies" (10).

To create a better future for themselves, Black males must change themselves in the present. Cosby and Poussaint state that Black males are "emotionally detached," except when they "explode in the kind of rage and violence that make no sense to anyone, not even themselves" (11). The anger that Black males feel stems not from society at large but from "what their so-called friends and family have done and continue to do to them" (11). While many commentators blame whites and society at large for the problems among poor Blacks, Cosby and Poussaint suggest that the locus of the problem lies in the Black community itself. Rhetorically this fits with their position that poor Blacks must engage in self-help. If the problems stem from pressures outside the Black community, then there is little that poor Blacks, and specifically young Black men, can do to change their lot in life. However, if the problem is centered in the Black community, and in Black men in particular, then they are imbued with the agency to affect their own lives.

There is a fine line between stating that victims have the power to become victors and blaming them for their position as victims. It is likely that Cosby and Poussaint mean to suggest that while poor Blacks are not responsible for the social conditions that forced them into poverty, they are responsible for the actions they take, which keep them mired in poverty generation after generation. Listening to rap music that glorifies the culture of poverty, including ignorance, violence, and the degradation of women, is one of the ways that poor Blacks are "handicapping themselves in the game of life" (13). Engaging in sexual intercourse and having children that they cannot support and often refuse to acknowledge play a major factor in the creation and maintenance of intergenerational poverty. About this phenomenon, "there is less shame and embarrassment" (14) in Black communities than there used to be. The authors suggest that "some black women simply don't want to marry the fathers of their babies because these men appear to have little else to offer beyond their sperm" (14). Yet these same women "can unknowingly transfer their rage toward their sons—just because they are male" (19). This would suggest that Black women do desire more from Black men than they are receiving, and ultimately their disappointment turns to anger. While Greeson (1995) discussed Black male abandonment of Black women in favor of interracial relationships and the feelings of betrayal this engendered, what we see here is another form of abandonment and the breaking of bonds due to the inability of Black men to fulfill an economic role as providers.

Cosby and Poussaint desire to create better social norms among the Black poor, starting with a reconstruction of the Black family. They write, "The fact that a black father is unemployed or underemployed should not disqualify him as a parent in the mother's eyes" (21). Moreover, "No matter how useless or hopeless a father may think he is, his role is simply to *be* there" (24). Yet this advice does not square with comments the authors make earlier in the text. As they admit, "Because so many black men are unemployed, underemployed, and incarcerated, they are not proposing marriage, and if they did, their proposals might not be taken seriously. A father takes care of his children. These men have trouble taking care of themselves" (15). As Eugene Robinson (2010) observed, "The decline of marriage and the rise of single-parent households are society-wide phenomena, albeit with their greatest impact among African-Americans" (133).

The question of whether Black women are smart or unintelligent for the choices they make in regard to less desirable Black males is up for debate.

What cannot be debated is that Black women are making choices and exercising their own agency. Cosby and Poussaint are attempting to change the choices that Black women are making to ones they believe are better. Yet if poor Black men "have trouble taking care of themselves" (2007, 14), then one should wonder how good they will be at taking care of their offspring. It is doubtful whether simply being there will in fact be enough, given that this is not the case for middle- or upper-income Americans of any race. The authors want to see young Black men get married and "assume their responsibilities as men" (15). However, these responsibilities must certainly go farther than putting a ring on a woman's finger and staying in an apartment that he does not contribute to maintaining. As the authors note, "Working fathers can teach their sons about the necessity of hard work and about the need to show up on time and stick to a job" (7). This statement shows that what is really asked of Black males is to do more than simply show up at the house. Black men need to leave home regularly to go to work, or it won't be possible to maintain a home. Black women already bear much of the responsibility for taking care of their children, and it is unlikely that they also want the responsibility of taking care of their baby's daddy as well.

POOR PEOPLE AS POOR PARENTS

While the authors call on both Black women and men to play a greater role in the lives of their children, they are also critical of the ways in which many parents fulfill their roles. Cosby and Poussaint's aim is to save the children. Yet one source of danger from which they seek to save children is their own parents. Parents are in fact advised to protect their children from bad parenting. If children are the potential bright spots of the future, then their parents are the dark corners of the present, under which these same children fail to find the light they so desperately need. As Cosby and Poussaint write, "Every last one of our children is gifted in some way. It's just that no one has helped each of them discover and nurture his or her own particular gift" (102).

A reasonable reading of this passage is to see it as a rebuke of parenting among Blacks, particularly low-income Blacks, who are undoubtedly a source of shame for Cosby and Poussaint. The authors feel shame for the actions of poor Blacks, even if poor Blacks do not feel shame for themselves. Du Bois (1995) observed that Black leaders "are ashamed and embarrassed because of the compulsion of being classed with a mass of people over whom they have no real control and whose actions they can influence only with difficulty and compromise and with every risk of defeat" (78). One potential reason why poor Blacks may lack a sense of shame is that whatever problems they experience may be displaced onto society, thus putting poor Blacks in the position of being victims. As Feagin (2000) noted, "Within American society, African-Americans have been dominated and exploited in much larger numbers than has any other group" (3). Yet Cosby and Poussaint's desire to turn poor Blacks into victors also means that these same individuals must be seen as possessing the ability to make changes in their own lives and, more importantly, possessing the responsibility for doing so. If poor Blacks are in part responsible for their own condition, then they must also accept the shame that comes with failing to improve it. As was noted earlier, the actions of poor Blacks were deemed to be shameless, as those who possessed a sense of shame would either not commit egregious acts or try somehow to make up for them.

Poor Blacks, it seems, have not learned the proper value system and behavioral patterns that go along with it. As Sowell (1999) argued, "Cultures have consequences. Ignoring those consequences . . . does nothing to benefit the less fortunate, and in fact tends to freeze them into their backward position while the rest of the world moves forward" (75). Although parents are responsible for teaching their children, the schools these children attend also share some responsibility for their plight. Schools often fail to educate Blacks, while society is quick to incarcerate them. A school-to-prison pipeline exists for many poor Blacks. As Cosby and Poussaint note, "Teachers have to realize that they may very well be the last stop before a child winds up institutionalized—the last hope even" (109).

Nevertheless, Cosby and Poussaint still believe that the primary responsibility for ensuring a child's education belongs to his or her parents. They state that a parent should "keep asserting yourself until the children get the services they need" (107). The significance of education must be transmitted from parent to child, even if parents do not possess an adequate education, because "school will mean nothing to a child if she doesn't hear from you how important it is" (115).

Unfortunately, poor Black parents are unlikely to convey this message in the Standard English that mainstream society deems acceptable for advancement in both the educational system and the workplace. While acknowledging that Ebonics "is a legitimate dialect" (117), the authors see the failure of poor Blacks to learn to speak in a manner that the majority of Americans can understand as reason for their lack of social mobility. The authors note that "for black males especially, there seems to be a correlation between a high drop-out rate and a deep attachment to Black English" (119).

Worse still, when given advice by their elders on how to improve their lot in life, many Black youths fail to heed this advice owing to a lack of respect for the wisdom older Blacks can impart. This too, the authors believe, is the fault of Black parents. In remonstrating with these parents, the authors state, "You must teach your kids not only good manners but also the cultural value of treating people with respect" (123). In Cosby and Poussaint's rhetoric there is little difference between remonstration and education. Black parents must be educated about the many reasons they ought to be ashamed, one of which is the total lack of control they appear to have over their children.

Instead of educating their children, many Blacks, like other Americans, have turned this responsibility over to the purveyors of mass media. As the authors observe, "These media have dominated so many homes that some have called them a 'third parent,' but not a very helpful one" (135). Yet even the idea that media constitute a "third parent" is based on the presumption that a child has two parents in the home. As Cosby and Poussaint note earlier, this is not the case for many Black households, in which single mothers are the primary and possibly the only caregivers. What the authors ask of any parent is to monitor and control the media consumption of his or her child. While acknowledging that the task is akin to "taking a crack addict's pipe away" (137), they neverthe-less see this as necessary if black youths are to attain an adequate education that does not involve "edutainment." As Meyrowitz (1986) argued, television does more than entertain; it also provides people with a glimpse of social norms and values that exist outside their immediate environment. Yet while Meyrowitz noted the positive effects this could have on society, much of our contemporary discussion focuses on the negative outcomes.

Television is seen as a purveyor of violent messages and stereotypes that have a detrimental impact on the development of Black youth. This idea relates to Gerbner's 1998 work on cultivation analysis. Specifically, Cosby and Poussaint note a gangsta rap industry whose culture "promotes the moral breakdown of the family" (143). Black youths, they argue, "are being swept up in decadence and glorified self-hatred" (145), and the blame for this lies with their parents. Everything from promiscuous sexual behavior to the HIV epidemic, obesity, and rampant consumerism can be traced back to television, according to the authors. Despite the power of television and the executives who create the programming it carries, the ultimate blame must rest with parents if Cosby and Poussaint are to move their readers toward a new role as victors.

The victory, I suggest, is ultimately over themselves and their own poor choices and harmful behaviors. As parents, as individuals, poor Blacks are seen as having made bad choices. They have agency, but they lack the wisdom to use it effectively. This is where Cosby and Poussaint come in. They dispense the wisdom of the elders to Black parents who themselves were never properly raised. These parents, once enlightened, can then shine the light down onto their children.

SPEAKING TRUTH TO THE POWERLESS

Cosby and Poussaint attempt to teach the many all at once in the hope of creating a new meme that will circulate throughout the Black underclass. Yet the Black underclass is unlikely to read this text, given the inadequate education that many lower-income Blacks receive in their school systems. The book's true audience is more likely the Black middle and upper class, those individuals who make up the Talented Tenth. As Eugene Robinson (2010) noted, "To the extent that it reached African Americans, the book connected with Mainstream readers" (197). This text allows members of the Talented Tenth to speak truth to those without power, even if the powerless refuse to listen. Whether they listen, I contend, is not the point. The point is only that the words are spoken.

The words must be spoken, as providing leadership of the race is the duty of the Talented Tenth. What is interesting is that leadership in this context amounts only to showing which direction those less privileged should walk. It does not entail leading them down the path. The Black middle class and upper class have long since left the Black poor behind. Fulfilling their "duty" at this point amounts solely to leaving a recorded message behind, even though few are likely to listen to it. The Talented Tenth, for the most part, speaks to itself and for itself. It has become separate and distinct from the Black poor.

Each group in some ways has developed into a separate class based on income and education. These class differences form nearly impenetrable walls, making it difficult for the groups to communicate with each other and understand the other's behavior. As Hochschild (1995) observed, "African Americans are becoming more disparate politically and demographically as well as economically and socially" (50). The Talented Tenth has become white in the eyes of the Black poor, and the Black poor are simply poor as well-off Blacks seek to claim the moniker of "Black" for themselves. If, like Chris Rock, they cannot create a linguistic separation, then like Touré (2011), the Black middle class attempts to redefine Blackness for itself (161) as a means to illustrate the differences that exist among us. According to Eugene Robinson (2010), Blacks now comprise four distinct subgroups with different levels of education, income, values, and goals.

Differences among the Talented Tenth and the Black poor show up in the area of health and the choices that individuals make that endanger it. While Cosby and Poussaint acknowledge the role of societal discrimination and mistreatment of Blacks as factors creating distrust toward the health-care system, they nevertheless see these as aspects of the past that Blacks must educate themselves to overcome. The authors admonish those with poor health, stating, "When you put off seeking treatment for things like cancers and diabetes, you flirt with disaster. Once again, the word *victim* shows up" (169).

Nonetheless the authors do not really see these individuals as victims at all but rather as individuals who have made poor choices. These individuals may then seek to convince themselves and others that they are not responsible for the choices they have made. Cosby and Poussaint urge people around these individuals to embrace a tough-love approach. They advise, "When he gets around friends or family and starts playing the victim, we cannot indulge him any longer" (169).

The authors draw a sharp line between the past and the present in America. In the past, Blacks were victims of the Tuskegee experiment and "Mississippi appendectomies," but Blacks in the present are seen as being to blame for their own failures to seek and gain appropriate medical care. Even if one ignores the fact that many Americans cannot afford health insurance, the Black poor are still blamed for failing to demand better health care when they fail to receive it. Moreover, their increasing need for health care is seen as their own fault as well.

Poor Blacks are seen as victimizing themselves and their children owing to a lack of parenting. The authors caution, "Don't give your kids money and expect them to buy something nutritious. They won't" (170). Parents are seen as abdicating responsibility for their children and instead attempting to place it on the children or on individuals in the school system. Yet, as the authors state, "The cafeteria won't train your child. You can. We're talking about parenting here. We're talking about not leaving your child unprotected" (170).

Black parents are depicted as being at fault for leaving their children subject to everything from obesity to diabetes to HIV and AIDS. Poor Black women specifically come under fire for failing to "talk to their doctors about how to protect their babies from becoming infected," as well as having sex with a man who "refuses to put on a condom" (179). These poor choices subject their children to the poor health that they will live and perhaps die from at the hands of negligent caregivers.

Black parents in this instance have replaced the negligent parties who conducted syphilis experiments on Black men and made reproductive choices for Black women without their authorization. Black parents, specifically poor Black parents, can be said to be conducting experiments on their own children. In a time when the dangers of smoking are well-documented and widely known, Cosby and Poussaint still find it necessary to advise Black parents not to "expose children to second-hand smoke" (181). The only reading of such behaviors is to see them as negligence. Poor Black parents are willingly exposing their children to unnecessary health risks. As the authors state, "We can play victim all we want, but it does not make us one bit healthier" (190).

Playing the victim, as we know, is quite different from being a victim, and in this instance we are once again shown one of the ways in which poor Blacks victimize themselves and even their own children. It appears that the move from victim to victor has more to do with overcoming inner demons than conquering outer ones. Black Americans, rather than whites, are now seen as most responsible for their own condition. This contrasts starkly with Randall Robinson's (2000) focus on the impact of slavery and segregation in his call for reparations. Blacks may not have created the conditions they face, but in the eyes of Cosby and Poussaint, they are responsible for maintaining them.

This line of thought is evident in the authors' discussion of crime in the Black community. As they note, "Poverty, fatherless homes, and the lack of good parenting all aggravate it" (191). The Black community, they argue, is under siege, but "now the attack comes from within the village" (193). Blacks, rather than whites, are now responsible for the problems within the Black community, and the solution is for us to "change our societal values to ones that build community rather than destroy it" (193).

POOR PEOPLE'S PROBLEMS

Still, the notion of a Black community is a strained one and, I believe, a fictional one. As Eugene Robinson (2010) argued, we should speak not of a Black community but of Black communities. This idea fits better with our ability to understand the separation that exists between the Talented Tenth and the Black poor. The Talented Tenth have for the most part been integrated into American society, while the Black poor stand apart from it. The only togetherness that exists in many quarters is a rhetorical one, as the Talented Tenth and the Black poor no longer share the same neighborhoods to the extent that they did during segregation.

It is the Black poor who are subject to the increasing rates of violent crime that Cosby and Poussaint seek to address. While their writing speaks of crime as a problem for the Black community, it is in fact more prevalent among a specific segment of the Black population. As bell hooks (2000) argued, "class matters" (7), because "there have always been diverse caste and class groups among African-Americans" (89). Cosby and Poussaint (2007) at one point even acknowledge that "the homicide problem is so out of control that some pundits have suggested that these killings are part of the 'culture' of the black poor" (196). Whether one believes that this behavior has cultural roots that are class based is less important than that one sees that these behaviors are in fact located among the poor in contrast to the middle class. Some behaviors are more class specific than others, even if the authors attempt to discuss them as a Black problem.

The problems of the Black poor are only a "Black problem" to the extent that the Talented Tenth see it as their duty to guide and improve the conditions of Blacks as a group. The Black poor in many respects are no different from the white poor, just as the Black middle class is similar to the white middle class in many respects. The crucial distinction between the Black middle class and the white middle class is that the latter has no rhetoric suggesting that it has any obligation to help poor whites. Whites see each other as individuals, whereas many Blacks see themselves as members of a group first and foremost. It is for this reason that members of the Talented Tenth find it difficult to focus on uplifting themselves rather than continuing to focus on the quixotic and perhaps harmful idea of racial uplift. To do otherwise would open them up to charges of selling out (Kennedy 2008).

Cosby and Poussaint write with the belief that the Talented Tenth and the Black poor occupy the same social world. The authors lament that "a gated community does no good if the problem is within the gates" (197). This is perhaps ironic, since the Black middle class moves out of traditionally Black neighborhoods and integrates what used to be all-white neighborhoods. Neighborhoods that are gated have gates to keep out not only the Black poor but also the white poor, precisely for the reasons that the authors bring up in their text. Gates are used to keep problems on the outside, and in the twenty-first century, what we see are perhaps attempts at class purity more than racial purity. If, as the authors suggest, "responsibility begins" at home and "that's where the responsibility also ends" (200), then like their white counterparts the Black middle and upper class see their first responsibility to be protecting their own offspring and the fruits of their own class status.

Cosby and Poussaint argue, "In short, African Americans need to care more about each other" (218). Yet one can argue that class now matters more than race in creating a sense of identification in America. This makes old notions of racial loyalty difficult to swallow and, for some, harder to espouse with a straight face. As with an old religious injunction, individuals may utter the words while at the same time understanding that a disconnect exists between the words and the world in which they live. As Burke ([1950] 1969) observed, "Identification is affirmed with earnestness precisely because there is division" (22).

Ultimately Cosby and Poussaint admit that it really is all about class. While their discussion is presumably about problems that affect the Black community, the reality is that the problems of which they speak belong exclusively to the Black poor. As the authors note, "We are talking about Black people in poverty. If you fit that description, we are talking to you" (221). Yet I contend that rather than talking to the Black poor, a more accurate description of the conversation is that Cosby and Poussaint are talking *about* the Black poor. Although there is a possibility that individuals located in the Black underclass may read their text, it is unlikely. The real readership of Cosby and Poussaint's work is the Black middle and upper class. It is these individuals who are more likely to seek an understanding of just what is wrong with the Black poor and what, if anything, separates the Black middle class from them.

The short answer to the question of why the Black middle class is integrating while the Black poor are separating is values. As the authors note in their discussion of Black youth, "What they watch on TV, what they listen to, how they dress, how they think—all of this conspires to lock them in poverty" (22). Moreover, the absence of fathers and a two-parent home is seen as the primary reason why the necessary values are absent in the first place. According to Cosby and Poussaint, "Many of the issues that the black poor struggle with are similar to those that the poor in America struggle with, regardless of race" (223). Specifically, these issues stem from a culture of poverty that perpetuates values that are inconsistent with attaining a middle-class existence. This is why the authors advise parents to "please remind our young people that there is no shame in hard work" (225). Only individuals who have become disconnected from the job market would need this reminder.

One should wonder how well poor parents can teach their children middle-class values when many of them have "found a way to live off the government unproductively" (227). Cosby and Poussaint's rhetoric does not blame the victim, because the authors do not see poor Blacks as victims. Rather, they are individuals who have failed to make proper choices in life, and their choices have consequences for both themselves and their children. According to the authors, poor people have been led to believe that it is acceptable "to deny personal responsibility for self-defeating behaviors" (235).

While admonishing the poor for their behaviors, the authors see fit to also castigate Black lawyers and business professionals, who they believe "have not yet learned to pool their talents for the mutual benefit of businesspeople and the black poor" (239). They are admonished for "working in predominantly white businesses and corporations" (239) when they could instead "play key roles in the economic advancement of black communities" (239). It is this final remark that underlies Cosby and Poussaint's belief in the idea that successful Blacks owe a debt to the Black community, an argument Randall Robinson (2003) made earlier in his work. While the Black poor are encouraged to emulate the agency of the Black middle class, the Black middle class is scolded for not using its agency to benefit the Black poor.

If poor Blacks have not helped themselves, it is unlikely that they can take credit for the success of the Black middle class. The Black middle class of today is composed of autonomous individuals who do not engage in the self-sacrifice that would be required of Du Bois's Talented Tenth. While Battle and Wright (2002) drew a distinction between the Talented Tenth (college-educated Blacks) and the Black middle class in their study, they found that Blacks with higher incomes and "those who supported notions of self-reliance . . . were less likely to feel middle class Blacks were helping poor Blacks" (670). A likely reason why the Black middle class does not engage in self-sacrifice is that they embrace the idea of self-help to the same extent as the white middle class. This explanation differs from the one West offered in seeing the Black middle class as deficient and decadent (1993b, 36). Members of the Black middle class do not see themselves as owing anything to the Black poor, who they believe possess the responsibility to help themselves. At best, the federal government may be seen as having some responsibility for helping to alleviate the conditions of the Black poor, given that slavery, segregation, and discrimination have played, and may continue to play a part in, curtailing their options in life.

CONCLUSION

My critique of Cosby and Poussaint's book suggests that the Talented Tenth see themselves as guilt free in the same way that middle-class whites bear no responsibility for poor whites. Members of the Black middle and upper class find it difficult to believe in the promise of America for itself while at the same time denying that success is unattainable to anyone with the desire to achieve it. Life chances are not equal, but all individuals do possess agency and with it the ability to create a better life for themselves and their families.

Cosby and Poussaint's rhetoric, while ostensibly a self-help book for the Black poor, ultimately functions as an explanation for why the Black poor remain poor. It delineates the values that separate the Black middle class from the Black poor and, perhaps contrary to the authors' intentions, frees middle-class Blacks of any obligation to poor Blacks. The Black man's burden that the Black poor represent for the Black middle class is no more. The Black middle class no longer functions, if it ever did, as the Talented Tenth that Du Bois envisioned. Instead the Black middle and upper class can at best point the way toward a better life for the Black poor, yet even the giving of advice is more self-serving than obligatory. If members of the Black middle and upper class attempt to leave a road map for the Black poor, then they do so only out of a residual memory for the obligations that the Talented Tenth once embraced and the burdens they once carried. No longer must one Black function as his or her brother or sister's keeper. Instead each Black individual is seen as responsible for keeping his or her own house in order. Those who don't will find themselves living apart from other Blacks who move to better locations in an age of integration.

Cosby and Poussaint's text functions as a self-help book to the extent that it diminishes the macro or larger systemic factors at work and instead enhances the micro or individual factors that contribute to success in America. If micro or individual factors are what make the difference in one's life, then self-help is indeed possible and even mandatory. Yet this work, I believe, is odd as self-help books go in that rather than making ostensible readers feel better about themselves and their prospects, it would likely do the opposite. Poor Blacks, if they do pick up a copy of the text, are likely to walk away feeling worse about themselves and the many failures that the authors point out. While urging poor Blacks to transform themselves into victors, the authors attempt to strip them of any notion that they are victims in America. Randall Robinson (2000), Bell (1987, 1993), and Feagin (2000) all position Blacks as victims of slavery, segregation, and continued discrimination. In contrast, Cosby and Poussaint take a position that has much in common with the Black conservative rhetoric of Steele (1991, 1998), McWhorter (2000, 2003), and Sowell (1999, 2005), rhetoric that aligns itself with that of white neoconservatives.

Rather than discuss the crimes of slavery, segregation, and continued discrimination as the primary causes of failure among poor Blacks, Cosby and Poussaint choose to see poor parenting and poor choices as the major hurdles to be overcome if poor Blacks are to fare better in the race of life. Poor parenting, in the eyes of the authors, is a form of Black-on-Black crime made worse because this crime begins not just at home but in the home. Poor Black children, it seems, are not even safe from their own parents.

The societal shame that we as a nation might feel for the existence of the underclass and our failure to improve their condition is supplanted by a rhetoric of personal shame. Members of the underclass are told that they should bear a personal shame for their very existence, and it is the absence of this shame that is a marker for their lack of responsibility for themselves. Those who have a sense of responsibility for their own condition would feel shame at not having improved it.

No matter what external factors exist, the solution for Cosby and Poussaint must always be internal when it comes to poor Blacks. This is the only way in which their rhetoric of self-help has any chance of working. Yet this lets not only society but also the Talented Tenth off the hook in regard to fulfilling any historical debt or obligation to the Black poor. I argue that their rhetoric does work, but not on the audience they suggest. It is the Black middle class that most benefits from the soothing balm that Cosby and Poussaint provide. It is the shame of their failure to fulfill Du Bois's mandate that is washed away as the authors provide them with reason enough to wash their hands of the Black poor.

CHAPTER 4

Identification, Division, and the Rhetoric of Black Disunity

America is a nation that proclaims its motto *E pluribus unum*, "Out of many, one." Yet that proclamation always rang hollow in the ears of the nation's Black population. At first they were considered no more than chattel; then, after finally being granted their constitutional rights as citizens, they suffered the injustice of segregation, which Woodson (1933) declared "a sequel to slavery" (102). Some, such as Bell (1993) and Feagin (2000), argued that racial prejudice and discrimination are not abnormalities but were present at the nation's founding and an integral part of all facets of its institutions and people.

Perhaps because Blacks were also deemed the permanent "other" and separated both physically and existentially from other Americans, they came to see themselves as a cohesive racial group. Whether this perspective was forced on them or freely chosen, the idea that Blacks were a unified group and that unity should be a goal to continually strive to maintain was taken as a given. The conditions under which Blacks were forced to live for over three hundred years no doubt reinforced this belief as the possibility of integration with other Americans remained a dream even after King's speech and the passage of legislation. However, over time, as American institutions began to open their doors and let a few Blacks trickle in, the possibility of greater identification with whites and America as a whole became possible. A growing Black middle class and even the existence of wealthy Blacks strained the bonds that had once kept Blacks together, united by segregation and poverty. Now the distinctions among Blacks became more evident, and the idea that Blacks should put the advancement of the group ahead of individual concerns was challenged. Notions of racial loyalty and debt to the race were no longer the powerful motivators they once were for many Blacks. In the twenty-first century, the sense of "oneness" that Blacks once had is no more.

Eugene Robinson's work *Disintegration* posits that Blacks no longer constitute a cohesive racial group in the United States. Rather, Blacks are now made up of four distinct subgroups: the Transcendent, Mainstream, Emergent, and Abandoned. Robinson begins his examination of the state of these Black Americas today by recounting the enormous power and influence attained among Blacks who have transcended traditional barriers to advancement for Blacks in the land of opportunity. The change in the status of many Blacks in America is now so profound that he states that "Black America, as we knew it, is history" (4). Robinson observes that the "four black Americas are increasingly distinct, separated by demography, geography, and psychology" (5). Yet his explanation for what he calls "disintegration" among Blacks boils down to not much more than that the times have changed.

After the success of the civil rights movement, Blacks with the opportunity and skills have in many ways integrated on all levels, including the highest levels of business and politics. Although these individuals may still give lip service to the idea that Blacks make up a unified group, Robinson states, "Perhaps we should begin to think of racial solidarity as a luxury item" (11), given that most middle-class Blacks no longer hold this view. Besides the passage of time, class status is also offered as a reason for disintegration. Yet I find that neither the passage of time nor differences of class can adequately explain the disintegration among Blacks. As Robinson notes for much of American history, "Solidarity was essential; the privileged few could not, would not, sell out the underprivileged many" (20). If Blacks held strong and stayed together for so long, then factors such as time and class differences, both of which were always present, prove inadequate as determinants for the changes seen in the last forty years. Something different, something more, accounts for the rise of a rhetoric of Black disunity that seeks to replace the rhetoric of Black unity that held sway throughout slavery and segregation. I argue that this rhetoric of Black disunity can best be understood through the lens of identification and division.

In the past, the desire for Blacks to identify with one another regardless of any apparent differences was strong owing to their obvious division from white America. Yet after the civil rights movement, the success of many Blacks marks a new chapter in American history. What we now find is that many Blacks have integrated into American society to such an extent that they can now identify more with white Americans than with each other. As Shelton and colleagues (2016) observed, many Blacks see themselves as increasingly similar to whites while at the same time different from other Blacks. The authors stated, "It appears that these respondents feel that variation within the Black community now exceeds that between Blacks and Whites—the two most historically antagonistic racial groups in the US" (95). Identification among Blacks is no longer based on race, as class and position in society are now seen as more important factors. Shelton and colleagues (2016) found, "As income increases, study participants across all categories are less likely to declare that middle class and poor Blacks are 'more similar,' holding all other variables constant" (92). Class and position were always present among Blacks, but they were previously never put forward as a reason for division among Blacks. The rhetoric of Black disunity is in fact a marker for the success of integration. Yet I note that it is also indicative of a profound change among Blacks in regard to notions of racial solidarity and advancement in America. The individual, rather than the group, is now deemed most important, and the individual is no longer defined by his or her location within the group. If what Robinson observes is correct, there is no longer a unified group to which one can belong, but at least four separate and distinct groups. Shelton and colleagues (2016) came to a similar conclusion in their study, finding that "widely recognized sources of diversity drive contrasting beliefs about conditions for Blacks in society and commitments to the sense of peoplehood" (94). If, as Robinson (2010) writes of the present, "the black American experience is nothing more or less than an integral and necessary component of the American experience" (23), then it is not surprising that Blacks may begin to see themselves and their experiences as American with no more need to include the adjective "Black" as a necessary descriptor. As Shelton and colleagues (2016) stated, "Thus, it appears that favorable evaluations of race relations undermine commitments to black unity and solidarity" (95). The times, it seems, have changed, as factors such as class, native-born Black versus recent immigrant, generational cohort, and assessments of race relations all play a role in determining Blacks' sense of whether they are a cohesive racial group or not (Shelton et al. 2016).

SEGREGATION, IDENTIFICATION, AND THE ILLUSION OF "ONENESS"

Robinson's discussion of the way things were in Black America emphasizes that what kept Blacks "integrated" as a group was their racial segregation from white America. Despite the author's discussion of the achievements of more successful Blacks during this period, what one comes to understand is that segregation, rather than racial loyalty, kept Blacks together both physically and philosophically. As the author observes, "Racial apartheid, imposed and enforced by others, ironically had fostered great cohesion among African Americans, binding together social and economic classes that otherwise might have drifted apart" (43). During the era of segregation, Blacks had little choice but to stand fast as members of a racial group, given that there was no place for them as individuals in the broader society.

Yet just as racial segregation kept the doors of opportunity closed to Blacks, so the coming period of racial integration opened those same doors (hooks 2000). As Blacks were given a chance to move forward as individuals, the need to focus on anything that might be called racial loyalty diminished. On the basis of Robinson's account, one wonders if such a thing as racial loyalty really existed at all, or if it was simply self-preservation in the face of white oppression. To draw from Burke's ([1945] 1969) discussion of the pentad, once the scene of racial segregation changed to one of integration, so did the agent's (Blacks) sense of themselves and what it meant to be Black. Looking at the scene as dominant over the agent, one realizes that the need for racial loyalty was predicated on the scene of racial segregation. A change in the scene led to a corresponding change in the agent. No longer facing a homogeneous scene of racial oppression, Blacks no longer had need to see themselves as members of a homogeneous group. Shelton and colleagues (2016) raised this question, asking, "If Blacks' history of second class citizenship is the glue to racial cohesion, then what does the future hold when many within their ranks now attribute racial inequality to Blacks themselves rather than the legacy of racial discrimination?" (95). Still, the rhetoric of Black unity prevailed for decades. As Burke ([1950] 1969) stated, "Identification is affirmed with earnestness precisely because there is division" (22). Division among Blacks was always present, yet these differences were downplayed, as the confines of segregation made them irrelevant to anyone outside the Black community.

While Robinson laments the "disintegration" that took place among Blacks, this change is understandable in the context of integration with the wider society and in particular with whites. Given a chance to attend predominantly white institutions, work among whites, and live in previously all-white neighborhoods, Blacks who were poised to do so walked through a door that they had fought for so long to open (hooks 2000). Yet the benefits of integration were not equally distributed among Blacks, as the existence of the underclass, or what Robinson calls the Abandoned, makes plain. Nevertheless, one would only lament disintegration among Blacks if one misses the fact that the racial bond between them existed primarily due to outside pressure. Once those forces were removed, what appeared to be a single molecule broke apart into various atoms.

The flip side of lamentation is celebration, just as the counterpart to division is identification. The possibility for Blacks to integrate, and in Burke's language to identify, with whites and vice versa brings the division among Blacks to the surface. The distinctions among Blacks were always there, as previously noted. What was lacking was a reason and perhaps a motive for expressing them. In celebrating the freedom of integration, Blacks are no longer bound to each other as they were during segregation. Shelton and colleagues (2016) noted that their "findings suggest that beliefs about race relations take precedence over other factors in shaping Blacks' beliefs about racial unity and solidarity" (95). Shelton and colleagues found that "optimistic assessments of race relations inspire beliefs that deemphasize commitments to Black unity and solidarity" (93). It is this unbinding that Robinson is writing about. The perhaps misplaced assumption that Blacks would continue to identify as a cohesive racial group under new circumstances that no longer require or enforce such identification becomes readily apparent.

Evidence of disintegration began before the death of Dr. Martin Luther King Jr. and the subsequent riots that took place throughout the country. Once de jure segregation was no more, Blacks moved into areas where housing covenants could no longer be enforced. It would appear that many Blacks had always desired to move freely about their chosen city but lacked the opportunity to do so (Wilson 1997). Yet what Robinson notes is that with the arson that took place after King's death, there was little reason for middle-class Blacks to remain in the segregated neighborhoods of old. The business districts of those communities were razed to the ground, and with them any reason potentially mobile Blacks had for remaining put. Poor and less educated Blacks who remained "became increasingly isolated from mainstream values, mores, and aspirations" (Robinson 2010, 58). Loury (2002) suggested that past and present racial discrimination "disadvantages blacks by impeding their acquisition of skills" (125). Opportunities that individuals might have had to attain well-paid work in manufacturing and ensure their children lived a better life also disappeared as automakers shifted production to new locales. This last part is interesting because while the flight of the Black middle class is to be noted, others such as Wilson (1997) placed more emphasis on the disappearance of jobs and the effect this had on displaced workers.

Those Blacks who were poised to benefit most from integration began to publicly cross other boundaries as well. Laws against interracial marriage were overturned as Blacks and whites began to mingle not only in schools and neighborhoods but also within households as well. Robinson holds up Barack Obama as a shining example of one such union and the difference this makes in regard to how Obama sees the world in comparison to someone like Robinson himself. Robinson (2010) believes that mixed parentage makes "residual bitterness" toward whites impossible (70) and thus creates a different relationship with white America than exists for many Blacks.

A second grouping that Robinson calls the Emergent consists of Blacks from Africa and the Caribbean. They too have a different relationship with America, seeing it less as a land of oppression than one filled with opportunity. Highly educated in their home countries and willing to work hard even if they have to start at the bottom, they labor to create a stepping-stone for their children, who prosper in their new home. This group no doubt has less in common with the native-born Black population, as their experiences with America and white Americans may be vastly different.

LIFE IN THE MIDDLE

In discussing the Mainstream, or the Black middle class, Robinson argues that "we live in two worlds" (77). Yet a closer examination of the text reveals that this is not entirely true. I would go so far as to state that it is not even mostly true. Although Robinson states that "a great deal of Mainstream black life is lived exclusively, or almost exclusively, among black people" (77), his own work shows the extent to which this is no longer true. He himself notes that Black millennials do not feel "the pull of racial affinity" (77) in the way their parents do. Furthermore, the majority of Blacks attend majority-white institutions for college rather than historically black colleges and universities (HBCUs). Even residential segregation, to the extent that it exists among the Black middle class, is now more a factor of choice or one's income than a matter of law or societal discrimination. As Robinson himself notes, he moved to a racially integrated neighborhood in Virginia thirty years ago. Why, then, does he spend much of one chapter discussing Prince George's County, "the most affluent black-majority county in the nation"? (79). He does so to argue that Blacks live in a different world from whites. His text, however, reveals that it is Blacks who now must try to do so if they desire to maintain a sense of racial solidarity.

The Black Mainstream that Robinson describes is in fact hindered not by white America but by its own choices. In Prince George's County, Blacks chose to settle there knowing that they would be buying homes in a predominantly Black area rather than an integrated one. As Robinson notes, "They were willing to make compromises and sacrifices" to do so (81). Yet the Mainstream did so after choosing to "abandon the city," moving to the suburbs to escape crime and "participate in the project of creating a black community like none other in the nation" (80). While the author does not emphasize this point, it is obvious that this new community is based more on class than on race. If race were what mattered most, then the Black Mainstream could have remained in the city. Yet rather than do so, they moved to Prince George's County to live among other middle- and upper-class Blacks. They did so knowing that the consequences of this form of self-segregation meant that their children would attend schools that were not as good as those they could otherwise have attended. They did so knowing that the major retailers and celebrity chefs would choose to set up shop in whiter or more integrated neighborhoods. Still, to Prince George's County they went. If, as Robinson notes, the Mainstream feels disrespected, then it is ironically enough because they have failed to derive the same benefits of self-segregation that whites did and some still do. Robinson states that "a sense of separate but not-quite equal" leads the Mainstream to seek "solidarity in numbers" (81). Yet I believe that it is in fact the desire to maintain a degree of Black unity, even if class based, that further creates a sense of being separate but not equal.

Blacks fought to integrate the mainstream of American society. What one actually sees in Prince George's County is an example of what happens when Blacks attempt to turn away from integration with white America. One cannot be both separate and equal in American society, at least not if one is Black. If one desires equality, then one cannot be separate from mainstream society, for it is only through integration with society that one can find equality. Home values in segregated Black communities are lower than they are in white communities. Major retailers and celebrity chefs choose to set up shop in areas that either are integrated or at least provide them with access to the larger white mainstream. No matter how much money the Black Mainstream possesses, it is not enough to lure capitalist enterprises to abandon the larger market that exists in mainstream society. Blacks succeeded in opening the doors that allowed for integration. What they cannot do now is to self-segregate and then expect that such self-inflicted wounds will not have consequences.

Robinson spends some time discussing the period of segregation in American history. He does so in part to note the differences that existed between the white world and that of Blacks. These differences are no longer as vast as they once were for the majority of Black people. The other reason he focuses on segregation is to note how far members of the Black Mainstream have come in so little time. The Mainstream that Robinson speaks of is no longer as different from the white majority as perhaps some would like it to be. In fact, this presents the real problem for Robinson and others, despite his protestation that the Black Mainstream lives in a different world from that of whites. What we really find in Robinson's text is the lengths to which Blacks must go to maintain the trappings of a Black identity that could be taken for granted during earlier periods when the distance between Blacks and whites on a social level was insurmountable. Now Robinson finds himself discussing the separate world of HBCUs during homecoming week and Black fraternity and sorority life—neither of which is representative of the experience of most Black Americans today, given the success Blacks have had in integrating majority-white institutions. To remain within a separate and wholly Black world is not just a choice but one that requires a degree of effort as well.

Robinson's lament that most Americans, and especially white Americans, fail to notice the existence of a Black Mainstream is based on the idea that the two worlds are still separate. Yet it is not that the majority of whites fail to notice a separate Black middle class but rather that the Black middle class has so thoroughly integrated into the middle class. What Robinson seeks is for people to acknowledge a separate Black world that in fact no longer exists. Blacks do not have their own middle class apart from white America. The Black Mainstream is now a part of mainstream America. Robinson still operates from a framework based on the model of segregation, in which two worlds could exist side by side and unequal. What he now posits is that two worlds still exist, only in this one they are more or less equal. However, the idea of two worlds existing at all is passé. If two worlds exist, they are based on class rather than race. The Black middle class now has more in common with the white middle class than it does with the Black underclass (Hochschild 1995). This is something that Robinson notices, given the nature of his book, yet he fails to come to terms with the fuller implications of that realization. Robinson is incorrect in arguing that "we tend to keep so much of the Black Mainstream experience to ourselves" (2010, 99). One only has to look up to realize that the Black Mainstream is now part of the American mainstream, and is acknowledged as such at least on an individual level, in ways that would have been unthinkable in the mid-twentieth century. If America is a land of opportunity for individuals, then it is as individuals that Blacks now make their mark on the American landscape.

Robinson sees Blacks of his generation as struggling to hold on to the idea of blackness, of a Black world, for both themselves and their children. He writes that assimilation "is where the black Mainstream is headed—not this generation, perhaps, but surely the next" (103). On this subject, he has missed the boat entirely. The Black Mainstream is not headed to assimilation; it has thoroughly integrated American society already. Blacks did not assimilate into the American mainstream. Their presence and contributions changed the meaning of "mainstream" America. Tocqueville (2002) was right in stating that Blacks could not be assimilated. We have not been assimilated. Blacks did, however, succeed in integrating themselves into American society to produce something new, just as jazz melded aspects of African rhythms and classical music. Robinson (2010) notes that "what we once thought of as 'proprietary' black culture has spread beyond any narrow racial context. Black became not just acceptable but cool" (103). For this reason, Robinson's admission that "race doesn't matter as much to our children's generation in the same way it does to ours" (104) points to the fusion of two worlds that were once separate. There is no longer a Black world apart from a white world. There is only one world, where parents such as Robinson may now worry that their sons and daughters may choose to marry individuals who are not Black despite their parents desire that "African American history and culture not only be revered but also perpetuated" (105). The false assumption in this case is that race and culture must always go hand in hand or that there exists anything like racial purity in America for Blacks in general. Robinson writes, "Mainstream black America, then, seems in many ways a paradoxical place" (105). Yet "paradoxical" is perhaps not the right word. The attempt to maintain a mainstream Black America apart from white America is perhaps better termed quixotic. Robinson jousts with imaginary windmills and attempts to maintain a separate Black world that no longer exists.

What we see in HBCUs and the Boulé is a desire to hold on to the vestiges of what once was, and what once was necessary. It is not, however, a reflection of the world as it exists today and the status and location of the Blacks in it. The majority of Blacks are just as much a part of the mainstream as are white Americans. Yes, differences in income and wealth may still exist between the two, but the social world of Blacks and whites now overlaps almost entirely. Some people may still attend segregated churches, but many others do not. While segregated neighborhoods still exist, so do integrated ones. Even Blacks who live in segregated neighborhoods may find that they attended the same universities and work in the same institutions as their white counterparts. If separate worlds still exist, then they are more a function of class than race, which is why Robinson finds himself discussing the distinctions that now exist among Black Americans.

LIFE AT THE BOTTOM

The Abandoned that Robinson speaks of constitute the underclass of Black America. He begins his discussion with the example of Hurricane Katrina and the ways this disaster put the dire circumstances of the group on display for the nation to see. While many understood that the underclass exists in the abstract, the visceral nature of the images shown on television screens across the nation were hard to ignore. According to Robinson, "The nation felt a deep sense of shame, at least for a while" (111). Yet what was put on display was more the result of both race and class than it was of race alone. Those left in the inner city suffered from broken homes, a broken school system, and now broken levees.

What Robinson finds in New Orleans when Hurricane Katrina hit is but one example of the Abandoned in America. Across the nation, individuals are living lives in which single-parent families are the norm, along with substandard educations, joblessness, and a high likelihood of incarceration. It is here that we find the class division and possibly distinctions in values that separate the Black Mainstream from the Abandoned. As Robinson observes, "The single-parent, female-headed household—once considered a shameful way to live—became commonplace, then normal" (119). The very structure of families separates the two groups and contributes to differences in the life prospects for children growing up among the Abandoned in contrast to the Mainstream (Cosby and Poussaint 2007).

The plight of the Abandoned is not a new subject, and their situation today is more chronic than acute. What is interesting is that the Mainstream no longer appears to feel any responsibility for the conditions of the Abandoned. While Robinson notes that some members of the Mainstream volunteer or start organizations meant to aid less fortunate Blacks, it is more common that members of the Mainstream take an out-of-sight, out-of-mind attitude when it comes to the Abandoned. The Mainstream, like the white middle class, is reminded of the Abandoned when they are depicted in motion pictures or in fleeting images on television screens. No longer do the two groups live side by side, as class, rather than race, is the most important factor both in where one lives and with whom one identifies.

LIFE AT THE TOP

Robinson's (2010) discussion of the Transcendent takes the discussion of class and its importance to new heights. Here we are introduced to captains of industry, but what is different about these captains is that they are Black. As the author observes, they have "the kind of power, wealth, and influence that previous generations of African Americans could never have imagined" (140). While Robinson mentions a number of such individuals, two in particular stand out. The first is Oprah Winfrey, whose climb from poverty to untold riches is a true American success story. What makes her story even more interesting is that it is based on her ability "to convince white Americans that she understood their lives and had their interests and well-being not just in her mind but in her heart" (141). Winfrey's story and that of America's first Black president, Barack Obama, intersect in that she supported his candidacy long before, and in contrast to, many traditional members of the civil rights establishment, along with members of the Transcendent class. Obama, like Oprah, rose to power on wings that were neither Black nor white. As Joseph (2013) observed, Obama "is the king of the exceptional multiracials; he is proof positive that mixed-race can indeed lead to successful race transcendence" (159). It is this lack of seeming to be a "race man" that made Obama suspect in the eyes of the Transcendents, according to Robinson.

In the past, to be a Black politician was to be directly connected to the needs and interests of the Black community. Obama, however, while claiming his Black heritage, does not make it central to his identity as a politician. Joseph (2013) wrote, "Being painted as post-racial means that he is a new model minority" (166). Moreover, "Being multi-racial or perhaps more specifically, not being 'all black,' means that such subjects are not threatening in the same way" (168). While still a relative unknown in political circles, Obama dared to dream that the highest office in the land could be his. This dream appeared quixotic to many Transcendent Blacks, who Robinson (2010) argued "knew from experience that the way African Americans got attention and redress at the highest levels of American politics and government was by working with and through sympathetic white politicians" (145). Not only did Obama seek to displace the virtual representation of white politicians who looked after their Black wards; he also sought to make his politics race neutral rather than race specific. This is something that the Transcendent class on the whole found unpalatable and unrealistic. Yet we fast-forward and find that Obama not only won the Democratic nomination but also the general election. He also won reelection in an America that now sees a Black occupant in the White House as the fulfillment of Dr. King's dream. Granted, many inequities still exist between whites and Blacks, but no longer are Blacks denied access to the highest office in the land. Joseph (2013), however, saw Obama's election differently, stating, "What the historic election of Obama shows is not that race and race politics are dead, but rather that multiraciality, and in particular mixed-race African-Americanness, resonates with the non-Black population" (158).

What Obama represents is not the traditional idea of a "race man" but rather the idea that a man can be seen as a man regardless of race. It is because of race that many deserving individuals throughout American history have been denied the opportunity to rise as high as their talents might otherwise carry them. Now we find that Obama and others have integrated into the mainstream to such an extent that there is little difference between their lives and the lives of high-achieving whites. It is here that the connection between the Transcendents and the rest of Black America appears to be broken. The Transcendents no longer need exist to provide leadership to the race, as Du Bois (1986) argued for. Rather, they can now provide leadership to the entire nation, and to do so often requires that they pursue race-neutral rhetoric and policies.

Joseph (2013) noted Obama's "mediated perception as a figure who is able to transcend the perceived burden of his Blackness" (159). Robinson (2010) states that for individuals like Obama, their "experience of being black in America is radically different from that of their elders" (159). They live in a world where they are no longer outsiders but consummate insiders (162). They are insiders whose experience of the world is based on their mastery of it rather than a remembrance of slavery and segregation, as Randall Robinson (2000) argued for in *The Debt*. The lives of this new generation of Transcendents differ not only from the rest of Black America but also from older Transcendents. It is in their separation from this older generation of Transcendents that one truly sees how wide the chasm has grown between the Black elite and other Blacks. Transcendent Blacks no longer exist to lead Black America but rather can now lead America in general. According to Joseph (2013), Obama's "specialness comes not from him being alone but from him being representative" of all Americans (159). Joseph observed, "Mixed-race is a marker of 'us' more than perhaps any other time in U.S. history" (159). Obama's election signaled this turning point in history and the extent to which the old bonds of racial unity and obligation are no more.

LIFE IN TRANSITION

The experience of being brought to America as slaves separated Blacks from other racial groups who came of their own volition. Yet immigrants from the Caribbean and Africa do not share in the same racial history of oppression as other Blacks. Rather, their experience of coming to America is quite different, and their perspective on the country and their place in it differs as well. Robinson observes that African immigrants are the most educated of all groups entering the country. While they may not have the ability to put their education to use at the same level as they did in their home countries, this high level of achievement provides a platform on which their children build. Moreover, given that little effort is made to distinguish new Black immigrants from native Blacks whose ancestors suffered the horrors of slavery, affirmative action programs and scholarships are available to recent arrivals as well. As Eugene Robinson (2010) notes, both college attendance and attendance in elite colleges are higher for immigrant Blacks than for any other group, including whites (169). The children of Black immigrants are more likely to have two-parent families that "are generally not just intact but also highly educated" (170). These children are also more likely to have attended private school, coming from families with a "history of education and a reverence for learning" (170). Descriptions of this group differ little from those of other immigrant groups such as Asians who have attained success in their new country. Everything about the way Robinson describes African immigrants and their children points to them being separate and perhaps seeing themselves as better than native-born Black Americans. As Robinson notes of the African immigrants, "Optimism comes easily and with a certain sense of entitlement. All or some of this gets passed down to the next generation" (171). One does not need a degree in sociology to know that such a description bears little relation to anything that has been written about native-born Blacks and their experience in America.

Echoing Randall Robinson, Eugene Robinson also sees the presence of a cultural history as something that separates African immigrants as well. They "know who they are and where they came from" (174), which is a statement than cannot be applied to native-born Blacks whose ancestors were stripped of both their cultural identity and their history (R. Robinson 2000). The presence or absence of a cultural past makes a difference in regard to how one sees oneself in the present and one's prospects for the future. African immigrants, Eugene Robinson (2010) observes, can choose to separate themselves from other Blacks by maintaining their cultural heritage. He summarizes this in stating that "there can be different shades of black" (176), a distinction that was not allowed for at an earlier time in American history.

Another area where questions of identification and division arise is the one-drop rule. This rule governed our understanding of racial identification in this country for much of its history; however, that is starting to change. With an increasing rate of interracial marriage between Blacks and whites, we find ourselves dealing with questions of racial classification in ways that defy the notion that anyone with a single drop of Black blood is considered Black. Joseph (2013) related how the push to add a multiracial option to the census in the 1990s had its roots in some white women not wanting their mixed-race children identified as Black (xvi). Eugene Robinson (2010) spends time discussing American celebrities who are biracial or multiracial and the extent to which they may choose to identify as Black or not. Noting the impact of desegregation not only on the public-school system but also on the public's understanding of race and its importance, Robinson notes that race means less to young people today than it did to their parents. Living in a world that he refers to as "anti-racial," these children, he believes, will bring about a world that is neither Black nor white but rather beige (182–83). Like President Obama, their relationship to white America will be different from that of individuals such as Robinson who are not biracial. Having never experienced Jim Crow segregation and having family members who are white changes their relationship to both whites and America as a whole. The line dividing Blacks from other Americans "becomes fuzzy and hard to pin down"

(190). In short, biracial individuals now have a choice to identify with America in a way that was historically denied to Blacks for most of the country's history.

LIFE AT ODDS

Identification between most of the groups Robinson discussed and America as a whole is all but complete. Rather than a unified group constituting Black America, one sees that the majority of Blacks are either integrated into the mainstream or on their way to doing so. However, the one group that stands apart is the Black underclass, whom Robinson refers to as the Abandoned. It seems that they are abandoned not only by white Americans but perhaps by other Blacks as well. The idea of Black unity no longer holds sway in the post–civil rights era as class becomes a stronger marker of identity than race. Robinson goes so far as to say that the Black middle class is now "liberated from the separate and unequal nation called black America that existed before the triumph of civil rights" (193). Yet this liberation creates division, because as "the Mainstream have risen, the Abandoned have fallen" (194).

Given that the Mainstream and the Abandoned are separated by both income and geography, they have less and less in common. Between the two groups "there is a failure to communicate, much less comprehend" (197). What Robinson argues is that more must be done to provide members of the Abandoned with a vehicle into the Mainstream. He discusses the culture of poverty that grips the Abandoned, and echoes Cosby and Poussaint (2007) in deriding the separate system of values that seems to hold sway in their communities. According to Robinson (2010), only members of the Abandoned who are capable of "being duplicitous—being literally two-faced" (205) are able to survive where they are at long enough to get where they are going.

The conditions under which the Abandoned live are so antithetical to the success that the Mainstream enjoys that Robinson echoes earlier calls for a Marshall Plan for the inner city. Yet he admits that the American people may not have the will to target policy to specifically address the needs of poor Blacks, and he notes that some members of the Mainstream deride President Obama for his race-neutral policies. One policy that Robinson argues ought to be changed to help the Abandoned is affirmative action. He believes that members of the Transcendent should be exempt from it, and perhaps even the Mainstream should be as well, if this is the deal that must be made to uplift the Abandoned. Cashin (2014) argued for the nation to rethink affirmative action along class lines as well. Yet in Robinson's attempt to uplift the Abandoned, his policy prescription underlines the divide between this group and other Blacks.

Robinson (2010) notes that "some politicians are going to have to fall on their swords" (221) to help the Abandoned. It would appear that he believes that sacrifice is necessary from the Transcendents and perhaps more importantly the Black Mainstream as well. Yet this is unlikely to occur voluntarily, as it pits groups of Blacks against each other. If, as Robinson notes, "the Mainstream's gains are historic, but they are precarious" (211), then it is unlikely they will be willing to endure a period of benign neglect on the part of the government. Rather, they will continue to support a program that helped many members of this group make the climb into the middle class. Members of the Mainstream are unlikely to risk the future of their own children in an attempt to help those of the Abandoned. Class, in this instance, will most likely play a stronger role than race, as will the basic human tendency to look out for one's own family. To ask that the Mainstream put the interests of the Abandoned ahead of its own is quixotic and perhaps no more likely to occur than Du Bois's Talented Tenth sacrificing itself for the Black masses. Du Bois himself later realized the folly of assuming that this would occur (Gates and West 1996). What Robinson's text does in noting the various groups among Blacks is to outline the division that exists within what some call Black America.

The notion of Black America is perhaps antiquated, as what we really have are Blacks who have integrated into American society and others who have not. Those who continue to be on the outside suffer the consequences of division, while those who are on the inside reap the benefits of identification with other Americans, specifically white Americans. Touré (2011) went so far as to say that the ability of Blacks to put whites at ease and show love for them equates to greater success in society (178). Robinson's discussion of both Oprah and Obama illustrates this point. Those who seek to transcend race stand at odds with those who seek "to make blacks powerful qua blacks so as to defeat whites" (Dickerson 2004, 200). In the twenty-first century, one sees a greater push toward Black individualism than one has seen in the past (Touré 2011), and some see this as long overdue.

A REMEMBRANCE OF THINGS PAST

Still, the notion of racial solidarity is a hard one for many Blacks to let go of, including Robinson. He notes that when giving a nod to other Blacks in passing, "it feels satisfying" (E. Robinson 2010, 223). Yet in describing why, his words indicate that this sense of satisfaction may stem more from a recollection of what was, rather than what is. He goes on to wonder whether Blacks still have a shared sense of racial identity and a feeling of racial solidarity. These two things went together in the past, but as one looks closer at Robinson's writing, one sees that the garment is now torn in two. In fact, Robinson's entire text posits that Blacks no longer have a shared sense of racial solidarity, no matter how much he may fondly recall what having one felt like in the past. Even the notion of race, he admits, is a social construct, and "racial identity has always been fluid, based not on objective reality but on perception and self-image" (226–27). That being the case, racial identity is subject to change and is no more real than we choose to allow it to be. This is not to say that society cannot enforce notions of race (Appiah and Gutmann 1996), but within that same society, the importance of race and definitions of it can change over time. López (2014) observed that just as southern Europeans became white, so efforts to include Latinos and Asians "may contribute to a long-term transition in the very definition of who counts as white" (216). This is the juncture we find ourselves at in the present.

Whereas in the past, race mattered more than class, today it is ever more apparent that class is more salient to individuals and perhaps more important to them than race. Even in dividing up Black America into four groups, one can easily see that these groups for the most part are based on class. Robinson (2010) himself notes that "the separation perceived by so many African Americans is both economic and cultural" (226). When nearly 40 percent of Blacks no longer see themselves as part of a single race, and personal responsibility trumps discrimination as an explanation for whether one gets ahead in America, something has changed. What has changed is the notion that to be Black is somehow different than to be American. Blacks, for the most part, have successfully integrated into the mainstream.

Robinson observes that in the past Blacks were a unified group with a shared agenda. That agenda revolved around the basic rights and opportunities that Blacks were denied because of race. A sense of racial solidarity or identification was tied to a very real division from the rest of American society. Moreover, since the division was very much economic in nature owing to the social consequences of ostracism and mistreatment, to be Black was for the most part to be identified with being poor (Steele 1991). Blacks stood outside the mainstream social circle and therefore had little choice but to oppose the establishment. Yet as Robinson (2010) notes, "Today, Black American's fundamental rights are secure" (229). While racism and inequality still exist, it would be difficult to argue that Blacks are still considered something other than American.

Robinson seeks but does not find the sense of racial solidarity and a shared agenda that existed in the past because there is no longer a need for such. This is something that I believe he fails to realize when he laments the lack of consensus on "the big, concrete, and urgent concerns that some black Americans now face" (230). The key word in that quote is "some." In particular, the issues

Robinson is most concerned with are those that face the Black poor, or the Abandoned. He notes that "ultimately the goal is for the Abandoned to become the Mainstream" (231). Yet what he misses is that the group he terms the Mainstream among Blacks is simply part of mainstream America. It's not about the needs of the Abandoned being different from those of the Mainstream; rather, they differ from those of mainstream America in general. What we are really discussing here is class, and specifically poverty. Robinson wants the government to do something about Black poverty, but this is no more likely than the government doing something about poverty in general (Glaude 2016, 23). The main issue is not that the Abandoned are poor Blacks but that they are poor. One no longer finds a Black leader or a Black agenda because at this point what we have are leaders who are Black promoting agendas that favor a social class more than a racial group.

In the end, Robinson harks back to Du Bois's notion of a Talented Tenth and a debt to the race that he believes still remains unpaid. I believe that he focuses less on the dream of Dr. King than on Du Bois's notion of racial obligation, loyalty, and debt. Robinson (2010) suggests that until the plight of the Abandoned is resolved, race will remain "the defining attribute of African Americans" (236). Yet his own book points to the idea that this is no longer the case, as class has moved ahead of race in American society. Still, Robinson argues that "race still separates us, preoccupies us, and defines us" and "there remains one black racial identity" shared by African Americans (236). This sense of racial identity, however, seems rooted in a sense of racial solidarity that Robinson earlier admitted no longer exists. He argues that all Blacks are tethered to the Abandoned and that we can feel no true sense of escape or "begin to un-hyphenate ourselves" (237) until their situation changes for the better. It is, however, a grave error to suggest that because the Abandoned are poor and still outside the circle of mainstream America, the rest of us must remain hyphenated Americans, unable to simply be American. Robinson's sales job falls flat, as the problem is not that the other groups he notes among Blacks are hyphenated Americans but that they are simply Americans. It is his notion that Blacks still share a racial identity that was rooted in racial solidarity due to discrimination and economic exploitation. Racial identity and racial solidarity were tied together, and when the need for racial solidarity lessened, so too did the sense of racial identity and its importance. Robinson appears to do a decent job of noting the changes that have taken place in American society in the post–civil rights era. Yet it is perhaps his nostalgia for the past that prevents him from accepting the implications of the very changes he observes. There is nothing on which to base a claim of racial identity anymore in a world where everyone knows that race is a fiction, and there is little difference between Americans who share the same social class. The Black Mainstream that Robinson writes about is not fundamentally different from the mainstream in general, nor are the Transcendents different from those with similar economic and political power in general. In attempting to describe the divisions within Black America, what Robinson really does is to succeed in noting the extent to which most Blacks are firmly identified with American society. The notion of Black America is difficult to sustain in a world where Blacks are simply thought of as Americans, and there is little to point to that separates all but the poorest Blacks from other citizens. Identification is the end of division. As Blacks are allowed to identify with whites and mainstream society in the absence of de jure segregation and discrimination, Blacks are no longer outside the circle but part of it.

CONCLUSION

In the post–civil rights era, we find ourselves facing the division among Black Americans and pondering what it means for the future. While noting that four separate groups exist among Blacks, Robinson still tries to assert that Blacks are united by a shared racial identity and their ties to the Black underclass, or what he terms the Abandoned. Yet, as I have pointed out, his own work shows the ways in which that is not the case. Blacks who are deemed the Transcendents, such as Oprah, Obama, and others, illustrate the importance of class and moreover extreme wealth in society. The Transcendents in many ways live in a world that, if it is not truly color-blind, at least aspires to the idea of a color-blind world: a world where race is either irrelevant or at the least matters less than the amount one has in one's bank account. Race for the Transcendents is not the overarching factor in their lived experience as it is for others. They live as businesspeople who happen to be Black, as politicians who happen to be Black, in a world where blackness can easily be an afterthought rather than the first thought that they or anyone else around them has on a given day. The Transcendents as a group would not even seem to aspire to make race relevant but rather seek to make it irrelevant. As a group, they have no reason to emphasize race when for so long throughout American history it is their identification with a racial group that would have kept them from reaching the heights they have achieved. No, these individuals have every reason to want people to look past their racial identity and see them as a person, an individual and no more.

Similarly, recent Black immigrants and individuals of biracial identity within the Emergent class have similar reasons for de-emphasizing race. Given the level of education that recent immigrants bring with them and the success of their children in attaining admission to prestigious universities and occupations after graduation, their experience is unlike that of native-born Black Americans. If anything, immigrants have every reason not to identify with native-born Blacks. Such identification gains them nothing, and it would lose them the advantage of having whites and others see them as better than native-born Blacks. They speak, look, and act differently, in that they have no fear of being held back because of racism and are not scarred by the long history of oppression in America. Instead they see America as a land of opportunity, just as many other arrivals to Ellis Island and other points of entry did long ago and still do. For the native-born Black, America is the land of a dream deferred, even after the March on Washington and Martin Luther King Jr.'s speech.

Individuals who are biracial do not necessarily have the same relationship to the nation, either. No longer forced to hold to the one-drop rule and declare themselves Black, they are now free to declare themselves something different, even other. Du Bois (1969) spoke of a sense of twoness, being torn between a Black identity and an American one (45). Yet if Obama represents anything, it is the fusion of these two identities when he speaks of having a Black father from Africa and a white mother from Kansas. Obama does not have to choose, and this lack of choice became his ticket to the White House in an America that longed to see his election as somehow signaling that we had all finally moved beyond race. A postracial America was not true at the time of his election, and subsequent events in Ferguson and elsewhere have shown the extent to which little has changed, especially for poor Blacks in America. Yet Obama's election signals the extent to which it has changed for other individuals once singularly identified as Blacks. Perhaps we have now reached a point in time when white people can tell the difference between one Black and another. However, rather than that being a good thing, it may very well herald a new era when the color caste just has more dimensions rather than being abolished altogether.

The Black middle class, or the Mainstream, now enjoys many of the same perks and privileges as the white middle class. Yes, racial segregation still exists in the de facto sense, but with enough money, a Black family can purchase a home in places where decades ago they would have been barred by law. The majority of Blacks attend integrated colleges and universities rather than the HBCUs that still serve Blacks exceedingly well and that Robinson speaks of with such fond recollection. The Black middle class, as Conley (1999) noted, still lacks wealth despite having income, and the housing crisis of 2008 destroyed what little wealth many Blacks had invested in their homes. While the Mainstream is not entirely equal to their white counterparts in every way, they still have the opportunity to climb the educational and economic ladder in ways that remain unimaginable for most of the Abandoned in America.

The Abandoned by far are the group with the lowest level of identification with whites or America in general. They are the most likely to be unemployed, incarcerated, and suffer from poor health care. While at time to be Black was to be identified with poor Blacks (Steele 1991), this is no longer the case. Poor Blacks are left to their own devices with few resources and no bootstraps on which to pull. If disintegration is relevant, it is most relevant for this group, as they can no longer even count on other Blacks to rhetorically acknowledge any debt to them based on racial obligation. They are seen no longer as an example of America's crimes against humanity but rather as individuals whose failures are their own in a society that worships wealth and denies the impact of systemic factors on the life chances of America's citizens, especially its Black ones.

Du Bois argued in the idea of the Talented Tenth that the most advantaged Blacks had an obligation to lift up those beneath them, and even at the end of the twentieth century, prominent African American scholars saw it as necessary to revisit his idea and discuss its continued relevance (Gates and West 1996). Yet Gates and West also noted Du Bois's own lack of faith in the idea decades after he espoused it. Du Bois's idea of the Guiding Hundredth was a revision of his previous theory, as he later felt that very few Blacks were willing to make the sacrifices he thought necessary for racial uplift (177). Moreover, around the same time that Du Bois was writing of his Guiding Hundredth, he noted the sense of shame that privileged Blacks felt in being lumped in with the masses, over whom they had no control, and receiving "no credit for social standing" (Du Bois 1995, 78). The Transcendents of today do receive credit for their standing and, in doing so, tower over not just the Black masses but the masses in general. Their identification with America and whites is complete, and the ties that bound them to the Abandoned are no more.

What we see in Robinson's discussion of disintegration is evidence of the renunciation of a singular Black identity. Yet this monolithic sense of blackness cannot be renounced without also casting aside the notion of racial obligation that went along with it. No more are the Talented Tenth bound to uplift the Black masses. At this point, the most they might do is leave a few bread crumbs pointing the way toward a better life. At worst, they castigate the Black poor for their failures and, in doing so, thoroughly identify with the white American obsession of victim blaming. It's not that the Black poor don't make poor life choices (J. Williams 2006), but rather that poor Blacks aren't any different than poor people in general. America has long sought to argue that there was something wrong with Black people. When they could no longer say that it was Blacks in general, the argument shifted toward a culture of poverty and a focus on the underclass. Yet what Americans consciously avoid is the truth that systematic factors contribute to, and in many ways have an overwhelming impact on, the circumstances and life choices of the poor. To do otherwise would be to acknowledge that every American, both past and present, bears some responsibility for the disparities in equality, fairness, opportunity, and justice that exist in our society. It is much easier for most Americans to simply separate themselves from poor people and say that it is their own fault and that we are so much better than they are. We have reached a stage when Blacks now publicly proclaim distinctions among themselves for all to hear. In doing so, they attempt to show that they too are better than the Abandoned. You see, we are just like you, and not like them. Members of the Talented Tenth can now identify with whites rather than poor Blacks. It is a sign that the times have changed, but perhaps not in all ways for the better. Burke ([1950] 1969) wrote that identification implies division (23), and in achieving greater identification with whites, the majority of Blacks now express the extent to which they are divided from the Abandoned. "Abandoned" may be just as apt a term as "the underclass" for describing the Black poor. They were never more alone than they are today, and that perhaps is the greatest tragedy of all.

CHAPTER 5

Divided Loyalty: Race, Class, and Place in the Affirmative Action Debate

Sheryll Cashin's book *Place, Not Race: A New Vision of Opportunity in America* provides more than a different way to look at affirmative action policy in the United States. I argue that a closer reading of the text in light of Du Bois's notion of the Talented Tenth provides us with a new understanding of the conflict that now exists between the Talented Tenth and members of the Black lower class. While Du Bois posited that the role of the Talented Tenth was to provide leadership and lift up the masses of Blacks, I find that Cashin's text provides evidence that the Talented Tenth may work alongside whites to keep poor Blacks in their place at the bottom of the social hierarchy. West (1993b) wrote of the selfishness he perceived among members of the Talented Tenth. In doing so, he was echoing Du Bois (Gates and West 1996), who lost faith in the Talented Tenth for similar reasons and instead placed his faith in an even smaller group he deemed the Guiding Hundredth. Yet neither the Talented Tenth nor a Guiding Hundredth has emerged as a group lacking in selfishness or a sense of self-preservation. Rather, both traits seem to be so characteristic of humans in general that even the idealistic notion of racial loyalty is not enough to overcome them.

Members of the Talented Tenth seek to pass on their privileges to their own progeny in the same way that members of the white middle and upper classes seek to do. As Cashin (2014) notes, affirmative action provides similar benefits to well-off Blacks in the same way that legacy admissions provide benefits to privileged whites. Both well-off Blacks and whites now unite to defend their privilege against poor Blacks who seek entrance into institutions of higher education. As Cashin asks, "Is this what America has come to—a country in which advantaged people of all colors look at growing inequality and are reduced to invoking numerical standards that block out others, and complaining when those others do gain access?" (x). The answer, it appears, is yes. Yet more important for my purposes, this answer points to the extent to which the Talented Tenth no longer fulfills its mandate to lift up the masses but instead may actively work against them to ensure that they stay down. As Battle and Wright (2002) observed, the possibility always existed that "those called on to help save the group would perversely become active participants in the exploitation and underdevelopment of the people they were called to save" (655). Although these authors argue that the Talented Tenth have fulfilled their role in providing leadership of the group in contrast to the Black middle class, which they do not see as synonymous with the former, the fact remains that the Talented Tenth may nevertheless hoard access to valuable educational resources for their own children. The affirmative action debate betrays not only the division between Blacks and whites but also the division that exists between Blacks as a group, if they can still be thought of as one at all. Class in this instance shows itself to be a much more important factor than race among Blacks themselves.

CLASS MATTERS

Early on in the text, Cashin relates a conversation with a student that revealed to her the "honest tribal talk" (xii) that whites have among themselves about affirmative action. She referred to her student, in a positive sense, as a race traitor in that he spoke truths about whites and their opinions that minorities are seldom privy to hearing. I believe that the term "class traitor" might apply to Cashin herself, and I use the term in a positive sense to denote one who reveals truths about the class divisions that exist among Blacks in America. Cashin's argument for place, not race, is antithetical to the current interests of the Talented Tenth, who benefit from affirmative action policies as they exist today. In arguing that place should take precedence over race, Cashin attempts to "help those actually disadvantaged by segregation" (xv). In doing so, she takes the side of the Black lower classes, the masses that Du Bois believed the Talented Tenth were supposed to lift up. Cashin seeks to fulfill Du Bois's historical mandate, and in this sense, she remains loyal to the group's initial charge. Yet at the same time, she betrays what is revealed as the group's interest in protecting the gains it has made and securing a place for its progeny, even at the expense of poor Blacks. The Talented Tenth want to defend affirmative action, but not for the purpose of lifting up the Black masses. Rather, defending affirmative action ensures at the least that the Talented Tenth do not fall, and at its best provides an opportunity for their privileged children to rise to even greater heights than they have achieved. The Talented Tenth want affirmative action of a particular kind, one still based on race rather than place, as the latter would no longer be advantageous for them.

What Cashin points out is that whites oppose affirmative action in general in a society where white males see themselves as victims. Even white females such as Abigail Fisher file lawsuits when the benefits of gender-based affirmative action are not seen as providing the same ones as those believed to exist for racial minorities. As Holmes (2007) observed, "While most white Americans purport to hate discrimination, an increasing number question or downright reject progressive policies that would redress discrimination" (36–37). Whites, as Cashin (2014) notes, believe that Blacks and whites are equal. She writes, "It is hard for non-blacks to see blacks as disadvantaged and needing affirmative action when examples of black success are ubiquitous, from Obama to Oprah to Jay-Z, not to mention black bosses non-blacks may report to" (xiv). The success of the Talented Tenth ironically works against continued attempts to uplift the masses of Blacks. Whites see the gains made by what Eugene Robinson (2010) termed the Transcendent and the Mainstream groups among Blacks and believe that they have no more cause to help the Abandoned. Moreover, Cashin (2014) points out that whites "don't see black poverty, because they are removed from the deprivations of ghetto neighborhoods" (xiv). The Black masses are not just out of sight but out of mind for the majority of white Americans. Black success is front and center to the extent that whites today believe that equality exists between the two groups. A twisted example of this is that on television and in film, "even a dark-skinned brother is now allowed to seduce a pale woman, the ultimate suggestion of black equality" (xiv). Given that for so long whites wrote laws and engaged in violence to prevent miscegenation or even the thought of it, they now see even fictionalized representations of this taboo as signs that racial equality is at hand.

Blacks have their problems when it comes to race as well. Continued Black support for affirmative action does not translate into a desire to fulfill Du Bois's historical mandate of uplifting the masses. Rather, Cashin's argument in favor of place rather than race shows the extent to which the Talented Tenth's desire for the status quo of affirmative action blocks efforts to uplift less privileged Blacks via the educational system. She desires to "help those actually disadvantaged by segregation" (xv). She notes, "Race is also overinclusive in that it can capture people with dark skin who are exceedingly advantaged" (xvi). Far from the Talented Tenth helping those less fortunate than themselves, it appears that they benefit from what Cashin deems "underlying systems of exclusion that propagate inequality" (xvi). In an effort to help the Black poor as well as poor people in general, Cashin turns away from race-based notions of uplift and instead calls for a multiracial coalition to address continued inequality. In doing so, her rhetoric provides evidence that bonds of racial solidarity that were believed to exist not only between the Talented Tenth and the Black poor but also within the Talented Tenth itself are broken. In their place, Cashin seeks to replace them with King's idea of a beloved community, where race no longer separates one person from another. She argues against an emphasis on race that "makes it mathematically impossible to build multiracial alliances for sanity and common sense" (xx). For more than a century, the notion that Black advancement would come through racial loyalty and sacrifice held sway. Even at the turn of the century, Gates and West (1996) sought to revisit Du Bois's idea of the Talented Tenth and dedicate themselves and others to fulfilling this dream. Yet Cashin's call to replace Du Bois's idea with that of Dr. King signals that perhaps one dream may replace another. In this new vision, the future of the race relies not on race but on place. Rather than racial loyalty, we see the abandonment of it in favor of cross-racial alliances that can more effectively speak to the challenges we face as a nation in the twenty-first century.

BLACK AND WHITE PAWNS

To lift up the Black masses, Cashin's work points, oddly enough, to the need to consider the economic situation and feelings of the white working class. Whites see themselves as having lost ground, and though they may not admit to feelings of racism toward Blacks, they undoubtedly do feel resentment. Greeson (1995) observed that "increasingly, whites experienced themselves as oppressed victims of an uncaring authority and cited efforts on behalf of Blacks, Hispanics, Native Americans, and other ethnics as 'reverse racism'—the birth cry of modern white racial recovery rhetoric" (9). Having seen their incomes decline while the status of at least some minorities appeared to rise, the white working class moved from being staunch supporters of the Democratic Party to becoming a bulwark of the Republican Party. Yet in this transition, they are still pawns, just as they have always been. As Du Bois once noted, white sharecroppers and Black sharecroppers were in the same boat economically. Yet privileged whites sought to prevent them from forming the cross-racial alliance of which Cashin now speaks. Poor whites were told that their white skin made them better than Blacks even while privileged whites did little to raise poor whites' economic prospects. This feeling of racial superiority made whites feel better psychologically, even if it did little for them economically.

Du Bois (1933, 1995) noted the extent to which whites failed to unite with Blacks on the basis of class:

> And while Negro labor in America suffers because of the fundamental inequities of the whole capitalistic system, the lowest and most fatal degree of its suffering comes not from the capitalists but from fellow white laborers. It is white labor that deprives the Negro his right to vote, denies him education, denies him affiliation with trade unions, expels him from decent houses and neighborhoods, and heaps upon him the public insults of open color discrimination. (541)

Over time, the status of white Americans did rise, especially after World War II. These whites had good union jobs, stable incomes, houses, and, for many, college educations with the help of the GI Bill. For white America, this was as good as it got. As Katznelson (2005) observed, "New programs produced economic and social opportunity for favored constituencies and thus widened the gap between white and black Americans" (23). Yet times of plenty were followed by recession, the demise of labor unions, and rising income inequality as the nation shifted toward more predatory forms of capitalism. Caught in the middle, the white working class began to seek salvation in the Republican Party and a politics of race (Mayer 2002) that fueled their resentment and gave them an easy scapegoat for all their problems (López 2014). White support for government policies meant to raise the status of Blacks declined along with the economic fortunes of working-class whites themselves.

Poor Blacks have generally struggled in any time period, but after the civil rights movement, some Blacks did see their educations and incomes rise with new opportunities, as bell hooks (2000) pointed out. Yet, as hooks observed, this exacerbated the class divisions that existed among Blacks (xx). Blacks with the ability to do so left urban enclaves, as Wilson (1997) noted, leaving behind deserts where very little flourished. Middle-class Blacks fled urban environments on the heels of whites who had left earlier. Neither group is to blame for what was left behind; rather, both sought to protect themselves and their families from the possibility of changes to their economic fortunes. Scholars and politicians on both the right and the left began to coalesce around the notion that a culture of poverty (Moynihan 1965) existed in the inner city, and that Blacks themselves were to blame for many of the problems that plagued their communities.

The courts, rather than being a palliative for these plagues as they had been in earlier times, instead became a refuge for whites who felt that the system no longer worked in their favor. As Cashin (2014) observes, "In fact, whites are more apt to perceive discrimination against themselves than against racial minorities" (10). Whites turned to the courts as well as to the ballot with referendums meant to roll back, if not eliminate, affirmative action measures seen as creating an unequal playing field, now tilted in the direction of minorities. The election of a Black man to the White House only increased whites' belief that Blacks no longer need special treatment from the government. It is whites who now see themselves as victims, as "levels of racial resentment toward Blacks have also risen since Obama became President" (11). Yet what, Cashin asks, is it all for? Who, if anyone, is helped by this politics of resentment? Neither working-class whites, she answers, nor even poor Blacks.

Poor Blacks, rather than benefiting from affirmative action, are instead pawns in a game played between white and Black elites. While Black elites seek to keep spots in the nation's top private universities with the added help of affirmative action, the prospects for the Black masses continue to decline. White elites, while railing against affirmative action, nevertheless find it a useful tool to stoke the fire of racial resentment among the white working class and win elections, even while doing little to help the working-class whites who vote for them and policies that favor the rich. What is interesting is that issues like affirmative action "at the non-elite schools . . . seemed to play little to no role in admissions" (16). So whether they are depicted as welfare queens, super predators, or undeserving, the masses of poor Blacks are in fact pawns in a game played between white and Black elites. Cashin's work, while focusing on the relationship between Blacks and whites, also reveals much about the relationship that exists among Blacks themselves. The interests of the Talented Tenth and those Du Bois charged them with uplifting are in fact disconnected. Poor Blacks, Cashin argues, would be better served by policies and politics that move beyond race than by ones firmly rooted in it. The only people who still support affirmative action are Blacks, even though a large segment of the Black population does not benefit from it and may in fact be hurt by it, as the politics of white resentment grow stronger. The election of Donald Trump to the presidency, which Cashin did not anticipate (13), is a prime example of such resentment.

THE GREAT DIVIDE

The circumstances of middle-class Blacks and above are quite different from those of the Black poor when it comes to educational opportunity. As Cashin points out, "Place, although highly racialized, now better captures who is disadvantaged than skin color" (21). Cashin notes the advantages that members of the Talented Tenth can provide for their progeny to ensure that they have the means to attend schools that will allow them to develop their talents to the fullest. Whether by living in good neighborhoods with good public schools or possessing the means to pay tuition at expensive private schools, the children of the Black elite are advantaged in ways that poor Blacks can hardly imagine. Yet given both the public's own lack of support for both affirmative action in higher education and declining support for desegregation efforts at the primary and secondary level, poor Blacks are stuck in place at the bottom in regard to attaining a quality education and the economic and social opportunities that stem from it. The courts, having stopped short of what Cashin terms "radical integration," do little to move the needle toward greater inclusion of poor minorities into mainstream society. What is interesting is that, in making an argument in favor of helping the Black poor, Cashin turns her attention to the ramifications of place on whites and other groups as well.

In appealing to the interests of poor whites and the extent to which inequalities in education rooted in class affect them as well, she seeks a broader multiracial coalition as a means to lift up the Black poor rather than emphasizing traditional notions of uplift rooted in race and the Talented Tenth's debt to those less fortunate. The Talented Tenth, in Cashin's narrative, appear to be self-interested, doing their best to ensure advantages for their own children on par with whites, rather than lifting poor Blacks up to their level. As she states, "We are no different than other parents in our aspirations for our children" (32). Even among Blacks, place seems to take precedence over race as individuals seek to pass on the advantages they have accumulated to their own children. Self-sacrifice just isn't in the cards for Blacks or whites, so Cashin seeks to deal a new deck in which place, rather than race, becomes the new rallying cry of those seeking to move the country forward on the journey to greater equality and opportunity for all. To achieve that goal, she is willing to turn her back on race-based affirmative action, even if doing so undermines the Talented Tenth's ability to "trade on their skin to benefit from racial preferences" (40). Du Bois's idea of the Talented Tenth may have something in common with wealthy Republicans' belief in trickle-down economics. The belief that the success of those at the top would allow them to spread largesse to those below has not worked out in either case. Rather, advantages accrue for those at the top, while those at the bottom fall further behind.

Admission into elite institutions of higher education is limited for poor Blacks for a number of reasons. Yet in Cashin's argument, racism is not primary among them. Rather, factors such as class and geography play a much greater role than race in excluding poor Blacks from educational opportunities. In fact, Cashin argues that class and geography affect poor whites and others as much as poor Blacks. Members of the Talented Tenth, even when they tackle the issues related to the masses of Blacks, tend to focus on racism and its effects. Yet in attempting to aid poor Blacks, Cashin tackles the much broader issue of class and its effect on everyone, not just the Black lower class.

Arguing that class matters more than race is typically controversial, and the idea that the Black lower class could be most helped by policies that are race neutral is perhaps even more so. For Cashin, the best way to help poor Blacks is to admit that the interests of poor Blacks and those of the Talented Tenth are no longer aligned. Although her focus is not specifically on the relationship between the Talented Tenth and poor Blacks, she nevertheless realizes that it has an impact, stating, "I recognize that what am writing is sacrilegious in the civil rights community" (56). She relays an anecdote from a mixed-raced student at an Ivy League school who noted that he felt he had more in common with a working-class white student than wealthy Blacks. Class, in this instance, was a greater factor in identification than race. Moreover, Cashin sees wealthy Blacks as having more in common with their wealthy white peers than with other Blacks (42). To the extent that Blacks are excluded from elite institutions, it is not because of race but because of class. As Cashin notes, "Place creates disadvantages that are different in kind than racial discrimination. Place is not a proxy for race" (49). Race itself, as she points out later, is problematic as well, for reasons that have to do with both geography and socioeconomic status.

As Eugene Robinson (2010) argued, we no longer have one Black community but rather separate and distinct Black communities. Cashin alludes to this fact in her discussion of who is Black and what counts as Black in regard to affirmative action. Cashin discusses the group that Robinson calls Emergents, composed of both people who are Black immigrants from Africa and the Caribbean, and people of mixed racial ancestry. As Cashin (2014) observes, Black immigrants are the most educated immigrant group coming to America, and their children do exceptionally well in regard to education and economic advancement. The second group of Emergents, composed of people of mixed racial ancestry such as Obama, Mariah Carey, and Tiger Woods, have the option of choosing how much to identify as Black or not at all, if that is what they wish (E. Robinson 2010). Both Black immigrants and people of mixed race often enjoy educational and economic advantages that native Blacks who are poor do not, even if one does not consider cultural and racial reasons for why whites may favor them relative to native-born Blacks in the United States. As Cashin (2014) observes, "Black immigrants can trade on their skin color more easily than African American slave descendants" (51), thus benefiting from affirmative action policies that were originally meant to help the latter group. As a result, "the descendants of slavery might fare better under programs based upon segregation or structural advantage rather than race" (52). In sum, "optical blackness . . . masks the struggles of those who are limited by the places they are relegated to" (55). At the end of the day, as Cashin notes, "less advantaged blacks are competing with higher-income blacks, and so on" (61). As Landry and Marsh (2011) observed, "Middle class growth is fueled by both upward mobility from the working class and what researchers call the inheritance of class, or the persistence of the children of middle-class parents in middle-class positions" (379). From this perspective, one can see the possibility that the interests of the working class in attaining a middle-class position, and that of individuals within the middle class in maintaining a similar existence for their children, may be in opposition. Rather than raising up the masses, middle-class Blacks may see progress as maintaining their own status and potentially elevating that of their children to even great heights. This, then, would give a new and different meaning to racial uplift than what Du Bois intended. The Black middle class could hoard educational advantages for their own children to the detriment of the lower classes. Far from being a mechanism for the social uplift of the Black masses, affirmative action redounds to the benefit of the Talented Tenth, solidifying class division rather than working to eliminate it.

FAIRNESS, OPPORTUNITY, AND THE STATUS QUO

In Cashin's eyes, universities and the system of higher education as a whole are complicit in keeping structural mechanisms in place that unfairly work against equal opportunity for poor students. Cashin expands her argument once again beyond race and instead tackles the structural disadvantage of place for students hailing from economically impoverished areas and backgrounds. She notes the examples of elite colleges such as Amherst and the ways in which a focus on place, rather than race, has in fact led to greater diversity among the student body while simultaneously avoiding the legal challenges that a focus on race would invite. Yet even at the schools she points to as success stories, students from poor backgrounds must first overcome long odds and achieve high grade point averages and test scores that are beyond the reach of most students from poor environments. As Cashin (2014) observes, standardized tests can "perform a gatekeeping function, because performance is tightly correlated with socioeconomic status" (70). While proponents of affirmative action focus on the impact of past racial discrimination on Blacks, Cashin instead takes a much broader view of the impact of geography and place and the ways in which living in a poor environment disadvantages not just Blacks but all Americans. In taking this broader view, she moves beyond the traditional focus on civil rights and instead engages in a larger discussion of fairness and opportunity in America. This is a discussion that poor individuals of all colors can benefit from and is much less likely to create animosity between racial groups, as the focus is not on race but on place. While poor Blacks will undoubtedly benefit from such a focus due to a history of racial segregation and lack of economic opportunity, the prospect of forming a multiracial coalition to fight for greater fairness in society exists. Wilson (1999) stated that African Americans would benefit most from such a coalition (66). Yet what stands in the way are institutions of higher education as well as privileged Blacks and whites who benefit both from legacy admissions and from current affirmative action policies.

It's an odd thing to consider that both rich whites and well-off Blacks may now support policies that disadvantage poor Blacks as well as poor whites. Yet as Hochschild (1995) noted, individuals of different races who share the same social class may have more in common than individuals who share nothing more than race (xx). While Cashin (2014) focuses on place rather than class, it is apparent that the configuration of loyalties today among the elite of both Blacks and whites works against Du Bois's belief that the Talented Tenth existed to ensure the social uplift of the Black masses. Cashin notes the extent to which test scores themselves are not meaningful and the ways in which a more holistic view of each college applicant would be both beneficial and more fair. Yet in challenging the way that universities select applicants today, I note that she pulls back the curtain on the Talented Tenth and the extent to which it does not fulfill its historical mandate and instead supports a status quo based on race from which its members and their children benefit. As long as race is a factor in college admissions, then the most privileged among racial minorities stand to benefit from such a system. Affirmative action in this instance performs the same role for Black elites that legacy admissions perform for white elites. It is interesting that one of the justifications that supporters of affirmative action make is that "it remains necessary to ensure the leadership class that emerges from very selective private and public colleges is diverse" (80). Yet if that leadership class among Blacks does not fulfill its historical mandate of racial uplift, then it fails to answer Du Bois's call. Moreover, if the mechanisms by which that same leadership class is created work to keep the Black poor down at the expense of the elite, then the entire system works against Du Bois's idea of racial uplift. Last, as Cashin points out in challenging Randall Kennedy's justification for affirmative action, there are poor children of every color "who are perfectly capable of competing, uplifting themselves, and being leaders" (81). This, more than anything else, is the most damaging not only to current justifications for affirmative action but also to those who seek to renew their faith in Du Bois's idea of the Talented Tenth.

Perhaps, at the beginning of the twentieth century, the need for such an idea of elite leadership made sense. Yet given the changes that have taken place in American society since the civil rights movement, the idea of leadership from above sounds elitist rather than altruistic. To say that poor people lack the ability to lead themselves sounds condescending. What Cashin points out is that poor people of all racial groups do not lack the ability to thrive but instead lack the opportunity to do so. At present they must play a game in which the dice are loaded against them while hoping that they can roll a seven. This may be one reason why Chrisman (2013) borrowed Gramsci's concept of the organic intellectual and applied it to the struggle of poor Blacks, arguing that we must draw "upon the intellectual, cultural and social resources of the people themselves to realize their educations" (69). Chrisman saw individuals such as Frederick Douglass and Malcolm X as examples of organic intellectuals who gained their knowledge outside of the traditional educational system (69) and advocated that we attempt to "stand the model of the Talented Tenth on its head" (68). Cashin (2014), however, does not turn wholesale against the idea of traditional higher education but instead seeks to increase the access that poor Blacks and others have to it. Access for the poor is often denied in a system that provides greater access to the haves than to the have-nots. Cashin asserts that "the goal of society should be to delink success from the status of one's parents" (86). Given that belief, she is not in favor of policies that benefit privileged elites, whether they are white or Black.

(NON)RACIAL UPLIFT

Cashin seeks to help individuals in our society who are marginalized for structural reasons such as place. While members of the Talented Tenth were tasked with raising up the Black masses, Cashin seeks to raise up everyone, regardless of race. She believes that the best way to help poor Blacks is to move beyond a politics specifically focused on race. Cashin urges people to form multiracial coalitions in which groups both recognize their own self-interest and see how their interests overlap in a system that often hurts not just poor Blacks and Latinos but poor whites as well. It is in her discussion of the interests of poor whites that she goes beyond the traditional focus on Black well-being characteristic of much civil rights discourse and the mandate of the Talented Tenth. A successful coalition, she argues, must "include some strange bedfellows" (100). For some time, whites have been seen as either an enemy or an obstacle to Black advancement. Yet in Cashin's work, whites working in concert with minorities become instrumental in challenging systemic inequalities that affect everyone in society, even if in different ways (104). If Blacks and other minorities fail to reach out to whites and seek common ground, they will "continue to lose whatever policy battle [they] are fighting" (106).

For Cashin, politics shifts from one based on the interests of a single racial group to one in which multiracial coalitions hold "elected officials of both political parties accountable" (106). Cashin's work goes not just beyond race but beyond party as well. Those leading the way in this new political environment are not the Talented Tenth but a group she calls "ardent integrators," defined as people who "move toward rather than away from difference, and they accelerate the racial enlightenment of those around them" (107). The goal of Cashin and these ardent integrators is "to unleash politics from the shackles of racial division" (14). In this, Cashin's work might be described as postracial, since mutual interest, rather than loyalty to a racial group, is the motivating force behind political and social action. In this brave new world, there is no need for the Talented Tenth that Du Bois conceived of long ago. Rather, ardent integrators push politics beyond the boundaries of race and in doing so liberate poor Blacks and the poor in general who are confined to a lower place in the socioeconomic hierarchy. The tacit alliance or stalemate between the white and Black elites is broken, as neither group would have a firm hold over their poorer brethren on the basis of racial loyalty.

Cashin believes that now is the time for Blacks, whites, and people of all colors to come together and "reinvent America" (110). Given the racial animosity of the past and the continued animosity that programs meant to address past discrimination engender, she argues that "jettisoning race-based affirmative action is the beginning, not the end, of creating a fair society" (111). Class, not race, is the issue for Cashin, as she states that "systems are rigged against all middle-income and poor people" (110). No one racial group alone can tackle this problem, even though what affects the majority will have an even greater effect on members of minority groups.

Blacks both past and present who sought racial uplift have tried to make Americans more aware of race and its importance in our lives. Yet to close the racial gap, Cashin argues that it is necessary to stop focusing explicitly on race in our social policy. Whites suffer too, she argues, and if their pain is not addressed, then there is no way to address the continued agony that poor Blacks suffer in a society that grants greater opportunity for the wealthy few than for the many poor. She believes that "the country is ripe for another leap forward," even while acknowledging that "each social transformation has been followed by a period of backlash" (112). The leap forward that Cashin advocates is to change how we respond to issues of race by not focusing on them as such at all. Instead, people of all colors are asked to unite and address issues of class.

Perhaps, in making this change, Cashin is truer to Du Bois's understanding of the social problem that faces America than many other commentators. Du Bois knew that America's race problem was really a mask for the issue of class, one that white Americans were not willing to address for themselves, let alone for the racial minorities who dwelt among them. Still, as Brown and colleagues (2003) observed:

> Since the inception of the United States, wealth and institutional support have been invested on the white side of the color line, leading to an accumulation of economic and social advantages among European Americans. On the black side, economic and institutional disinvestment has been the practice, resulting in a process of disaccumulation. (26)

Yet given the socioeconomic and demographic changes that have taken place since the civil rights movement, it is not sufficient to draw a line in the sand between whites and Blacks and assume that everyone on one side of the line is either wealthy or poor. Race, to use Cashin's (2014) words, "is too blunt an instrument and too costly politically" (112) as a means to address the problem of what it means to be poor and Black in America. If we can address what it means to be poor for all Americans, then perhaps being Black in America will not prove to be so costly for those who are just trying to pursue life and liberty in the land of the free.

CONCLUSION

Cashin's approach to creating a policy of affirmative action based on place, not race, relies on the formation of a multiracial coalition and acknowledges the need for whites' participation in a movement that will address their economic needs as well as those of minorities. In doing so, I believe she echoes the work of Dr. Martin Luther King Jr., who planned a Poor People's March on Washington for 1968, five years after the famed Marched on Washington. King saw the Poor People's Campaign as the next step in his thinking as he moved beyond a focus on civil rights and toward a focus on human rights. Individuals of all races suffered from poverty not only in America but also around the world. Yet King never lived to see the Poor People's March take place, as he was assassinated on April 4, 1968. Without King's leadership, the campaign did not go far beyond the march itself and the construction of a shantytown on the National Mall. The multiracial coalition that he sought to put together did not hold in the absence of his leadership. The campaign's ultimate failure was a lost opportunity not only in regard to fighting poverty but also to assembling a broad coalition that would move Black politics beyond a narrow focus on civil rights and racism. It's not that civil rights and racism aren't important but rather that violations of civil rights and racism stem from the self-interest of those who benefit from the unequal economic environment that racism is meant to support and perpetuate. Black leaders have for some time focused on race rather than place and in so doing have failed to continue the trajectory that King sought to place Black politics on before his death. As Holmes (2007) noted:

> Martin Luther King's dream of equality encompassed a broad vision that would aggressively address past racial discrimination and address economic deficiencies that all people of all races faced during his time.... Given the breadth of King's actual vision, then, affirmative action is itself problematic.... Its past implementation and current repudiation at once illuminate how material racism can be and how meager mainstream efforts to address it remain. (37)

As Cashin (2014) rightly points out, Black leaders' focus on affirmative action provides no bridge to the working class, as a campaign based on poverty would have, or a focus on place would do today. Given the inability of many whites to identity with Blacks on the basis of race and the failure to establish identification on the basis of class, a wedge exists between the two groups that politicians in the Republican Party have continued to exploit since Richard Nixon. Whites see Black advancement in any form as detrimental to, and in contrast to, their own advancement. Rather than seeing affirmative action and other policies as efforts to address past discrimination, whites instead see it as a form of discrimination in the present, aimed at them.

White racial resentment toward Blacks for both progress and failure exists as it has throughout the nation's history. Less than a century ago, as Robin Kelley (2002) observed, whites destroyed the property of Blacks and killed them in both Tulsa, Oklahoma, and Rosewood, Florida. They did so not because Blacks were failing to succeed but rather because they had succeeded. Jealousy over the economic success of Blacks engenders hate as much as any perceived failure of Blacks to overcome racial and economic oppression. The election of Donald Trump to the presidency signaled the resurgence of white racism in a society that a few ill-informed or intentionally misleading commentators tried to label as postracial after the election of Barack Obama. The resurgence of white nationalism in 2016 shows that it was always there and only grew stronger with the election of a man who, like many others, supports this viewpoint. The difference between Trump and many other Republicans is that his approach is blunter and less subtle than that of those who engage in dog whistle politics (López 2014) to gain election, be they Ronald Reagan or George H. W. Bush. The difficulty this leaves us with is the question of whether or not the multiracial coalition that Cashin believes is necessary can be created in an environment where the majority of the white population voted for a man who openly courted the support of white nationalists and made one of them, Steve Bannon, his chief strategist and senior counselor in the White House. Only time will tell, but Trump gives reason to doubt that a multiracial coalition is on the horizon in the near future.

If an alliance between Blacks and whites may be difficult to achieve, then what remains of the perceived alliance between the Talented Tenth and members of the Black masses or lower class? The debate over affirmative action would suggest that if such an alliance exists at all, it is fraying at the seams. Du Bois (1986) wrote:

> The Negro race, like all races, is going to be saved by its exceptional men. The problem of education, then, among Negroes must first of all deal with the Talented Tenth; it is the problem of developing the Best of this race that they may guide the masses away from the contamination and death of the Worst, in their own and other races. . . . From the very first it has been the educated and intelligent of the Negro people that have led and elevated the mass, and the sole obstacles that nullified and retarded their efforts were slavery and race prejudice; for what is slavery but the legalized survival of the unfit and the nullification of the work of natural internal leadership? Negro leadership, therefore, sought from the first to rid the race of this awful incubus that it might make way for natural selection and the survival of the fittest. (842–43)

The fact that Cashin is a woman writing in the twenty-first century about the problem of the color line is evidence that things are much different now than when Du Bois theorized about exceptional male leadership of the race before 1920, when women received the vote and were, at least on paper, citizens with the same right to suffrage as men. Still, Du Bois's quote points to the idea that education of the elite among Blacks must precede that of Blacks as a whole. It tells us that the Talented Tenth are the vanguard and the natural leaders among Blacks. However, the civil rights movement, along with the appearance of organic intellectuals such as Malcolm X, among others, suggests that leadership can rise from below and that the interests of poor Blacks are not necessarily the same as those of the Black elite.

The continued elevation and perpetuation of a Black leadership class into the twenty-first century with the help of affirmative action has done little to change the situation of the Black poor, as the interests of these two classes grow farther apart. Eugene Robinson (2010) even suggested that there is no such thing as a unified group of Blacks in this country, but rather that Blacks constitute four distinct groups with different levels of success and experiences in America today. Notions of racial uplift coupled with racial loyalty are questioned at a time when Kennedy (2008) can wonder about who is Black and what, if anything, Blacks owe to other Blacks. Randall Robinson (2003), after turning his gaze from the reparations debate, focused on what he believed Blacks owed to each other. Yet these notions of a debt owed to the race have all been subject to deferred payout, like the bad check King alluded to in his "I Have a Dream" speech. Kendi (2016) observed that "it is in the intelligent self-interest of middle- and upper-income Blacks to challenge the racism affecting the Black poor knowing that they will not be free of the racism that is slowing their socioeconomic rise until poor Blacks are free of racism" (504). While that may be true, it may also be true that middle- and upper-income Blacks see a world without race-based affirmative action as contrary to their self-interest as well. In such a world, they may fear that the socioeconomic rise of their own children would be slowed just as much as that of the children of poor Blacks is today. As hooks (2000) reminded us, "Class matters. Race and gender can be used as screens to deflect attention away from the harsh realities class politics exposes" (7). It is this screen, this veil, that Cashin seeks to lift, but in doing so, she exposes the class divide and different interests that exist among Blacks on the basis of class status.

Even if the Talented Tenth desired to fulfill the rhetorical mandate of Du Bois and had the ability to do so, it would still not solve the problems Blacks face in America. As Kendi (2016) noted, "Racist Americans have routinely despised those Black Americans the most who uplifted themselves, who defied those racist laws and theories that individuals employed to keep them down" (505). He went on to state that "power will never self-sacrifice away from its self-interest. Power cannot be persuaded away from self-interest. Power cannot be educated away from self-interest" (508). That being the case, we have to acknowledge that the self-interest of the Talented Tenth in the present may take them away from fulfilling their mandate to uplift the masses. Racial uplift for the Talented Tenth may be more about preserving their own position than about elevating the masses. This is what Du Bois himself eventually came to accept to some degree when he revised his theory of racial uplift from a Talented Tenth to a Guiding Hundredth, realizing that self-sacrifice was not something that most people would be willing to do.

Perhaps one of the biggest hurdles to the advancement of both Black politics and Black people is the idea that we can be held to a higher standard than whites or anyone else. If we are all human, then we are subject to the same desires, drives, and frailties as others. We are not superhuman but rather mortal beings seeking to secure our own survival and that of our progeny. We are no better and no worse than any other group, which is the most antiracist position we can hold. As Kendi (2016) wrote, "Black is beautiful and ugly, intelligent and unintelligent" (505). The continued farce that the interests of the black elite and those of the lower classes are the same is ugly. It would be intelligent for us to admit the truth and free both groups to pursue their own self-interest, even while admitting that these interests may run contrary to each other. The goal is not to disempower the Black poor but rather to acknowledge their own agency and ability to theorize and fight for themselves. They do not need to be led by a Talented Tenth, a term that in this day and age mocks and demeans the Black poor by default. For if we are talented, then what are they? The Black poor have excelled in sports, music, and any other field where they have been given a fighting chance. The changes that Cashin argues we should make in regard to affirmative action, basing it on place rather than race, would open up education as a road on which the Black poor too can walk or run to freedom and the fulfillment of their own American dream. While the journey may be long and the mountain high, I, like Cashin, believe that all of us are up to the task. It is a journey that we should begin with the utmost speed so that no one else's dreams have to be deferred.

CHAPTER 6

Blacks and the Rhetoric of Individualism

Touré's *Who's Afraid of Post-Blackness?* (2011) takes us into an examination of what it means to be Black in the post–civil rights era at a microscopic rather than a macroscopic level. Whereas Eugene Robinson (2010) was concerned with understanding divisions among Blacks at a group level, Touré's text goes deeper and notes the differences that exist among Blacks as individuals. Blacks have long thought it necessary to stick together as a means to combat white supremacy and the legacy of both slavery and segregation in America. The idea that a Black person could be seen simply as a person and not thought of as Black first was almost nonsensical, since racism and segregation ensured that one's individuality held little to no sway on the opinions of whites. Race, rather than character, was the defining feature for both whites and Blacks in America. Yet as hooks (2000) observed, the civil rights movement opened up doors for those Blacks who were already poised to walk through them. We now live in a time when we find ourselves examining the tension that exists between the individual and his or her racial group, rather than just the tension that exists between racial groups.

Kennedy's (2008) discussion of the rhetoric of selling out provides one way of dealing with this tension. As I argued earlier, I believe that the rhetoric of selling out functions to keep Blacks on their side of the color line. In Touré's work, we find the possibility that there are Blacks who seek to erase the color line altogether. What they seek is not just parity between racial groups but parity between individuals regardless of racial group. On the surface, this appears straightforward in that, in American society, all individuals ought to have the same rights regardless of race. This may be written into law, but on a social level, it does not address the identity politics that can take place within a racial group. A group can seek to police the behavior of individuals perceived to be members of that group. Kennedy's work offers an example of such policing. Individuals who are perceived to be members of a racial group are believed to be responsible to that group. The behavior of one individual is said to reflect on the group as a whole. This stems in part from the fact that Blacks, for example, were never seen as individuals in the eyes of whites but were seen as members of a racial group. Yet with the passage of time, some Blacks seek to break free of the confines of both white and Black America. They wish to live free of restrictions that attempt to tell them not only who to be but also how to be.

Greeson (1982) examined "the paradox of liberation—the pull toward liberation for both self and other with mixed motives" (14). Touré is one such individual dealing with this tension, and his book examines the lives of many others who, rather than trying to redefine what it means to be Black in a singular sense, wish to explore the plurality of ways in which individuals can enact their own notions of blackness. I argue, however, that the post-Black identity Touré advocates is more likely to be embraced by the Mainstream and Transcendent groups rather than the Abandoned, who continue to occupy a place at the bottom of America's social hierarchy, even among other Blacks. As I will show, problems with the post-Black identity exist. Still, some may see this as a trade-off they are willing to accept, especially if they see class as a more important marker for them than race. Touré's own work focuses on successful individuals who are atypical. These are individuals who not only survive but also thrive despite racism. Therefore they do not represent the average, nor can they be used to establish a new norm. Last, the post-Black identity is problematic for Blacks as a group and for individual Blacks as well.

POST-BLACK IDENTITY

Touré (2011) begins his discussion with the story of his first attempt at skydiving. As an individual, he thought it would be something worth trying. Yet when he encountered three Black men at a restaurant on the way to his first jump, he was told during conversation, "Brother, Black people don't do that" (1). Touré goes on to state that "as they saw it I was breaking the rules of Blackness" (1). While this particular rule seems arbitrary in relation to the types of violations Kennedy discussed, it nevertheless functions to keep Black people in their place. Yet as Touré points out in his discussion of the 555th Parachute Infantry Battalion, an all-Black unit of paratroopers during World War II, some lines have previously been crossed, even when segregation was rampant. The majority of Blacks, however, are likely unaware of the exploits of the 555th, and they are even more unaware that skydiving might help one "get closer to God" (4), as Touré experienced. Our notions about what Blacks do or don't do may be there to keep us safe or at least protect the group as a whole. Yet these same notions, Touré believes, limit the fields that Blacks may choose to explore, and what they do within a given field, and moreover limit the experiences that Blacks may have as human beings. When we attempt to police blackness and determine who is or is not Black based on an individual's choices, Touré argues that we "sell Blackness short . . . and limit the potential of Blackness" (5). In a post-Black world, we will be free to determine what blackness means on an individual level, and no longer embrace as a collective "the bankrupt, fraudulent, concept of 'authentic' Blackness" (11). To be post-Black, Touré writes, is to "not be restricted by Blackness. It means we love Blackness but accept the fact that we do not all view or perform the culture the same way given the vast variety of realities of modern Blackness" (12). Blackness, for Touré, is "whatever you want it to be" (12).

Touré takes the notion of post-blackness from the art world, a realm where artists began to define themselves as artists who were Black rather than as Black artists limited solely to exploring Black themes and Black life. Yet in his application of the term to Blacks in general, Touré makes an inductive argument that what is true for the particular holds for the larger population as well. The question is whether the freedom that artists may explore within the microcosm of art can exist in the macrocosm of society at large.

As Touré notes, Blacks have for some time felt the need to stick together in the face of white supremacy and societal racism. Yet with the success of the civil rights movement came a "shift from living amid segregation and civil war to integration" (21). In this larger world, many Blacks started to consider the possibility of thinking of themselves not primarily as members of a racial group but rather as individuals. Integration opened up the possibility that Blacks could do something that previously only whites could take for granted: to think of themselves in nonracial terms. Yet this freedom to explore one's individuality led to tensions among Blacks between what Touré labels "identity liberals" and "identity conservatives." Identity liberals "took Black identity to new places and challenged identity boundaries," while identity conservatives judge which Blacks "need to be shaped up or weeded out by any means necessary" (23). Identity conservatives see blackness in rigid terms and believe that individuals must live in ways that demonstrate their blackness and loyalty to the racial group. Failure to pass whatever litmus test is used constitutes a reason to have one's blackness questioned or, in more severe cases, be excommunicated from the group. Yet Touré questions these limited understandings of blackness and argues that no one can be kicked out of a racial group for not being Black enough. Rather, Blacks need to allow for the possibility that blackness can exist in any number of forms and that individuals are free to choose how and when they will express it.

Touré takes the work of William Pope.L as one example of a post-Black identity at work. Touré observes that Pope.L's work both uses and challenges negative depictions of Blacks at the same time in ways that may make other Blacks uncomfortable. As an artist, Pope.L is unconcerned with the reactions of white viewers, which, according to Touré, form a prison within which both Black artists and Blacks in general have labored for some time. Blacks have long feared the white gaze, and it is this fear that causes Blacks to police the actions and choices of other Blacks, thus subjecting Blacks to an additional level of monitoring. The Black gaze exists, Touré suggests, as an outcome of the white gaze. Yet to truly be free, Blacks must allow themselves to live as individuals, with all that this entails, because "unity is sometimes disguised as a weapon that someone can use to try to enforce social control" (31). In a post-Black world, artists, among others, are free to embrace integration and draw from both African and European traditions. Individuals may do so knowing that this is not a rejection of blackness but rather a different way of performing it. Yet such freedom still comes at a cost, as artists such as Kara Walker have experienced. Touré notes that her work "is also reviled by many artists" (33) because of the ways in which she explores masters, slaves, and plantation life. It is work that, in the words of Dr. Derek Conrad Murray, "is not trying to validate you or make you feel good about being Black" (35). Walker herself explains that, growing up, she "was just so ambivalent about learning how to be devout about Blackness" (37). This lack of devotion is what the identity conservatives Touré alludes to would find objectionable in Walker's work. Her desire to explore her own identity as an artist and as an individual puts her in conflict with an identity conservative's understanding of what it means to be Black and what is in the best interests of Black people as a group.

In a post-Black era, Touré states that some artists "have a general sense of removal from the sacredness of history that inspires a feeling of independence and individuality" (39). Rather than blackness and Black culture being separate from and challenging mainstream culture, both have become, in Touré's words, "more like Starbucks: located on every corner in every major city" (41). Blackness is no longer the sole province of Black people but is available to anyone "in a world that [understands] that subject matter as being cultural in a general way" (43). Artists began to see blackness as part of a "shared culture rather than as something that is private or must be preserved in a glass case" (43). Touré argues that this change is due to multiculturalism. Initially Blacks may have seen multiculturalism as beneficial, yet for the identity conservative, it comes at the sacrifice of a sense of ownership over the cultural productions of the group with which one identifies. Individuals who are not Black could explore Black art, and individuals identified as Black could explore areas previously seen as off-limits to Blacks even by other Blacks. The identity conservative would have trouble differentiating between buying into the culture at large and selling out to it. Yet if everything now exists in one big pot, and we can all eat from the same spoon, then what we make is up to us and belongs to all of us. Visual arts in particular, Touré argues, have the ability to "take chances with identity and aesthetics that even other artists can't" (53). Whether or not this freedom can be generalized to all Blacks is the question we are struggling with today. If, as former congressman Harold Ford suggests, "post-Blackness means being an American. Being as broad and as full an American as you can be" (56), then we have reached a point at which the antagonistic relationship between America and Blacks may be changing. Blacks would then have the freedom to see themselves as Americans first and Blacks second or at the least see the two as existing on the same plane.

FREEDOM AND THE LIMITS OF POST-BLACKNESS

Touré sees visual artists as standing at the vanguard of a movement to embrace greater individuality and believes that it is possible to extend post-blackness to the larger Black population. Yet the problematic nature of this extension quickly becomes evident. In Touré's discussion of Dave Chappelle and his show on Comedy Central, the freedoms and limitations of post-blackness become evident.

One of the first sketches Chappelle performed on his show involved the character of Clayton Bigsby, a blind Black man who was told throughout his life that he was white. As a result, Bigsby takes his white identity to an extreme and becomes a writer and leader in the Ku Klux Klan. A white friend and fellow Klansman helps Bigsby to keep his identity hidden from his readers in the white supremacy movement. Touré discusses this sketch as an example of Chappelle's liberation from the need to always portray Blacks in a positive light and put the needs of the group ahead of his own desire for individual expression. Touré notes that after a friend told Chappelle that the sketch was harmful to Black people, Chappelle offered up an apology that was anything but an apology. Chappelle shrugged, said "sorry," and then moved on with the sketch as planned. Touré observes that, in doing so, Chappelle declared his allegiance to comedy and his own individuality rather than to Blacks as a group. This was the first of many times that Chappelle's sketches pushed the boundaries of what some Blacks might have thought was permissible on national television.

Yet Chappelle's decision to push these boundaries ultimately brought him fame and a contract worth tens of millions of dollars from a network that originally attempted to prevent the inclusion of the Bigsby sketch in the show's first broadcast. Even Comedy Central executives were afraid that the sketch went too far. Chappelle threatened to walk away and give up his show from the outset if he was not allowed to pursue his artistic vision. Chappelle both prevailed with the network and won the approval of the public, but his commitment to his artistic vision did not come without consequences.

Like the Black mailman Clifton who made fun of the oddly named white family in the famous "N---ar Family" sketch, Chappelle ultimately found that the attempt to create comedic reversals in discussing racism in America might ultimately redound upon the performer. Just as Clifton at the end of the sketch declared, "Oh, Lord, this racism is killin' me inside" (64), Chappelle found it difficult to continue pursuing his artistic vision in the face of material success in a culture in which racism was still alive and well. Chappelle walked away from his show and retreated to Africa after reportedly hearing white interns laugh in a way that suggested they were laughing at him rather than with him during one of his sketches. Yet while Chappelle referenced this incident, as well as the network, as reasons for his departure, a fellow member on the show, Donnell Rawlings, suggested that Chappelle's break with the show came not all at once but over a period of time. Moreover, Touré suggests that Chappelle, rather than feeling he was being prostituted by the network, actually struggled with the possibility that he was both his own pimp and his own prostitute.

Chappelle's freedom to pursue his own individuality put him in conflict with his own values and desire not to sell out to white supremacy. As much as Chappelle wanted to be an individual, he nevertheless did not really want to do harm to Black people as a group in the process. Touré states that "it's Chappelle who's put himself in a position that he doesn't want to be in" (73), yet this place is exactly where Chappelle arrived at in pursuit of the individuality that Touré seeks to champion himself. As Touré observes of Chappelle, "The freedom of the post-Black era has scared him to death" (74). If this can be said of someone who Touré states "produced the clearest example of post-Blackness ever seen on television" (58), then the limitations of an attempt to extend post-blackness outside the realm of visual artists to all Blacks becomes evident. Blacks may pursue their individuality, yet they do so in the face of the potential costs to the group as a whole in a culture where racism is still a part of our day-to-day reality. Racism may not be as pervasive as it was in the past, but it is still there, as the election of Donald Trump to the presidency suggests. Blacks should be able to pursue their individuality on the same level as whites, but unfortunately the consequences of that pursuit are not the same. Blacks may be free to finally pursue their individuality, but it does not come without costs. Some individuals, such as Dave Chappelle, may decide that those costs are too high a price to pay if they make it difficult to respect oneself.

POST-BLACK IN THE WHITE WORLD

Touré spends time discussing his own struggles to embrace a post-Black identity in a culture in which issues of race still exist both overtly and covertly. As a young man, Touré grew up in Boston, and while experiencing the freedom that came from his parents' middle-class status, he also knew that there were parts of the city where his presence would not be welcome. While attending the prestigious Milton Academy, Touré experienced an environment that on the surface appeared to deal "with race and racism in an upfront and candid way" (79), yet over time it became evident that some of his classmates believed that even the most talented Blacks only advanced because of affirmative action. This was the first of many encounters with microaggression that Touré would experience in his life. He notes the difficulties he experienced in having whites question his credentials while participating in a writer's retreat, as well as questioning his ability to write on non-Black topics for magazines, and the exclusion of Black authors from the curriculum at Columbia University when he was pursuing his MFA in creative writing. Yet whites are not the only ones who interfere with the ability of a Black person to embrace a post-Black identity.

Blacks, Touré notes, are both a source of strength in a hostile world and an impediment for Black individuals who seek freedom from group norms and identity politics. At Emory University, Touré recalls that initially he hung out primarily with white students before later deciding to immerse himself in all things Black after his first year of college. While seeming to gain acceptance among Blacks, Touré notes that some Black students still remembered that he was not initially a bona fide member of the group during his freshman year. This later became an issue when a fellow student told Touré that he wasn't Black, causing the author to experience a moment of crisis when no other Black students came to his defense. The experience caused Touré to realize that not only whites but also Blacks could make it difficult for a Black person to define blackness in his or her own unique way.

When Touré writes that "I may be a work in progress but I will always be Black" (97), one senses the defensiveness the author felt and the insecurity he had to overcome when his blackness was questioned. This insecurity, I believe, stemmed in part from Touré's class status, his attending a prestigious private school with wealthy whites, and his own comfort level with having a majority of white friends during his first year of college. These facts left Touré vulnerable to being called a sellout in a way that someone from a different class background might not have been concerned with, because their connections to other Blacks and sense of identity would have been more firmly rooted in blackness. What another Black person might have laughed off, Touré could not, because at the time his own understanding of what it meant to be Black was limited, and thus he was potentially subject to the limitation that someone he may have perceived as being "blacker" placed on him.

As a young magazine writer, Touré struggled to define himself not just as a Black writer but as a writer capable of addressing any subject of interest to him in an industry that sought to limit him to writing solely about Black people. Touré observes that the magazine world was interested in him not as a post-Black writer but only as a Black writer. Du Bois (1969) wrote of double consciousness and the difficulties of being torn between being both an American and a Negro (45). Touré's (2011) attempt to fuse those identities is challenged, and he is forced to admit that "much of the world may not be ready for the post-Black liberty and complexity that so many of us feel within us" (102). This fact creates a dilemma for Blacks who seek to embrace individuality in a culture in which race and the importance of one's racial group are still seen as paramount, even decades after King's speech about his dream and the importance of character over color.

As much as Touré would like to live in a fully multicultural world, his own life provides evidence that this is not yet the case. In recounting a trip to Indiana to participate in a demolition derby, he "felt surrounded by intense hate" that pushed him "towards a nervous breakdown" (109). These feelings were not just in Touré's head, as young white men made it evident to the film crew that Touré was not welcome there, while using the most racist language they were familiar with to drive home the point. Bonilla-Silva (2001) argued that "actors in racialized societies, which I formally label *racialized social systems,* participate in race relations as either beneficiaries (members of the dominant race) or subordinates (members of the dominated race or races)" (11). Even in the twenty-first century, the young white men at the derby saw themselves as members of the dominant race and took issue with Touré's attempt to occupy the same social space and privileges that they did. Touré feared for his safety and wondered if he as a Black person would be targeted during the demolition derby. Only the intervention of a white woman accepted in the community provided Touré with a measure of safety before the derby started. While Touré (2011) speaks of setting aside his "defensive mistrust of all the whites around me in that little town" (109), allowing him to accept the woman's prayers and concerns, his own recollections of the environment show that he had a right to be concerned for his safety. What would have happened had this devoted Christian, whose grandfather was a leader in the Klan, not intervened? Would Touré's fears of winding up in a wheelchair as a result of pushing the boundaries of race too far become reality? While Touré uses the story to exemplify the need for Blacks to open themselves up to the possibility of help from good white people, the story illustrates the valid concerns that Black people may have in relation to hostile whites. Blacks have experienced this hostility before and have good reason to fear it. Brophy (2002) discussed the loss of life and property in Tulsa, Oklahoma, in 1921 stemming from white anger at Blacks' ability to succeed despite segregation. As Touré (2011) noted of the demolition derby, "Confederate flags were all over the place" (107). Just as Chappelle ran up against the potential limitations of a post-Black identity, Touré found himself facing the dangers of attempting to be post-Black in the face of traditional white supremacy. Blacks may decide to see themselves as individuals, but this does not mean that white people will see them this way as well. The potential losses may outweigh the gains for Blacks in this scenario, as Blacks have no ability to dictate how white people will respond to our own efforts at personal transformation.

Black freedom has been, and to some degree still is, limited by whites because whites are the majority group. We are not entirely free to do as we please without consequence. It is these consequences that the identity conservatives Touré discusses likely fear, and as a result the Black gaze and the white gaze cannot entirely be separated. Blacks police other Blacks and place limitations on each other as a consequence of the limitations that the larger white society places on Blacks as a group. Whether it is our decision to spank or not spank a child, or to eat watermelon in view of whites, Blacks find it necessary to think twice, because they know that they do not enjoy the same freedoms as whites. Touré tries time and again to push past the boundaries of both the larger society and those that Blacks impose on each other. Yet one cannot help but see this is a struggle for Touré, just as it would likely be for any reader attempting to live as he attempts to do, free from fear and excited about the possibilities of a post-Black identity.

Blacks may encounter difficulty realizing a post-Black identity because of the continued presence of racism in society. While racism today is not what it was in the past, this does not negate its effects on Black life. Racism has changed form, but this has made it more difficult for Blacks to know when they are affected by it. As Bonilla-Silva (2010) observed, "Compared to Jim Crow racism, the ideology of color blindness seems like 'racism lite'" (3). When Touré asked a number of successful Blacks what was the most racist thing that ever happened to them, the most common response was that it was probably something the individual was unaware of. Yet when respondents did note a specific incident, it was apparent to Touré that the effects of those incidents still lingered today for those who experienced them.

For some time, many Blacks labored under the assumption that if they achieved a measure of education and class success, they would be free from the effects of racism. Yet more often than not, Blacks wind up experiencing racism in new settings where they did not expect it. Having lowered their guards, they are left more vulnerable to the blows they sustain, even if those punches are not as hard as they were during segregation. As Cose (1993) wrote, "For the truth is that the often hurtful and seeming trivial encounters of daily existence are in the end what most of life is" (192). Touré's (2011) interview with the comedian Paul Mooney provided the term "n----r wake-up call," which signifies the moment when Blacks are reminded of the "societal limitations and the emotional assault that comes along with Blackness" (125) in this society. Whether it involves having one's intelligence doubted in school or at work, continually being questioned about one's credentials no matter what one achieves, or even being subjected to racial slurs on the sidewalk or in church, Blacks find it difficult to secure a safe space in America where they can feel at home.

While Touré claims that "in no story I heard was anyone permanently broken by racism" (139), he fails to understand that all the individuals he interviewed were successful. As a result, his sample suffers from survivor's bias. The reason he chose to interview these individuals in the first place is because they are successful. Yet these individuals stand out because they do not represent the average. The wounds, anger, and bitterness that Touré notes often change people (139) may be more than many Blacks are able to overcome. When Touré writes, "We revitalize ourselves like the phoenix—rebuilding our spirits and coming back stronger" (139), he ignores the fact that this strength of spirit does not apply to everyone. As Smith and O'Connell (1997) argued, "White racism is much less a barrier to black advancement overall than are a weak commitment to middle-class values and a paucity of skills, especially within the black underclass" (10). Touré takes the strength of the few to be indicative of the many, but this is not the case. He talks of successful Blacks who have overcome racism as if they can stand in for Blacks as a whole. Yet this misconception fails to recognize the power of racism and its detrimental effects on many Blacks.

Touré wants to give his readers a sense of hope and imbue them with the idea that we have overcome; but wishes are not the same as reality. A large share of the Black community still suffers from poor educational opportunities, poverty, imprisonment, poor health care, and early death in comparison to whites. Giroux (2010) observed of the American public that "a clear majority appears to have neither the will nor the stomach to challenge and transform deepening racial disparities in employment, education, housing, health, and mortality" (5). As

Touré notes, even the most successful Blacks may work their way to an early grave as a result of attempts to overcome racism through the strength of will alone, without the necessary social and environmental support. Conley (1999) found that "at all income, occupational, and educational levels, black families on average have drastically lower levels of wealth than similar white families" (5). John Henryism is not a solution to racism but another manifestation of it. Gates (1997) profiled various successful Black men and noted that "they are extraordinary men who may be taken as Representative in an Emersonian rather than a statistical sense" (xvi). As Touré (2011) notes, successful Blacks "may overcome and achieve but they will pay with their bodies . . . brought on by the extra effort of being at war with racism" (144). This being the case, then once again we find that the post-Black identity that Touré seeks to have readers embrace does not come without problems. Blacks cannot ignore racism, and when we attempt to overcome it alone, it literally kills us.

While Touré notes that the ways in which Blacks seek to cope with racism are not always healthy, and "Black cultural norms strongly encourage us to hold our pain" (144), this focus puts the cart before the horse. Even if Blacks had ideal coping strategies, it would not erase the fact that racism would still take a mental, physical, psychological, social, and economic toll on us. Our ways of coping with racism may make its effects worse, but attempts to deal with it stoically no longer work out well for us, either. As Dr. Jelani Cobb states, "It is literally destroying our community" (Touré 2011, 145). It is not possible for Blacks to embrace the post-Black identity that Touré advocates without the support of the very Black community that a post-Black identity might question or take one away from. The post-Black identity that Touré advocates puts individual Blacks out on a limb by themselves. Perhaps this is not new, as hooks (2000) wrote that our "sense of solidarity was altered by a class-based civil rights struggle whose ultimate goal was to acquire more freedom for those black folks who already had a degree of class privilege however relative" (91). Yet it is the strong roots of the Black community that have allowed individual Blacks to weather the storms of racism for centuries. Touré's goal seems admirable, but the evidence from his own life and that of the individuals he interviews raises questions about the possibility of most Blacks being able to live a post-Black life in the midst of a society that still suffers from racism.

COLOR, CLASS, AND CASTE

In an attempt to live the post-Black lives that Touré espouses, we will encounter issues of color, class, and caste that are brought up in his text. Color matters in that the color of one's skin matters not just to white people in a racist society but to Black people as well. Unfortunately, as Bonilla-Silva (2010) observed, "Colorism may become an even more important factor as a way of making social distinctions among 'blacks'" (197). While it has long been understood that whites may treat lighter-skinned Blacks more favorably, the same applies to Blacks as well. When Touré interviews Dr. Michael Eric Dyson, the celebrated professor speaks of the ways in which members of his own family as well as the Black community treated him in relation to his brother who was darker-skinned. The privileges of color accumulated for Dyson without him needing to ask as the social disadvantages and stigma of being too Black added up in a negative way for his brother. As Goffman (1974) noted, "Finally there are the tribal stigma[s] of race, nation, and religion, these being stigma[s] that can be transmitted through lineages and equally contaminate all members of a family" (4). Yet Blacks, while being stigmatized as a group, have at times sought to separate themselves from other members based on skin tone. Dr. Melissa Harris-Perry went even further than Dyson in admitting that her lighter complexion added up to social benefits and advantages in America. Cose (1997) observed, "That a lighter complexion may be related to success is not news to many blacks, who have long acknowledged—if not always openly—that color sometimes matters nearly as much as does race" (23). Yet all this favoritism takes place in a Black culture influenced by James Brown, Malcolm X, and the Black Panthers.

As a result of the militancy of the civil rights era, Blacks simultaneously embrace the ideas that light skin is good while at the same time believing that poor, darker-skinned Blacks are more authentic than their lighter-skinned cousins. While the light-skinned and advantaged among us reap the social rewards of their phenotypes, they at the same time can be wounded by accusations that they lack soul and are not Black enough or not Black at all. Some even spend their lives trying to learn more about what it means to be Black, and others succumb to stereotypes that cause them to embrace poverty and a life of low expectations for fear of being seen as sellouts or less Black. As Steele (1991) noted, "Being black and middle-class becomes a double bind when class and race are defined in sharply antagonistic terms, so that one must be repressed to appease the other" (96). This equation of blackness with poverty, and education with whiteness, proves harmful to Blacks who fall prey to this misconception.

Yet even those Blacks who overcome the misconception that educational achievement and success are somehow the province of whites may find themselves wondering if their success takes them away from the center of blackness. Tuck (2010) noted that "during the 1990s, African Americans moved to the suburbs at a faster rate than white Americans" (396). Surrounded by whites in their neighborhoods, schools, and jobs, Blacks may wonder if they or their children are sufficiently rooted in the Black community and cultural identity. West (1993a) suggested that "the repoliticizing of the black working poor and underclass should focus primarily on the black cultural apparatus, especially the ideological form and content of black popular music" (289). Musical and artistic tastes are sometimes taken as markers for rootedness, and some young middle-class Black children may decide to embrace hip-hop over classical music for fear of being seen as less Black than those residing in the inner city.

Caste comes into play in that if the poor Black is taken to be the real Black, then the farther up the educational and economic ladder Blacks climb, the less Black they will seem to be. As hooks (2000) observed, class "disturbs the illusion of racial solidarity among blacks, used by those individuals with class power to ensure that their class interests will be protected even as they transcend race behind the scenes" (8). While many Blacks such as Touré seek to redefine what it means to be Black—or, in Touré's case, post-Black—they may nevertheless wonder if their attempts are sufficient. Touré (2011) recalls embracing the word "n---a" in his twenties because "it seemed every Black man around me was using it" (167). While his use of the word bothered his parents, who had attempted to give him every advantage they could, this did not deter him. Touré found something in the word that made him feel more a part of the group and perhaps allowed him to rebel not only against white society but also to some extent against his class background as well. The word "n---a" is rooted in opposition to white society and the low status that Blacks occupy in the American social structure. Yet rather than avoiding the term, many Blacks have over decades embraced it, along with the overtones of fear and shock that it imbues in white people. Baldwin (1963) remarked, "You can only be destroyed by believing that you really are what the white world calls a n----r" (18). It is a word that today emanates from the streets, and its usage is more common among the Black underclass than the Black elite, even if Martin Luther King Jr. and Jesse Jackson are said to have used it at times. It is a word that, as Touré (2011) points out, signifies that "we couldn't end up with a position any lower than what we've had" (172) in American society. The use of the word is "anti-communal and anti-progress" (172).

The election of Barack Obama to the presidency, however, caused some Blacks to question the status of Blacks in society, as well as the continued use of the word "n---a." If some whites could find it in themselves to elect a Black man to the highest seat in the land, then what did or could that mean for the status of Blacks as a group? Tuck (2010) observed that "Obama's victory seemed to mark the final defeat of the power of white supremacist sentiment" (416). The subsequent election of Donald Trump to the presidency via a campaign that openly courted and was supported by white supremacists gave many Blacks pause in thinking that the soul of America had changed as much as we had hoped. As Coates (2017) wrote, "In Trump, white supremacists see one of their own. . . . To Trump whiteness is neither notional nor symbolic but is the very core of his power" (343). Yet the election of Obama was enough to cause Touré to decide that it was time to give up his use of the word "n---a" and instead embrace the term "post-Black." Unlike "n---a," which filled him with rebellious-ness, the term "post-Black" is, in Touré's (2011) words, "about empowerment, love, freedom and the American way" (173). Post-Black signifies the possibility that not all Blacks are at the bottom of the social hierarchy anymore. Yet while Touré may decide that post-Black is a better way to define himself, the question remains as to whether those Blacks Robinson refers to as the Abandoned will be so quick to redefine themselves as well.

POST-BLACK POLITICS

When we discuss the aspirations of Blacks to political office, the difficulties of a post-Black existence become evident. As members of the Mainstream and Transcendent class seek access to higher office, their ability to represent the interests of the majority of Blacks lessens. Norman Kelley (2004) discussed "the rise of 'symbolic politicians,' HNICs who aspire to the pretense of leader-ship without being accountable or presenting solutions" (9). In fact, as Touré and others note, loosening connections to the Black community is seen as an imperative if members of the more privileged classes of Blacks are to attain the votes of whites. The primary reason for this is that politicians who hap-pen to be Black can in no way make white voters uncomfortable. The easiest way to make whites uncomfortable is to remind them of the history of racism and its continuing effects in the present. Instead politicians who happen to be Black must focus on race-neutral issues and must never be seen as advocating for the interests of their specific minority group. Giroux (2010) noted, "Reluc-tantly or willingly, Obama has chosen to capitulate to the nation's collective refusal to address race and, more shamefully, its willful denial of ongoing racist exploitation, exclusion, humiliation, and violence" (72). Terrill (2015) observed, "Obama rarely speaks about race directly, generally does so only within the tight confines of a sanctioned civil rights movement narrative, and is soundly disciplined in the public sphere when he strays beyond this narrative" (152). Yet as Perry (2011) stated, "Not talking about race is actually detrimental to the project of addressing the practice of racial inequality" (191–92). While this silence benefits members of the Mainstream and Transcendent classes who seek higher office, the benefit to members of the Abandoned is questionable, if any benefit exists at all.

In discussing the pursuit of higher offices such as the governorship, Congress, or the presidency, Touré runs into a problem in his desire to spread the post-Black identity. If political office represents the height of post-Blackness, then the trade-off is that one must all but abandon the possibility of being a Black politician. One can be a politician who happens to be Black, but a Black politician is all but barred from success at the highest levels of government. Giroux (2010) remarked that "understanding the generalized ambivalence, where not open hostility, of most whites to any mention of race, Obama owes his electoral success in part to his efforts to ride the post-racial wave and to distance himself—generationally, politically, rhetorically—from civil rights advocates" (5). While white politicians do not need to abandon their identity as whites, Blacks seeking higher office must do their best to lessen their identification with Blacks while at the same time drawing on Blacks as potential voters. As Dr. Phillip Atiba Goff explained when discussing Black politicians, they must be Black while sending a message to white voters that "I'm not that kind of Black person" (Touré 2011, 187). Class status must be made salient, and race must be pushed as far as possible into the background. This fits with Hochschild's (1995) observation that "African Americans are becoming more disparate politically and demographically as well as economically and socially. . . . Well-educated blacks vote, campaign, organize, and petition at the same rates as well-educated whites" (50). White voters are made more comfortable when Black politicians emphasize their membership in the Mainstream or Transcendent groups among Blacks. These groups are seen as less threatening and do not remind whites in word or deed of the dire situation of the Abandoned.

As some of the interviewees Touré spoke with noted, the way a Black person presents himself or herself to whites is important. A politician who happens to be Black will speak in ways that lessen racial identification in his or her tone of voice and grammatical structure. A successful post-Black politician must show that he or she is a member of the Mainstream or Transcendent groups and evidence a comfort level with both standard English and mainstream white America. As a number of the interviewees mentioned, this can be done through one's educational credentials, but as Dr. Goff noted, more important is one's ability "to never make whites feel racist" (181). McWhorter (2000) provided an example of this ability in stating, "In short, black Americans are no longer a race of victims as a whole in the meaningful sense. . . . Instead, this is a race a fraction of whom are victims, and victims more as a result of historical than present-day racism—the people who remained behind for various reasons while most of the race moved upward" (216). Although Touré (2011) may not agree entirely with McWhorter, he does note that "the more love a Black person can find for whites . . . the further up the ladder he or she can climb" (178). Yet not all Blacks evidence this love for whites, as Dr. Melissa Harris-Perry points out. She stated, "Many Black people I know would be perfectly happy if they literally never saw another white person" (178). Touré himself noted that despite growing up around white people, "some voice deep in my mind told me that I shouldn't emotionally trust white people" (179). If this is the case for someone like Touré, then it shows the extent to which politicians who happen to be Black are different from many Blacks.

To become a member of the Transcendent group, it may be necessary to first transcend both racial identification and the sense of racial animosity and historical grievance that many Blacks hold for whites and American society as a consequence of slavery, segregation, and ongoing racial discrimination. One would need a belief system and rhetoric that points in the opposite direction of Randall Robinson (2000), who argued that "no race, no ethnic or religious group, has suffered so much over so long a span as blacks have, and do still. . . . It is a miracle that the victims . . . have survived at all, stymied as they are by the blocked roads to economic equality" (8). Earlier advocates for reparations such as Bittker (1973) argued that "to concentrate on slavery is to understate the case for compensation, so much so that one might almost suspect that the distant past is serving to suppress the ugly facts of the recent past and of contemporary life" (12). Feagin (2000) wrote, "In the United States racism is structured into the rhythms of everyday life. It is lived, concrete, advantageous for whites, and painful for those who are not white" (2). The ability to deny these facts is a type of mind game that is not an easy trick to master, and it is not one that every Black would be comfortable learning, given that it would require one to set aside both historical and present injustices.

At the end of the day, Touré's desire to extend the idea of post-Blackness beyond the art world runs into some serious complications, as he himself admits. Touré (2011) states, "In politics it seems to constrict what Black politicians can do for the Black community" (188). As the Reverend Jesse Jackson told him, "If the price we pay for getting the crossover vote is to miss base needs, it's too expensive" (188). Norman Kelley (2004) wrote that "today black elected leaders are a comprador class, i.e., intermediaries whose sole function is to channel black votes into the Democratic Party apparatus while the party ignores black needs and gears its programs to white suburban voters or Reagan Democrats" (17). Yet this kind of trade-off may be exactly what should be expected as members of the Mainstream and the Transcendent groups take advantage of their class privilege and their access to the white mainstream. In pursuit of their dreams as individuals and the ability to take advantage of their class status among Blacks, they may believe that the interests of the Abandoned and their own personal interests are not aligned. Even Du Bois abandoned his idea of the Talented Tenth in favor of a Guiding Hundredth, admitting, "My Talented Tenth, I could see, might result in a sort of interracial free-for-all, with the devil taking the hindmost and the foremost taking anything they could lay hands on" (Gates and West 1996, 162). West (1993b) remarked, "Most present-day black political leaders appear too hungry for status to be angry, too eager for acceptance to be bold, too self-invested in advancement to be defiant" (38). We saw this conflict of interest recently in Cashin's (2014) critique of affirmative action and her assertion that we should put place ahead of race, which at this point benefits the Mainstream's and the Transcendent's access to elite higher education more than it benefits Blacks as a whole, and in particular the Abandoned, who are losing the educational arms race.

EXTRAORDINARY AND ORDINARY BLACKS

While acknowledging the continued difficulties and inequality associated with racism, Touré (2011) observes that "we do have more of a shot now than at any time in Black history" (189). This is something that Touré feels many Blacks are slow to acknowledge, and their failure to see that the glass is at least half-full is holding them back. As proof of racial progress, Touré points to the increasing numbers of Black CEOs and politicians who are finding success in mainstream America. Kendi (2016), however, noted that in the past, extraordinary Blacks were not seen as "ordinarily inferior like the 'majority.' This mind game allowed racists to maintain their racist ideas in the midst of individual Africans defying its precepts" (97). Touré (2011) holds Obama's election to the presidency as the touchstone for what it is possible to achieve if we as Blacks are willing to dream on an epic scale. Yet the history of race and racism in America and our knowledge of it hold many of us back, according to Touré and some of the successful Blacks he interviewed. As Nelson George stated, "A Black president helps matters but we're still too deeply scarred by the things America has done and continues to do to us" (191). Dr. Melissa Harris-Perry remarked that Blacks "are deeply hurt by the fact that it (America) doesn't love us back" (192). As Dickerson (2004) stated, "Blacks may not be loved, but they cannot be denied, and it is long past time that black nay-sayers stopped telling them otherwise" (9). Still, Touré (2011) believes that despite the lack of identification that some Blacks have with America, or the problematic nature of unrequited love, we have no choice but to do the best we can "in a bad marriage with no possibility for divorce" (198). We must show our love for America and our identification with America, even if the country does not always love us back in the way we would like to be loved, if at all.

Touré argues that our tendency to reject America before it rejects us creates a self-fulfilling prophecy. In this sense, while the doors of opportunity do not equally present themselves for Blacks as they do for whites, Blacks are to some degree responsible for not taking advantage of the opportunities that do exist. Steele (1998) wrote, "It cannot be coincidental that in those areas of greatest Black achievement—music, literature, entertainment, sports—there have been no interventions whatsoever, no co-optation of agency, no idea that some 'opportunity structure' will enable blacks to participate" (60). Even more so, Touré believes that Blacks must create opportunities that others cannot imagine for ourselves, the way Obama did in running for the presidency. Yet I see Touré's rhetoric as akin to a gospel of wealth doctrine, in which we are told that if we only have faith, all of us can succeed and gain riches. As Kendi (2016) wrote, however, "Everyone who has witnessed the historic presidency of Barack Obama—and the historic opposition to him—should know full well that the more Black people uplift themselves, the more they will find themselves on the receiving end of racial backlash. Uplift suasion, as a strategy for racial progress, has failed" (505). Touré also ignores the fact that in America, not all whites succeed. There is a pyramid, and for much of America, Blacks have provided the base of that pyramid on which the success of others is achieved.

We have come to a point in history when some Blacks, such as members of the Mainstream, Emergent, and, as Touré likes to note, the Transcendents, can achieve success on levels previously unimagined. However, this does not mean that the pyramid no longer exists or that all Blacks can achieve if they only dream big enough. Yes, it is true that some Blacks can rise, even those who start at the bottom among the Abandoned. Yet to conflate the success of the Transcendents or the few members of the Abandoned who rise high enough to become members of the Transcendent class with the opportunities for Blacks as a whole is a serious error. The fact that Obama rose to the presidency did not fundamentally alter the systemic issues that members of the Abandoned face at the bottom of America's social hierarchy. Bell (1987) saw racism as a permanent feature of American society, written into the nation's foundation at a constitutional level. As even Touré admits, Obama dealt with racism and disrespect during his presidency, speaking to the fact that not all white Americans were comfortable with, or accepting of, the idea of a Black president.

Touré suggests that rather than fighting against the system, Blacks have an opportunity to force their way into positions of power if they are willing to play the game. While I do not deny that some Blacks can integrate institutions and rise higher than ever before, I do not believe that this is possible without the willingness of at least some whites to allow such a change to occur. It is not solely in the power of individual Blacks to overcome systemic inequities and institutional racism based on sheer will alone. It is, in fact, the work of Blacks as a group, protesting against systemic racism that pressures institutions to create opportunity for individual Blacks. As Shelby (2005) stated, "Historically, political unity among black Americans has contributed much to the cause of social justice" (ix). Still, Touré (2011) exhorts, "Let's be like Barack. Let's get what we want from America in spite of racism" (201). Yet as Perry (2011) noted, "Black American exceptionalism sustains American mythologies of perfect democracy and unfettered possibility" (128). This is problematic because not all Blacks are like Barack, and the ability of Blacks to overcome racism is difficult for the group as a whole and more so on an individual level. As Balfour (2011) wrote, "Du Bois replaces the conventional conception of individual exertion and reward with a more dynamic story of race and class" (30). Moreover, "The result of white dependency on such 'special protection' is a distorted sense of self-worth and an incapacity to comprehend the gap between professed ideals and unjust social practices and structures of power" (34).

A truly equal America would not require us to work ourselves to death like John Henry or push ourselves to exceptional heights like Obama. The privilege of whites is to be average and still attain the American dream. Touré confuses the opportunities available to the Transcendents with those available to other groups of Blacks. His desire for post-Blackness may work well for the Transcendent class, the Mainstream, and perhaps some members of the Emergent class. Yet for the bottom tier of Blacks, or the Abandoned, such calls could potentially resort in blaming the victims for their condition in an unjust system. Cosby and Poussaint (2007), while ostensibly offering poor Blacks a rhetoric of self-help, engaged in this sort of victim blaming, as Dyson (2006) pointed out. Blacks can no more force their way to the top of American society than whites can, because in America not all whites equally share in the bounty that centuries of racism have produced.

Touré's rhetoric justifies the individuality of the Transcendent class, nullifying any perceived debt to Blacks as a whole. Randall Robinson (2003) would take issue with such rhetoric, as he believes there is "a special responsibility upon more fortunate African-Americans" to aid those who are less fortunate (193). Touré's rhetoric may also appeal to members of the Mainstream and Emergent groups who desire to climb ever higher on the rungs of the socioeconomic ladder. Yet it will do little to help the Abandoned, whom Du Bois (1986) believed it was the responsibility of the Talented Tenth to raise up. Du Bois wrote, "The Talented Tenth rises and pulls all that are worth the saving up to their vantage ground" (847). Touré equates the elevation of the individual with the rise of the group as a whole, but this view ignores the fact that the opportunities that exist for the few are not necessarily available to the many. It also ignores the fact that a few can rise at the expense of the many, for in elevating individuals like Obama, some whites proclaim not a post-Black but rather a postracial country. America is no more post-Black than it is postracial, even if we can all agree that it is no longer the same country that it was before.

CONCLUSION

Touré takes the notion of post-blackness from the art world. The question is whether the freedom that artists may explore within the microcosm of art can exist in the macrocosm of society at large. The answer, I believe, is no. The post-Black identity Touré advocates is more likely to be embraced by the Mainstream and Transcendent groups than by the Abandoned. I see at least four problems with the post-Black identity that Touré advocates in relation to both Blacks as a group and Blacks as individuals, and I will discuss each of them in turn.

The first difficulty is that the post-Black identity problematizes the relationship between the self and the group among Blacks. Du Bois argued that the Black self was indebted to the group, and it was the role of the Talented Tenth to provide leadership of the race. As elitist as this idea was and still is, it nevertheless provided a connection between more privileged Blacks and those who were less fortunate. Touré, however, seeks to break this bond, believing that the freedom that artists enjoy can be extended to Blacks as a group. He believes that each Black individual can be free to define blackness on his or her own and be free of any restrictions or limitations on his or her choices. Touré himself eventually chose to move from embracing the term "n---a" to seeing himself as post-Black. He defined "n---a" as "rebelliousness," as opposed to "post-Black," which for him meant "empowerment, love, freedom and the American way" (173). Touré's own change in preference between the two terms and his definition of them illustrate the distinction between identification with the Abandoned and with the Mainstream or Transcendent groups.

"Post-Black" expresses the latter two groups' embrace of an American identity and an attempt to resolve the tension of double consciousness that Du Bois (1969) spoke of. For Du Bois, "One ever feels his twoness,—an American, a Negro; two souls, two thoughts, two unreconciled strivings; two warring ideals in one dark body, whose dogged strength alone keeps it from being torn asunder" (45). Yet Touré seeks to privilege an American identity over that of a Negro. Rather than be at war, Touré seeks peace through submission. The Negro must be redefined so as to be almost meaningless, since for Touré (2011), blackness "is whatever you want it to be" (12). In contrast, Du Bois (1969) wrote, "He would not bleach his Negro soul in a flood of white Americanism. . . . He simply wishes to make it possible for a man to be both a Negro and an American, without being cursed and spit upon by his fellows, without having the doors of Opportunity closed roughly in his face" (45–46). Touré seeks opportunity by stressing an American identity over that of a Black identity so much so that he seeks to redefine himself and others as post-Black, as if blackness is something we can move beyond or set aside at will. As Joseph (2013) stated, "The racist notion that blackness is a deficit [is something] that black and multicultural people must overcome" (7). Touré's rhetoric is a rejection of Du Bois. The individualism that Touré advocates in the twenty-first century is what Du Bois feared would happen at the turn of the twentieth. Du Bois feared that privileged Blacks would elevate themselves at the expense of the many with no concern for them or sense of indebtedness to them.

The second difficulty is that what Touré advocates could be seen as promoting selfishness over sacrifice. Greeson (1982) observed, "Generally, the self-interest of the oppressed person, like that of people in general, is felt to be secondary to that of the collectivity. Thus he is expected to negate, or sacrifice, this generic self-interest or firstness tendency, by placing it second" (18–19). Greeson continued:

> Violation is ultimately a matter of individual versus collective hegemony. Further, while a "unifying ideology" may indeed be a comprehensively shared concern, there is a paradox of liberation involved herein which may generate and place in contention for ultimate hegemony a privately integrative or compelling program which challenges any and all collectivity held unifying ideologies. (41)

Time and again, we see that the artists Touré profiles choose their own artistic vision, freedom, and desires ahead of the perceived interests of Blacks as a group. Pope.L's work both uses and challenges negative depictions of Blacks at the same time in ways that may make other Blacks uncomfortable. Kara Walker's work "is also reviled by many artists" (Touré 2011, 33) because it is work that, in the words of Dr. Derek Conrad Murray, "is not trying to validate you or make you feel good about being Black" (35). After a friend told Chappelle that one of his first sketches was harmful to Black people, Chappelle shrugged, said "sorry," and then proceeded with the sketch as planned. In each of these instances, we see artists more concerned with their own artistic vision than with any ramifications of their work for Blacks as a group. We allow for a degree of selfishness and even narcissism in artists, but to argue that all Blacks as individuals should behave in the same manner is problematic. Greeson (1982) suggested that "betrayal among the socially oppressed can be conceptualized as expressions of 'spoiled sacrifices' and a felt violation of the codes shaping the original efforts at sacrifice" (106). Moreover, "The 'freedom' one may seek as a human being (individual) is not necessarily the same as (or realizable in terms compatible with) the 'freedom' sought as a member of a socially devalued collectivity" (129). These are the key points that Touré fails to understand, and there is evidence for this lack of understanding in Touré's own work.

The third reason that Touré's advocacy of a post-Black identity fails shows in the individuals he profiles to support his argument. We have already seen the reception that the work of Pope.L and Kara Walker received from some Blacks. Yet even if these artists were willing to endure alienation and separation from the Black community, this does not mean that everyone is. Dave Chappelle walked away from a successful show and tens of millions of dollars because the stresses of a post-Black identity were too much for him to bear. Touré (2011) stated that "it's Chappelle who's put himself in a position that he doesn't want to be in" (73), but this place is exactly where Chappelle arrived at in pursuit of the individuality that Touré seeks to champion. As Touré observed of Chappelle, "The freedom of the post-Black era has scared him to death" (74). If this can be said of someone who Touré states "produced the clearest example of post-Blackness ever seen on television" (58), then the limitations of an attempt to extend post-Blackness outside the realm of visual artists to all Blacks becomes evident. Touré noted his own struggles with trying to define a post-Black identity. He recalled the places in his hometown of Boston where he dared not go; his struggles to pursue a post-Black identity in college and his dismay at having another Black person call him out on it; and the difficulties he experienced when attempting to be a post-Black writer in a magazine world that was not interested in a post-Black identity, along with his experiences at a writers' retreat, as well as in graduate school at Columbia. While praising Obama and stating that we should all be more like him, Touré nevertheless admits that Obama dealt with racism and disrespect during his presidency that spoke to the fact that not all white Americans were comfortable with, or accepting of, the idea of a Black president, much less a post-Black one.

As a candidate and as president, Obama gave a nod to the civil rights movement of the past, but he could not outwardly embrace civil rights advocates in the present. To win the presidency, Obama was even forced to distance himself from his longtime pastor and friend Reverend Wright when the latter's rhetoric proved too militant for white Americans to stomach. The rules are different for whites and Blacks. Trump did not disavow the endorsement of a Klan leader during his run for the presidency. Trump was openly racist, whereas Obama felt it necessary to remain race neutral. No tension between self and group exists for whites as it does for Blacks. Whites never have to choose between being white and being accepted as American.

Fourth, the difficulty of a post-Black identity is that Blacks enjoy freedom within limits. They are limited by the power of whiteness to constrain blackness and Black identity. We are not creatures of our own making and never have been. Whiteness was always defined against blackness. As Hale (1998) remarked of emancipation after the Civil War, "American culture already associated dark skin with bondage, the very opposite of self-determination, the value that sat at the symbolic center of American identity" (18). So any efforts to create a post-Black identity will likely be met with resistance from whites, who have the option to accept or reject such attempts at redefinition.

Whites know that Blacks cannot be allowed to redefine themselves without a corresponding change in what it means to be white. On a small scale, Dave Chappelle experienced this when he heard white interns laugh in a way that suggested they were laughing at him, rather than with him, during one of his sketches. Chappelle had no power to force his interpretation of the material or his intentions on a white audience. They were free to interpret or reinterpret his sketches in a manner of their choosing, even in ways that reinforced stereotypes about Blacks and worked to uphold white supremacy. Touré asks: Who is afraid of post-blackness? Perhaps most Blacks should be in the face of continued white supremacy. Chappelle initially was not, but when confronted with how deep racism in American society goes, he booked the first ticket to Africa in an attempt to escape and get in touch with his roots. Touré (2011) himself was afraid, as he discussed when recalling his experience at the demolition derby, confronted by white supremacists, fearing for his safety, "surrounded by intense hate" that pushed him "towards a nervous breakdown" (109). Touré could not handle the heat and hate all on his own. As he admitted earlier, "Much of the world may not be ready for the post-Black liberty and complexity that so many of us feel within us" (11). Touré's book contains six instances of racism that he experienced. Selling a post-Black identity is hard when one's own life provides evidence of the difficulty of the struggle to attain it.

Touré's suggestion that we must love America no matter how we are treated is equivalent to telling a battered spouse to love her partner no matter how much domestic violence she endures. White Americans' embrace of this stance is evidenced in their reaction to Colin Kaepernick's taking a knee during the national anthem and the Black Lives Matter activists taking a stand against police shootings of unarmed Blacks. Touré believes that we have no choice but to do the best we can "in a bad marriage with no possibility for divorce" (198). We may not be able to, or even want to, leave America, but that does not mean we have to love America. Even when we do, we may find it difficult to love America on the same level and in the same way that whites do. Our love has often gone unreciprocated, and the country we love has never treated us with the level of equality and respect that we deserve.

We are Americans, but we are never allowed to forget that we are Black and what that means to white Americans. While Touré notes that artists began to see blackness as part of a "shared culture" as a result of multiculturalism, one must ask whether white Americans really see America as a shared culture. The answer so far from many white Americans is no. They acknowledge the existence of other cultures and groups but still see America and Americans as white. Until that changes, whites have the power to limit blackness and any redefinition of what it means to be Black. The coin of the realm is two-sided, and Blacks do not have the power to socially construct a new reality all on our own. Touré's advocacy of post-blackness fails in part because America has failed to provide life, liberty, and the pursuit of happiness for all its citizens regardless of color. Our nation is not postracial, and we cannot be post-Black.

CONCLUSION

As this work draws to a close, I will provide a short synopsis of the rhetorics of Black unity and Black disunity discussed earlier. I will then discuss how both types of rhetoric ultimately point to the divided state of Blacks in the post–civil rights era. Given Bitzer's 1968 observation that all rhetoric is a response to a situation, I have no way of knowing what shape or direction this discourse will take in the future. Nevertheless, I will provide some guidance based on what I can see at present.

RHETORICS OF BLACK UNITY

While Du Bois believed that leadership comes from the top down rather than from the bottom up, there are times when we hear the voices of those at the bottom of America's racial hierarchy. Coates, in his work *Between the World and Me*, seeks to provide readers with an understanding of the gap that exists between whites and Blacks. Yet I argue that his work reveals a great deal about the distance that separates members of the Mainstream and Transcendent groups of Blacks from the Abandoned or underclass. It is a work that is quite revealing of the changes that have taken place in the post–civil rights era among Blacks.

Coates seeks to establish fear as the force that unites all Blacks together. Violence against the Black body has a long history in America and continues to this day. Coates argues that all Blacks live in fear and that the fear stems from three sources. The first is white society and in particular the police force. The second is Black parents who may behave violently toward their children in an attempt to prevent them from becoming subject to police violence later in life, though this is not the only reason why Black parents may do so. The third is Black youths who engage in violence toward each other for simply being in the wrong place at the wrong time or looking at someone in the wrong way. What all these sources of violence have in common is that they are omnipresent in the lives of poor Blacks. While Coates seeks to argue that the fear of violence is something that unites all Blacks, I argue that his text reveals this to be more a preoccupation of the Abandoned than of members of the Mainstream or Transcendent groups.

People write primarily from their own perspectives, and Coates's perspective stems from seeing life from the vantage point of the underclass. It is life as seen from the bottom, looking across the divide that separates the life of white Americans living "the dream" from the nightmare Coates saw outside his front door growing up in Baltimore. Even when Coates moved to New York City, he took this perspective with him, and it is likely that the neighborhood where he first lived was not much different from the one he had left. Coates never knew a life free from fear, a life filled with possibility rather than limitations. While Coates's perspective is true for himself and members of the Abandoned, he makes the mistake of believing that all Blacks equally share it.

Coates first learns that this is not the case when he meets Prince Jones's mother. She is a doctor who dreamed of her son going to Harvard or Yale. In this encounter, Coates still seeks to equate the violent death of Prince Jones at the hands of a Black police officer with that of other Blacks. Yet what is more revealing is how extraordinary Prince Jones's life and death were, given that this is not something that his mother or he ever envisioned. Moreover, Prince Jones's mother had every expectation that the officer who killed her son would be punished. In this she reveals the extent to which she is a member of the Mainstream and believes that justice, fairness, and the rule of law will prevail. These are not beliefs that Coates shares or has ever shared, given his upbringing among the Abandoned.

Coates's preference for the philosophy of Malcolm X over that of Martin Luther King Jr. reveals not just a difference of opinion about the efficacy of nonviolence but also a difference in class. Violence circumscribes the lives of the Abandoned in a way it does not for those of the Mainstream and the Transcendent classes in the post–civil rights era. Blacks and whites do not just live in separate neighborhoods; from Coates's perspective, they live in separate worlds. Yet this separation exists among Blacks as well, as Prince Jones was killed by a Black police officer who saw himself as protecting and serving the residents of Prince Jones County, who themselves were members of the Mainstream among Blacks.

While Coates seeks to remind us of the importance of race, members of the Mainstream, like their integrationist predecessors, continue to try to move the country past the issue of race so that issues of content and character can come to the fore. The election of Barack Obama represented, at least on a political level, the achievement of that dream, even if more remains to be done socially and economically. The Mainstream and the Transcendent have become part of American society in a way that the Abandoned have not. Members of the Abandoned are still seen as the other even by other Blacks, as we saw in Cosby and Poussaint's discussion of the underclass in their book. Well-off Blacks can now afford to pay police to protect them from what they see as the wrong kind of Blacks: the Abandoned. Class, we come to understand, is as much a factor as race in the post–civil rights era as the separation between the Abandoned and the Mainstream becomes clear to us, even if that was not Coates's intent in his work.

Attempts to keep Blacks unified as a group are rhetorical in nature, which should not be surprising, given that one's identity as a Black person is largely symbolic, though rooted in a shared history of oppression. I argue that Kennedy's work *Sellout: The Politics of Racial Betrayal* is an attempt to police the boundaries that separate whites from Blacks, though in the post–civil rights era, this policing originates from within the Black community, unlike in the past, when whites did so from without. As Burke ([1950] 1969) observed, calls for unity are most often heard during times of division, and hooks (2000) noted that the civil rights movement made it possible for some Blacks who were poised to do so to move ahead, breaking the bonds that had connected them to the Black community as a whole and in particular poorer Blacks. Individuals like Kennedy seek a way to prevent the dissolution of the Black community from happening as Blacks embrace the freedom to make their own choices as individuals regardless of the effect their choices may have on Blacks as a group. In employing the term "sellout," Blacks seek to keep other Blacks on their side of the color line, thus restricting their choices to gain greater identification with white Americans and the mainstream. In using or advocating the use of the term "sellout," Kennedy and others desire to force Blacks to put race first and their identity as Americans second, given that racial patriotism and racial loyalty are seen as requirements for continued membership in the Black community.

Yet the determination of who is or is not Black is problematic for Kennedy, and though he admits that the answers are uncertain, he nevertheless settles on an essentialist notion similar to the one-drop rule that whites imposed on Blacks for much of American history. Kennedy, to use Appiah and Gutmann's (1996) terminology, embraces a race-conscious rather than a color-conscious notion of racial identity. Kennedy uses skin color as a determinant of who is presumably Black and argues that this blackness comes with obligations to the racial group that must be met. In this sense, he is in keeping with Du Bois's notion that the Talented Tenth owe a debt to the race, only Kennedy extends this notion of debt to all Blacks. Blacks who fail to fulfill their obligations to the group are subject to excommunication from the group, and this ostracism serves as a reminder to other Blacks of the consequences of placing oneself above the group, even if no choice was involved in claiming membership in the group.

The choices that Blacks can make as individuals in the post–civil rights era are problematic for Kennedy and others in that any choice that appears to move one toward whites and away from Blacks is grounds for applying the term "sell-out." These choices are numerous and include attaining an education; achieving middle-class status; talking white, acting white, and marrying white; or simply being liked or admired by white people. As Kennedy (2008) states, the problem of selling out is a problem of "blacks who attain success in a multi-racial setting" (7). So, unfortunately, Blacks find themselves in the position of being accused of selling out if they embrace the goals of the civil rights movement and successfully integrate into the larger society from which Blacks were previously segregated. The term "sellout" seems to embrace the idea that poor Blacks are the real Blacks and that success or anything to do with it is non-Black. While Blacks like to claim individuals who achieve success in mainstream society, that very success renders them suspect and brings up the possibility of them being accused of not being Black enough, forgetting where they came from, or which group they are said to belong to. Poor Blacks don't have to struggle with the question of whether or not they are sellouts; only Blacks who achieve some measure of success are asked to question whether or not their buying into mainstream values and behaviors makes them somehow less Black.

The rhetoric of selling out functions as a mechanism of social control based on an essentialist notion of race. It ignores the fact that Blackness is a sociological construct that whites created, enforced, and maintained for their own advantage as they engaged in racial cartel behavior (Roithmayr 2014) for their own benefit and to the detriment of individuals labeled Black. In seeking to maintain a line in the sand that separates all things Blacks from everything white, Kennedy does so to the disadvantage of the most successful Blacks. He offers them no perceived benefit to embracing their Black identity and placing it before their identity as Americans, other than maintaining their racial bona fides in the eyes of others who might seek to judge them and the choices they make. While seeking to enforce greater identification among Blacks, Kennedy's rhetoric has the potential to create division instead. The more one seeks to define and control Black identity, the fewer people one will find who ultimately claim it, especially in a multicultural world where individuals have the opportunity to work, live, and sleep alongside other Americans whose skin color and ancestry differ from their own. Using rhetoric as a weapon, Kennedy tries to play the role of a forceful unifier. Yet because of his instance on a race-conscious mentality for all, he does more to divide individuals who might otherwise choose to be color conscious based on a shared history of struggle.

Cosby and Poussaint's book *Come On, People: On the Path from Victims to Victors* provides the authors' prescription for what is wrong with the Black underclass. Ostensibly, the work is a self-help book meant to provide poor Blacks with the tools they need to lift themselves up out of poverty and into a middle-class life. Yet I argue that the book's true audience is the Black middle class, or what Eugene Robinson (2010) termed the Mainstream among Blacks. Rather than a guide to help poor Blacks lift themselves up, the work functions as an explanation for why they are down. The authors do not see poor Blacks as victims at all, at least in regard to American society and racism being the primary explanations for why poor Blacks remain poor. Instead, poor Blacks are seen as individuals who have made poor life choices. These are choices for which they are to be held accountable and, according to the authors, ought to feel shame. Only in recognizing and changing their own poor life choices can poor Blacks move forward on the path from self-inflicted wounds to becoming victors or winners in life.

As I noted earlier, Cosby and Poussaint's diagnosis of what ails poor Blacks would fit nicely with the work of Black conservatives and would play well with members of the Republican Party. It blames Black males for not being there for their children without any discussion of systemic factors such as a failing education system and the prison-industrial complex. It blames poor Black women for having sex with poor Black men and in turn producing poor Black children whom these mothers will do a poor job of taking care of. Cosby and Poussaint proffer conservative values such as respect for one's elders, marriage, and hard work as solutions to the problems that plague poor Blacks. The solutions are all aimed at individuals, because the authors see poor Blacks as responsible for keeping themselves mired in poverty, even if systemic factors contributed to them being poor in the first place.

Yet, as I note, the work's real function is to absolve the Talented Tenth of any obligation or responsibility toward the Black poor. What Cosby and Poussaint do is to rhetorically erase the debt that Du Bois created through his own rhetoric. The sense of obligation that Blacks are said to owe each other is no more. That *Come On, People* is a self-help book is the most telltale sign of its anti–Du Boisian nature. Du Bois believed that racial progress came from the top down and that the most educated and successful Blacks had the responsibility and the means to lift up the masses of Blacks. What Cosby and Poussaint argue is that poor Blacks have the responsibility and the means to help themselves if only they adopt more mainstream values and behaviors. The Talented Tenth's only role in this process is to castigate poor Blacks for their failures and to remind them when they have strayed from the path of righteousness, given that they are suffering the wages of sin.

Cosby and Poussaint's work appears to be based on the idea of Black unity. They see themselves as having the obligation to help the Black poor. Yet this form of help stops at speech and does not involve action beyond writing a book that notes how and why poor Blacks are responsible for their own fate. As I argue, Cosby and Poussaint position themselves as fathers to the race and the Black underclass in the role of children who need of guidance. Yet if they are fathers, then their approach is that of a strict parent, rather than a nurturing one. These are parents who can look at their children and say that what they are is of their own making and has nothing to do with their parents. More-over, Cosby and Poussaint see the Black poor as something less than or even un-American, given the behaviors they describe them as engaging in, while simultaneously arguing that the Black poor have the agency to help themselves. This is not the role that Du Bois saw for the Talented Tenth; this is something else. This is the work of what Robinson labeled Transcendents, speaking on behalf of themselves as well as the Mainstream to absolve themselves of their own shame at not fulfilling Du Bois's mandate to uplift the race.

What Cosby and Poussaint provide to the mainstream is a soothing balm that allows them to take comfort in their own middle- or upper-class status while washing their hands of the Black poor. The work speaks to the fact that Mainstream and Transcendent Blacks now have more in common with whites of similar class status than they do with poor Blacks. Cosby and Poussaint see poor Blacks through the same eyes as the majority of white Americans. Du Bois saw poor Blacks differently, even nobly at times, despite the economic degradation they were forced to endure. Cosby and Poussaint's book, if read by the Black poor, would make them feel worse about themselves. As self-help books go, this would be an odd outcome. It is Mainstream and Transcendent Blacks who would be most helped psychologically from reading this work, as it would alleviate any sense of guilt or shame that they might feel about their own class status and lack of ability or desire to help Blacks less fortunate than themselves. Although it begins from the standpoint of Black unity, Cosby and Poussaint's book ends in disunity, pointing to the many ways in which poor Blacks are not like Mainstream and Transcendent Blacks, and why we no lon-ger have to shoulder the Black man's (or woman's) burden of uplifting them.

RHETORICS OF BLACK DISUNITY

One of the more interesting facets of rhetorics of Black disunity is the hesitance of Blacks to engage in it or fully see it for what it is. A telling example is Eugene Robinson's book *Disintegration*. Robinson posits that there are four distinct groups of Blacks in America—the Transcendent, Mainstream, Emergent, and Abandoned—but he laments this fact and longs for a time when Blacks had a greater sense of racial identity and solidarity. While Robinson sees the passage of time and class differences as an adequate explanation for disintegration, I believe that integration and greater identification with white Americans provide a better one. Identification among Blacks is no longer based on race and is more a function of class. The very groups that Robinson identifies are for the most part drawn around class lines. What we see is that members of each group, with the exception of the Abandoned, have integrated into mainstream society and are succeeding both educationally and economically in ways that were previously unimagined.

The Transcendent class among Blacks, of whom Oprah and Obama are Robinson's main examples, integrate by showing an ability to take the needs and concerns of white Americans into consideration. Their ability to do so has made this class of Blacks rich and politically powerful. Oprah, for example, backed the presidential aspirations of Obama long before other Black Americans, and her support went a long way toward helping him be acceptable in the eyes of many whites. The other factors that helped were the fact that he is biracial, pursued race-neutral politics, and has a Harvard law degree. While a billionaire and a president do not by themselves signal a postracial America, they do point to the fact that race no longer impedes the ability of some Blacks to attain economic and social success. Yet, as noted earlier, individuals in the Transcendent class often pursue a race-neutral strategy that makes them something other than the leaders of the race that Du Bois desired. Instead, members of the Transcendent class have every reason to continue to push for race to eventually be irrelevant in American society, because for so long it was their membership in a racial group that was used to discriminate against them.

The Mainstream Blacks that Robinson identifies attend majority-white institutions rather than HBCUs on the whole and can live and work alongside whites as never before. They can even marry whites in an era when many of the offspring of such unions can identity as biracial or multiracial rather than Black. Even members of Generation X and millennials who are not biracial do not see race as nearly as important as their parents do, a fact that Robinson finds upsetting. Yet, as I argue, the rhetoric of Black disunity is a marker for the success of integration. Content, character, and class have become more relevant than race for younger generations when choosing their friends and marriage partners, especially for those who grow up in integrated neighborhoods, attend integrated schools, and move on to integrated workplaces.

The Emergent group, composed of both biracial people and immigrants from Africa and the Caribbean, also shapes identities that point to different kinds of Blacks, from different places, who are even more educated than many white Americans. While still benefiting from affirmative action, they are more likely to attend private schools and go on to attend elite institutions of higher education, displacing native-born Blacks in the process. Instead of being seen as one and the same, they see themselves, and are seen by others, as different from native-born Black Americans. They are more likely to see America as a land of opportunity rather than oppression, and in this outlook, they have more in common with white immigrants than the descendants of Black slaves.

While Robinson (2010) still attempts to claim that "race still separates us, preoccupies us, and defines us" and "there remains one black racial identity" (236), his own work points us to the opposite conclusions. Issues of class are now as important, if not more important, than race for all but the Abandoned. It is only members of the Abandoned or the Black underclass whose lives are still primarily defined by a history of slavery and segregation, lives lacking the upward mobility that is found in the other groups of Blacks Robinson identifies. Although Robinson argues that the plight of the Abandoned will continue to make race "the defining attribute of African Americans" (236) until it is resolved, what we may in fact be seeing is a new era when the color caste has more dimensions rather than being abolished altogether.

Members of the other three groups can identify as American and no longer need see themselves as hyphenated Americans unless they choose to do so. Robinson's nostalgia for the past prevents him from seeing the implications of his work and the changes he observes among Blacks. Members of the Mainstream, Transcendent, and Emergent groups can now identify more with white Americans than with members of the Abandoned. The end of de jure segregation made it possible for Blacks to identity with white Americans, yet it also provided an opportunity for the divisions that exist among Blacks to be made plain for all to see. Robinson's work points to the renunciation of a single Black identity and possibly to a future in which even the Black identities that Robinson outlines fade away as well. Yet with the loss of a unified racial identity, notions of racial solidarity and racial obligation also become things of the past. As members of the Talented Tenth identify more with whites, their relationship with the Abandoned changes as well, and perhaps not to the benefit of the Abandoned, who find themselves increasingly alone both geographically and existentially.

Cashin's *Place, Not Race: A New Vision of Opportunity in America* focuses on affirmative action, an issue that divides both whites and Blacks. Yet I argue that a closer look at the text reveals the extent to which affirmative action separates the interests of the Talented Tenth from the Black underclass. To use Robinson's terminology, it divides members of the Mainstream, Transcendent, and Emergent groups from the Abandoned, as the three preceding groups can each take advantage of affirmative action in ways that the Abandoned do not. Moreover, Cashin goes further in showing the ways in which members of the Mainstream, Transcendent, and Emergent groups benefit from affirmative action at the expense of the Abandoned. Du Bois's Talented Tenth were charged with lifting up the Black masses, yet today we find that members of the Talented Tenth have redefined racial uplift as securing their own class status and that of their children, rather than helping members of the Black underclass to rise. What is more revealing is that Cashin argues that the interests of the Black elite and those of white elites are aligned in ways that allow affirmative action to operate along similar lines as legacy admissions do for white elites. Class matters more than race in this instance as the old bonds of racial solidarity and racial loyalty that Du Bois and scholars like Kennedy argue should exist among Blacks are broken.

Given that these bonds are broken, and policies such as affirmative action now work against the uplift of the Abandoned while simultaneously fueling racial animosity among whites, Cashin argues for changes that would substantially alter the status quo. Rather than focusing on race, Cashin argues that we should focus on place, which would reveal the extent to which the interests of poor whites and those of the Black underclass are aligned. Just as the Black elite and the white elite can find common ground in place, Cashin suggests the possibility that poor Blacks and whites can do so as well. Place, rather than race, is a better marker for who is disadvantaged in America today, and class issues come to the fore in Cashin's work.

A focus on place and issues of class brings to the fore a new group of Cashin's invention that she names ardent integrators. These are people who would push for multicultural alliances that move us beyond the ties of racial loyalty that existed in the past. If Du Bois's Talented Tenth have failed to fulfill their historical mandate to uplift the Abandoned, then Cashin sees an opportunity to create a new group that would work toward fulfilling this task, not just for Blacks but for whites and others as well. Cashin's rhetoric reveals her to be more in line with Dr. Martin Luther King's vision than that of Du Bois, in that King's focus shifted from civil rights to issues of poverty and an attempt to unite poor people regardless of race in fighting for their economic rights. To secure a stronger foothold economically, education is vitally important today, and so an affirmative action policy based on place becomes a means to secure economic ends.

Yet in pushing to change the ways in which our society provides educational opportunity, Cashin also seeks to change the relationship between the poor of all races. Her work reveals the extent to which the bonds of racial loyalty that were presumed to exist between the Talented Tenth and the Black underclass are broken. It also challenges Du Bois's notion of racial leadership from above with the Talented Tenth at the vanguard. Instead Cashin argues that the Black poor can lead themselves and have the talent to do so. What they lack is the opportunity to fulfill their promise educationally at the highest levels.

In pushing for a focus on place rather than race, Cashin's work does not state that we are living in a postracial America where race no longer matters. Yet in arguing in favor of place and seeking to create a group of ardent integrators and multicultural coalitions based on class, she puts forth a new vision that could lead to a more postracial way of Americans interacting with each other. Affirmative action today provides no bridge to the white working class. In arguing that place should take precedence over race, Cashin creates this bridge. At the same time, she reveals the wedge that exists between the Talented Tenth and the Abandoned. The Black elite are no longer asked to be selfless in ways that whites are not. Instead, Cashin's work allows everyone to follow his or her own self-interest but notes the ways in which the interests of the Mainstream, Transcendent, and Emergent groups among Blacks are no longer aligned with those of the Abandoned.

Touré in *Who's Afraid of Post-Blackness?* puts the self-interest of individuals in the Mainstream, Transcendent, and Emergent groups on full display. If Du Bois (1969) argued that "the problem of the twentieth century is the problem of the color-line" (54), then Touré in the twenty-first century seeks to erase that line altogether but does so in ways that I believe are problematic and unworkable. Touré attempts to extend the notion of post-blackness from its origins in the art world to the Black population at large. Yet in doing so, he fails to see that what may be possible for artists who define themselves as artists first and Blacks second is not necessarily possible for Blacks as a group. This is a rhetoric of individualism, and it is a rhetoric that is more appealing to members of the Mainstream, Transcendent, and Emergent groups than it is to members of the Abandoned. It also reveals the extent to which these groups are attempting to separate themselves from the Abandoned and break the bonds that Du Bois believed should tether the Talented Tenth to the Black masses.

The notion of a debt to the race has long been a staple of Black thought from Du Bois to Randall Robinson. Yet what Touré (2011) seeks to do is to free individual Blacks from what he sees as the shackles of collectivity and allow them to embrace a post-Black future in which blackness is "whatever you want it to be" (12), and Black culture is "more like Starbucks" (41), no longer the sole province of Black people but available to anyone. Blacks have long sought to define themselves and their group as a people, given that they were stripped of much of their history and culture. Now Touré seeks to have each and every Black person define what it means to be Black for himself or herself. This, however, would render the term "Black" meaningless. Moreover, treating Black culture as if it were a Starbucks and available to anyone is problematic in a country that has a history of appropriating the culture and works of Black people without giving them any credit for their contributions to America.

Still, Touré turns to visual artists, Dave Chappelle, and politicians such as Obama to make his claim that Blacks can embrace a post-Black identity successfully. However, the examples that Touré provides, even those from his own life, point to the difficulties Blacks have in embracing a post-Black identity. Blacks cannot be post-Black in a country that is not postracial, and America is not close to achieving that state, not by a long shot. The visual artists that Touré profiles produce works that are often reviled by other Black people, as these artists choose to put their own artistic vision ahead of any loyalty to Black people as a group. Individuals like Dave Chappelle find that their attempts to challenge American culture and identity from a post-Black perspective can be reinterpreted by whites in ways that support white supremacy and negative depictions of Black people. Politicians like Obama find that they can succeed only by distancing themselves from Blacks to the extent possible and pursuing race-neutral politics in ways that never remind people of America's past and present discriminatory practices. Touré's rhetoric may free individual Blacks to see themselves as Americans first and Blacks second (if at all), but it does little to help members of the group as a whole, and it does the least to help members of the Abandoned, who are the most affected by America's history of racial discrimination.

Touré's rhetoric relieves members of the Talented Tenth of their historical obligation to uplift the masses of Blacks. Instead it allows them to redefine uplift in terms of their own individual advancement rather than the advancement of Blacks as a group. Touré's rhetoric is the antithesis of Du Bois, and it is everything that Du Bois feared would happen when he envisioned the downside of the Talented Tenth. Scholars like West (1993b) have remarked on the selfishness that exists among members of the Black middle class and the political elite who are more interested in themselves than any notion of racial uplift.

When taken outside the confines of the art world, notions of post-blackness are unworkable. Blacks cannot be post-Black in the face of white supremacy. Whites have always defined themselves in relation to Blacks and cannot allow Blacks to redefine themselves without a corresponding redefinition of what it means to be white. The reaction of some whites to the Obama presidency during his term of office bore the marks of racism. The election of Trump to the White House represented a resurgence of white supremacy in reaction to an intelligent and dignified Black family occupying a space where many whites felt Black people did not belong, no matter the content of their character. In Trump we see that a white man with disreputable character can be president, but a Black man with an impeccable reputation will be opposed and disrespected for eight years straight.

What makes the idea of a post-Black identity possible is the existence of a strong Black identity and a Black community from which individuals can find safety and shelter in the face of racism. Yet if one attempts to break the bonds of community that Blacks possess, however frayed they may be, then we are left with nothing but individuals who are unmoored and ungrounded. Even Robinson did not go so far as to preach the degree of individualism that Touré put forth. Robinson argued that there were four different groups of Blacks, but he did not go so far as to argue that there was or should be nothing that connected one Black person to another. Our nation is not postracial, and we cannot be post-Black. Perhaps if and when the connection between American identity and white supremacy is broken (Olson 2004), Blacks will be able to simply be Americans. Yet until that day, we remain on the other side of the color line, not by choice but by design, and it is not wholly within our power to erase that line, no matter how much some might wish it to be true.

BROKEN BONDS

What we see in the rhetorics I have critiqued is the importance of class both in the perspective each author provides and in the extent to which Blacks are identified as a single racial group with common interests. With the exception of Coates, each of the authors sees the world from the perspective of the Mainstream, Transcendent, or Emergent groups of Blacks rather than from the perspective of the Abandoned. Only Coates provides a view from the bottom, although this does not make his vantage point any truer than another or any falser. It is simply the perspective that he can provide, given where he comes from, having grown up among the Abandoned and not yet thoroughly identified with the Mainstream despite his success. For the most part, as Blacks begin to change their class status, they no longer see Blacks as a unified group, for better or for worse. Cosby and Poussaint look down on the Black poor and urge them to change their ways and adopt middle-class values and behaviors. Cashin seeks to empower the Black poor by allying them with poor whites based on a rhetoric of place (or class), rather than along racial lines that would continue to link them to others who share the same racial identification as Blacks.

The role of the Talented Tenth in all of this has shifted in that members of the Mainstream and Transcendent groups no longer see it as their responsibility to lift up poor Blacks. Cosby and Poussaint blame the Black poor for not doing more to change their own circumstances, and seem to believe that castigating the Black poor for their situation is the best way to help them. The responsibility for lifting the masses lies with the masses themselves, according to these authors, and as such, the members of the Talented Tenth are absolved of their own guilt at having failed to achieve Du Bois's vision of racial uplift. Even Cashin turns away from the Talented Tenth in favor of a group she calls ardent integrators, who could potentially be of any racial group and align themselves based on their interests in advocating the importance of place over race in American society.

What we see is a redefinition of racial uplift from lifting up the poor to the Talented Tenth finding ways to lift themselves and their children. The continued success of the Mainstream, Transcendent, and even the Emergent groups among Blacks becomes the goal rather than uplifting the Abandoned. What one sees is an increase in the distance that separates the Abandoned from other groups of Blacks, rather than a lessening of that distance. Cashin strives to close the distance by acknowledging that the bonds of racial loyalty no longer hold. She believes that the only way to achieve racial uplift for the Abandoned is to change from a rhetoric of race to one that emphasizes place and builds bridges to the white working class in ways that acknowledge their pain rather than calling attention to their complicity and support for the racial status quo.

Integration, as I argued earlier, is both a sign of the civil rights movement's success and also the catalyst for disunity among Blacks in the post–civil rights era. Integration equals success equals disunity as one leads into the other. Put more simply, integration equals disunity, which is what hooks observed in *Where We Stand: Class Matters.* The changes that took place after the civil rights movement have created a moment in which Blacks, and in particular members of the Talented Tenth, are forced to grapple with not only what it means to be Black in America today but also what role members of the Talented Tenth are to play among Blacks as a group, if one or more groups are said to exist at all. What do Blacks owe each other? What do members of the Talented Tenth owe other Blacks? These are questions that Randall Robinson asked in *The Reckoning,* and Touré appears to revisit for himself in *Who's Afraid of Post-Blackness?* Both authors have very different answers to these questions, with Robinson appearing to adhere to Du Bois's vision of group unity and debt, while Touré seeks to chart a new course based on individualism and no sense of obligation to anyone besides oneself.

If for Du Bois in the twentieth century, the color line that separated whites from Blacks was the focus of his discourse, then for Blacks in the twenty-first century, issues of class that separate one Black from another are now a subject of concern. In the course of a century, the subject of Black discourse has changed, as disunity is both acknowledged and, for some, seen as potentially desirable. Although Cosby and Poussaint's work is ostensibly a work of Black unity, it says more about the division that exists between the Abandoned and other groups among Blacks. Cashin and Touré both produced works that point toward disunity, though the ways they deal with that division differ. Cashin seeks to create multiracial alliances, while Touré seeks to abolish the color line altogether in favor of each individual being free to pursue his or her own self-actualization, freed of the tethers of racial obligation and racial loyalty.

Those advocating Black unity do so in different ways as well. Coates attempts to divide the world into Black and white based on who lives in fear and who gets to live "the dream." Kennedy seeks to control the choices Blacks make through a rhetoric of social control based on who is or who isn't labeled a sellout. While I see Eugene Robinson's text as a work of Black disunity, given that he admits division among Blacks, he does so while lamenting the loss of unity that once existed and that he wishes could be so again.

Times change, and yet the alliance between Blacks and whites along class lines that Cashin proposes is one that leaves me skeptical of its possibility for success. The same possibility for a class-based alliance between poor whites and poor Blacks existed during Reconstruction, and poor whites chose racism over class solidarity. The current wave of white nationalism shown in the election of Donald Trump points toward more racism and less solidarity along class lines, at least at present.

A more likely scenario than class-based solidarity is a color/class caste among Blacks that still places members of the Abandoned at the bottom. Mainstream, Transcendent, and Emergent Blacks may occupy a middle ground like Latinos, or a higher ground like Asians, but only to the extent that they are seen as similar to, and enjoying the privileges of, whites. That may be seen as progress of some kind, but only to the extent that the individual is freed of any connection to a group- or race-based identity. It does not overturn the existing racial hierarchy but rather provides a more nuanced approach to it based on more, rather than less, distinctions between groups. Whether that counts as progress depends on one's perspective, but it would represent a break in the sharp divisions of the color line that Du Bois encountered and his successors dealt with for decades. What we can know for sure is that Blacks now stand divided in ways they had not been before the success of the civil rights movement.

REFERENCES

Abramowitsch, Simon. 2017. "Addressing Blackness, Dreaming Whiteness: Negotiating 21st-Century Race and Readership in Ta-Nehisi Coates's *Between the World and Me*." *CLA Journal* 60 (4): 458–78.

Appiah, K. Anthony, and Amy Gutmann. 1996. *Color Consciousness: The Political Morality of Race*. Princeton, NJ: Princeton University Press.

Asante, Molefi Kete. 2005. *Race, Rhetoric, and Identity: The Architecton of Soul*. New York: Humanity Books.

Baldwin, James. 1963. *The Fire Next Time*. New York: Dial Press.

Balfour, Lawrie. 2011. *Democracy's Reconstruction: Thinking Politically with W. E. B. Du Bois*. New York: Oxford University Press.

Banks, Patricia. 2010. "Black Cultural Advancement: Racial Identity and Participation in the Arts among the Black Middle Class." *Ethnic and Racial Studies* 33 (2): 272–89.

Battle, Juan, and Earl Wright II. 2002. "W. E. B. Du Bois's Talented Tenth: A Quantitative Assessment." *Journal of Black Studies* 32 (6): 654–72.

Bell, Derrick. 1987. *And We Are Not Saved: The Elusive Quest for Racial Justice*. New York: Basic Books.

Bell, Derrick. 1993. *Faces at the Bottom of the Well: The Permanence of Racism in America*. New York: Basic Books.

Beltrán, Cristina. 2010. *The Trouble with Unity: Latino Politics and the Creation of Identity*. Oxford: Oxford University Press.

Bittker, Boris. 1973. *The Case for Black Reparations*. New York: Random House.

Bitzer, Lloyd. 1968. "The Rhetorical Situation." *Philosophy and Rhetoric* 1:1–14.

Bonilla-Silva, Eduardo. 2001. *White Supremacy and Racism in the Post–Civil Rights Era*. Boulder, CO: Lynne Rienner.

Bonilla-Silva, Eduardo. 2010. *Racism without Racists*. 3rd ed. Lanham, MD: Rowman & Littlefield.

Brophy, Alfred. 2002. *Reconstructing the Dreamland: The Tulsa Riot of 1921; Race, Reparations, and Reconstruction*. New York: Oxford University Press.

Brown, Michael, Martin Carnoy, Elliott Currie, Troy Duster, David Oppenheimer, Marjorie Shultz, and David Wellman. 2003. *Whitewashing Race: The Myth of a Color-Blind Society*. Berkeley: University of California Press.

Burke, Kenneth. (1945) 1969. *A Grammar of Motives*. Berkeley: University of California Press.

Burke, Kenneth. (1950) 1969. *A Rhetoric of Motives*. Berkeley: University of California Press.

Carney, Kelly Walter. 2017. "Brother Outsider: James Baldwin, Ta-Nehisi Coates, and Exile Literature." *CLA Journal* 60 (4): 448–57.

Cashin, Sherryl. 2014. *Place, Not Race: A New Vision of Opportunity in America*. Boston: Beacon Press.

Charland, Maurice. 1987. "Constitutive Rhetoric: The Case of the Peuple Québécois." *Quarterly Journal of Speech* 73 (2): 133–50.

Chrisman, Robert. 2013. "Black Studies, the Talented Tenth, and the Organic Intellectual." *Black Scholar* 43 (3): 64–70.

Coates, Ta-Nehisi. 2015. *Between the World and Me*. New York: Spiegel & Grau.

Coates, Ta-Nehisi. 2017. *We Were Eight Years in Power*. New York: One World.

Conley, Dalton. 1999. *Being Black, Living in the Red: Race, Wealth, and Social Policy in America*. Berkeley: University of California Press.

Cosby, Bill, and Alvin Poussaint. 2007. *Come On, People: On the Path from Victims to Victors*. Nashville, TN: Thomas Nelson.

Cose, Ellis. 1993. *The Rage of a Privileged Class*. New York: HarperCollins.

Cose, Ellis. 1997. *Color-Blind: Seeing beyond Race in a Race-Obsessed World*. New York: HarperCollins.

Cruse, Harold. 1967. *The Crisis of the Negro Intellectual*. New York: William Morrow.

Dahl, Adam. 2017. "Black Disembodiment in the Age of Ferguson." *New Political Science* 39 (3): 319–32.

Dawson, Michael. 1994. *Behind the Mule: Race and Class in African-American Politics*. Princeton, NJ: Princeton University Press.

Dawson, Michael. 2001. *Black Visions: The Roots of Contemporary African-American Political Ideologies*. Chicago: University of Chicago Press.

Dickerson, Debra. 2004. *The End of Blackness: Returning the Souls of Blacks to Their Rightful Owners*. New York: Pantheon Books.

Du Bois, W. E. B. 1969. *The Souls of Black Folk*. New York: Signet Classic. Original edition, 1903.

Du Bois, W. E. B. 1986. *Writings*. New York: Literary Classics of the United States. Original edition, 1903.

Du Bois, W. E. B. 1995. *W. E. B. Du Bois: A Reader*. Edited by David Lewis. New York: Henry Holt.

Dyson, Michael. 2006. *Is Bill Cosby Right? (or Has the Black Middle Class Lost Its Mind?)*. New York: Basic Books.

Feagin, Joe. 2000. *Racist America: Roots, Current Realities, and Future Reparations*. New York: Routledge.

Gates, Henry Louis, Jr. 1997. *Thirteen Ways of Looking at a Black Man*. New York: Random House.

Gates, Henry Louis, Jr., and Cornel West. 1996. *The Future of the Race*. New York: Alfred A. Knopf.

Gerbner, George. 1998. "Cultivation Analysis: An Overview." *Mass Communication and Society* 1 (3): 175–94.

Giroux, Susan Searls. 2010. *Between Race and Reason: Violence, Intellectual Responsibility, and the University to Come*. Stanford, CA: Stanford University Press.

Glaude, Eddie S., Jr. 2016. *Democracy in Black: How Race Still Enslaves the American Soul*. New York: Crown Publishers.

Goffman, Erving. 1974. *Stigma: Notes on the Management of Spoiled Identity*. New York: Jason Aronson. Original edition, 1963.

Greeson, Aaron. 1982. *The Dialectics of Betrayal: Sacrifice, Violation and the Oppressed*. Norwood, NJ: Ablex.

Greeson, Aaron. 1995. *The Recovery of Race in America*. Minneapolis: University of Minnesota Press.

Greeson, Aaron. 2004. *America's Atonement: Racial Pain, Recovery Rhetoric, and the Pedagogy of Healing*. New York: Peter Lang.

Griffin, Rachel Alicia, and Bernadette Marie Calafell. 2011. "Control, Discipline, and Punish: Black Masculinity and (In)visible Whiteness in the NBA." In *Critical Rhetorics of Race*, edited by Michael Lacey and Kent Ono. New York: New York University Press.

Guerrero, Lisa. 2017. "New Native Sons: Ta-Nehisi Coates, Kiese Laymon, and the Phenomenology of Blackness in the Post-racial Age." *CLA Journal* 60 (4): 414–33.

Hacker, Andrew. 1995. *Two Nations: Black and White, Separate, Hostile, Unequal*. New York: Ballantine Books. Original edition, 1992.

Hale, Grace. 1998. *Making Whiteness: The Culture of Segregation in the South, 1890–1940*. New York: Pantheon Books.

Hochschild, Jennifer. 1995. *Facing Up to the American Dream: Race, Class, and the Soul of the Nation*. Princeton, NJ: Princeton University Press.

Holmes, David. 2007. "Affirmative Reaction: Kennedy, Nixon, King, and the Evolution of Color-Blind Rhetoric." *Rhetoric Review* 26 (1): 25–41.

hooks, bell. 2000. *Where We Stand: Class Matters*. New York: Routledge.

Hyra, Derek. 2006. "Racial Uplift? Intra-racial Class Conflict and the Economic Revitalization of Harlem and Bronzeville." *City and Community* 5 (1): 71–92.

Joseph, Ralina L. 2013. *Transcending Blackness*. Durham, NC: Duke University Press.

Katznelson, Ira. 2005. *When Affirmative Action Was White: An Untold History of Racial Inequality in Twentieth-Century America*. New York: W. W. Norton.

Kelley, Norman. 2004. *The Head Negro Syndrome: The Dead End of Black Politics*. New York: Nation Books.

Kelley, Robin. 2002. *Freedom Dreams: The Black Radical Imagination*. Boston: Beacon Press.

Kendi, Ibram X. 2016. *Stamped from the Beginning: The Definitive History of Racist Ideas in America*. New York: Nation Books.

Kennedy, Randall. 2008. *Sellout: The Politics of Racial Betrayal*. New York: Pantheon Books.

Kim, Claire Jean. 2000. *Bitter Fruit: The Politics of Black-Korean Conflict in New York City*. New Haven, CT: Yale University Press.

LaMothe, Ryan. 2018. "Singing the Blues: Reflections on African American Men, the Emergence of Melancholic Selves, and the Search for Transformational Objects." *Pastoral Psychology* 67: 655–71.

Landry, Bart, and Kris Marsh. 2011. "The Evolution of the New Black Middle Class." *Annual Review of Sociology* 37.

Lewis, Thabiti. 2016. "How Fresh and New Is the Case Coates Makes?" *African American Review* 49 (3): 192–96.

López, Ian Haney. 2014. *Dog Whistle Politics*. New York: Oxford University Press.

Loury, Glenn. 2002. *The Anatomy of Racial Inequality*. Cambridge, MA: Harvard University Press.

Lusane, Clarence. 2001. "Unity and Struggle: The Political Behavior of African American Members of Congress." *Black Scholar* 24 (4): 16–27.

Mack, Katherine, and Jonathan Alexander. 2019. "The Ethics of Memoir: Ethos in Uptake." *Rhetoric Society Quarterly* 49 (1): 49–70.

Malcolm, Nigel. 2008. *One More River to Cross: The Therapeutic Rhetoric of Race in the Post-Civil Rights Era.* Lanham, MD: University Press of America.

Martin, Ben. 1991. "From Negro to Black to African American: The Power of Names and Naming." *Political Science Quarterly* 106 (1): 83–107.

Massey, Douglass, and Nancy Denton. 1993. *American Apartheid: Segregation and the Making of the Underclass.* Cambridge, MA: Harvard University Press.

Masuoka, Natalie, and Jane Junn. 2013. *The Politics of Belonging: Race, Public Opinion, and Immigration.* Chicago: University of Chicago Press.

Mayer, Jeremy. 2002. *Running on Race: Racial Politics in Presidential Campaigns, 1960–2000.* New York: Random House.

McDermott, Monica. 2001. "Class Structure and Racial Consciousness among Black Americans." *Critical Sociology* 27 (1): 1–28.

McPhail, Mark. 1994. "The Politics of Complicity: Second Thoughts about the Social Construction of Racial Equality." *Quarterly Journal of Speech* 80: 343–81.

McPhail, Mark. 1998. "Passionate Intensity: Louis Farrakhan and the Fallacies of Racial Reasoning." *Quarterly Journal of Speech* 84: 416–29.

McWhorter, John. 2000. *Losing the Race: Self-Sabotage in Black America.* New York: Free Press.

McWhorter, John. 2003. *Authentically Black: Essays for the Black Silent Majority.* New York: Gotham Books.

Meyrowitz, Joshua. 1986. *No Sense of Place.* New York: Oxford University Press.

Montoya, Roberto, Cheryl Matias, and Michelle McBride. 2017. "*Between the World and Me*: A Review." *Multicultural Perspectives* 19 (1): 53–57.

Moshin, Jamie, and Ronald Jackson II. 2011. "Inscribing Racial Bodies and Relieving Responsibility: Examining Racial Politics in *Crash*." In *Critical Rhetorics of Race*, edited by Michael Lacy and Kent Ono. New York: New York University Press.

Moynihan, Daniel Patrick. 1965. *The Negro Family: The Case for National Action.* United States Department of Labor, Office of Policy Planning and Research.

Olson, Joel. 2004. *The Abolition of White Democracy.* Minneapolis: University of Minnesota Press.

Perry, Imani. 2011. *More Beautiful and More Terrible.* New York: New York University Press.

Postman, Neil. 1985. *Amusing Ourselves to Death: Public Discourse in the Age of Show Business.* New York: Viking.

Rambsy, Howard, II. 2016. "The Remarkable Reception of Ta-Nehisi Coates." *African American Review* 49 (3).

Robinson, Eugene. 2010. *Disintegration: The Splintering of Black America.* New York: Doubleday.

Robinson, Randall. 2000. *The Debt: What America Owes to Blacks.* New York: Plume.

Robinson, Randall. 2003. *The Reckoning: What Blacks Owe to Each Other.* New York: Dutton.

Roithmayr, Daria. 2014. *Reproducing Racism: How Everyday Choices Lock In White Advantage.* New York: New York University Press.

Russell, Margaret. 1997. "Beyond 'Sellouts' and 'Race Cards': Black Attorneys and the Straitjacket of Legal Practice." *Michigan Law Review* 95 (4): 766–95.

Shelby, Tommie. 2005. *We Who Are Dark: The Philosophical Foundations of Black Solidarity.* Cambridge, MA: Harvard University Press.

Shelton, Jason E., Dante Bryant, and M. Curtis Brown. 2016. "We as a People: Assessing the Consequences of Various Sources of Diversity within Black America." *Phylon* 53 (2): 79–99.

Smith, Alexander, and Lenahan O'Connell. 1997. *Black Anxiety, White Guilt, and the Politics of Status Frustration*. Westport, CT: Praeger.

Smith, Derik. 2016. "Ceding the Future." *African American Review* 49 (3): 183–91.

Sowell, Thomas. 1999. *The Quest for Cosmic Justice*. New York: Free Press.

Sowell, Thomas. 2005. *Black Rednecks and White Liberals*. San Francisco: Encounter Books.

Steele, Shelby. 1991. *The Content of Our Character: A New Vision of Race in America*. New York: Harper Perennial.

Steele, Shelby. 1998. *A Dream Deferred: The Second Betrayal of Black Freedom in America*. New York: HarperCollins.

Stewart, Charles. 1997. "The Evolution of a Revolution: Stokely Carmichael and the Rhetoric of Black Power." *Quarterly Journal of Speech* 83: 429–46.

Stubblefield, Anna. 1995. "Racial Identity and Non-essentialism about Race." *Social Theory and Practice* 21 (3): 341–68.

Terrill, Robert. 2015. *Double-Consciousness and the Rhetoric of Barack Obama*. Columbia: University of South Carolina Press.

Tocqueville, Alexis de. 2002. *Democracy in America*. Chicago: University of Chicago Press. Original edition, 1835.

Touré. 2011. *Who's Afraid of Post-Blackness? What It Means to Be Black Now*. New York: Free Press.

Tuck, Stephen. 2010. *We Ain't What We Ought to Be*. Cambridge, MA: Belknap Press of Harvard University Press.

West, Cornel. 1993a. *Keeping Faith: Philosophy and Race in America*. New York: Routledge.

West, Cornel. 1993b. *Race Matters*. Boston: Beacon Press.

Williams, Dana. 2016. "Everybody's Protest Narrative: *Between the World and Me* and the Limits of Genre." *African American Review* 49 (3): 179–204.

Williams, Juan. 2006. *Enough*. New York: Three Rivers Press.

Wilson, William. 1997. *When Work Disappears: The World of the New Urban Poor*. New York: Knopf.

Wilson, William. 1999. *The Bridge over the Racial Divide: Rising Inequality and Coalition Politics*. Berkeley: University of California Press.

Woodson, Carter. 1933. *The Miseducation of the Negro*. Washington, DC: Associated Publishers.

INDEX

147

ABOUT THE AUTHOR

Photo by Sarah Hardin

Nigel I. Malcolm is associate professor of communication at Keene State College. He is author of *One More River to Cross: The Therapeutic Rhetoric of Race in the Post–Civil Rights Era*.

CPSIA information can be obtained
at www.ICGtesting.com
Printed in the USA
BVHW041551201122
652364BV00005B/9